'Gordon Lynch is a li   ake in the
present conflict between progressive spirituality and traditional religious
belief. He offers us a clear and comprehensive account of the historical,
sociological, economic, political and philosophical underpinnings of
left-leaning spiritual movements throughout the modern West. Lynch's
encyclopaedic knowledge of feminist theology, deep ecology, vigorous
human rights advocacy and anti-globalization campaigns give his
analysis of "the new spirituality" a range and profundity that is unique
in the field of religious studies. His book will likely be regarded as the
classic text about our contemporary western religious scene.'

Naomi Goldenberg, Professor of Religious Studies, University of Ottawa

'Gordon Lynch's mapping and analysis of "the new spirituality" is
genuinely ground-breaking and far surpasses the modesty of his
stated aims and the provisional nature of his conclusions. With a rare
combination of objectivity, insight and empathy, he identifies contours,
landmarks and defining features in the contemporary spiritual landscape
which have gone un-surveyed until now. Lynch's great contribution
to the spirituality debate is to demonstrate the theological coherence,
historical lineage and social conscience of progressive spirituality. His
book will give confidence, encouragement and hope to individuals
embarked on this path and will be an important springboard for further
professional and academic enquiry. Above all, Lynch challenges lazy and
catch-all critiques of spirituality as inevitably superficial, narcissistic and
consumerist. Here, at last, progressive spirituality is rescued decisively
from that amorphous and much-derided land where only dragons dwell
– The New Age.'

Eley McAinsh, Director, The Living Spirituality Network

'If you are interested in the progress of religion in the West, you cannot
afford to ignore this important book. It provides a particularly insightful,
informed and empathetic interpretation of the "progressive milieu".
Likewise, its carefully thought-through analysis of current thinking
regarding the new spiritual consciousness is cogent and stimulating. That
it is also written in an enviably accessible and lively style makes it a study
that both the seasoned scholar and the novice will benefit from and enjoy.
I cannot commend it highly enough.'

*Christopher Partridge, Professor of Contemporary Religion and Co-Director of
the Centre for Religion and Popular Culture, University of Chester*

'Unlike so much of the current writing on "the new spirituality",
Gordon Lynch's examination of the contemporary religious ferment is
sociologically astute, intellectually precise and carefully balanced. His
own sympathies place him squarely in the "progressive milieu" and even
ally him with much of the "progressive spirituality", but such alignments
are incidental to the incisive cultural analysis that Lynch offers. For
the major ideological constructs that drive the new spirituality – from
pantheistic ecology to feminism to liberal individualism to interfaith
ecumenism – Lynch is a sure guide. For its organizational bases and
collaborative networks, he serves as both cartographer and wary realist.
Lynch's book is important reading for anyone interested in the contours
and prospects of progressive religion in the twenty-first century.'

Leigh Eric Schmidt, Professor of Religion, Princeton University, author of
Restless Souls: The Making of American Spirituality

'Scholarship is still trying to come to terms with the recent proliferation
of new forms of spirituality, and this book represents an important
milestone on the way. Drawing on primary and secondary sources,
Gordon Lynch manages to give a lucid account of the nature,
development, social contexts and significance of what he labels
'progressive spirituality'. One of the great strengths of the book is its
ability to steer a steady course between the extravagant claims and
equally passionate denunciations which are regularly made of alternative
spirituality. Instead, Lynch offers a balanced assessment which is clear
enough to serve as an introduction, and nuanced enough to advance our
understanding.'

Linda Woodhead, Professor of Religious Studies, University of Lancaster

The new spirituality

An introduction to progressive belief in the twenty-first century

Gordon Lynch

I.B. TAURIS

LONDON · NEW YORK

Published in 2007 by I.B.Tauris & Co Ltd
6 Salem Road, London W2 4BU
175 Fifth Avenue, New York NY 10010
www.ibtauris.com

In the United States of America and in Canada distributed by
Palgrave Macmillan, a division of St Martin's Press
175 Fifth Avenue, New York NY 10010

ISBN 978 1 84511 413 8 hardback
ISBN 978 1 84511 414 5 paperback

A full CIP record for this book is available from the British Library
A full CIP record for this book is available from the Library of Congress

Library of Congress catalog card: available

Typeset in Palatino Linotype by Steve Tribe, Andover
Printed and bound in Great Britain by TJ International Ltd, Padstow

Contents

On the other hand, I also believe that our own spiritual traditions [in the West] will have to undergo some radical changes in order to be in harmony with the values of the new paradigm. The spirituality corresponding to the new vision of reality I have been outlining here is likely to be an ecological, earth-oriented, post-patriarchal spirituality. This new kind of spirituality is now being developed by many groups and movements, both within and outside the churches… We are embedded in the multiple alternative networks of what I have called the 'rising culture' – a multitude of movements representing different facets of the same new vision of reality, gradually coalescing to form of powerful force of social transformation.

Fritjof Capra[1]

This is a vision of life energy that calls us all into life-giving community from many strands of tradition, culture and history. This common theology, I believe, must also call us to stand shoulder to shoulder and arm in arm to oppose the systems of economic, military and ecological violence that are threatening to undo the very fabric of planetary life. This, as Thomas Berry has said, is the 'great work' of our generation.

Rosemary Radford Ruether[2]

The source of spiritual vision is deep within us; within the heart, mind, soul and spirit. In our era we are seeing a shift of authority away from outside authorities to within the individual. There is no centralized and orthodox version of deity to which all must subscribe; instead we have the spiritual reality of today, which is *pluralism*: there are many paths, many ways, many visions of the Divine. What members of this new spiritual community share is a common commitment to the Sacred Quest – for wholeness within and for social, community and planetary responsibility. However, each one of us is free to experience our own religious symbols and to create a personal spirituality based on understanding the true nature of the holistic universe.

Vivianne Crowley[3]

Without the transcendent and the transpersonal, we get sick, violent and nihilistic, or else hopeless and apathetic. We need something 'bigger than we are' to be awed by and to commit ourselves to in a new, naturalistic, empirical, non-churchly sense, perhaps as Thoreau and Whitman, William James and John Dewey did.

Abraham Maslow[4]

We need a new God.

Neale Donald Walsch[5]

Introduction

There is an increasingly widespread perception that western society is undergoing one of its most significant religious transitions for many centuries. Book titles such as *The Spiritual Revolution*, *The Death of Christian Britain* and *Tomorrow's God* all suggest some kind of religious ferment. 'The times they are a-changin'', sang Bob Dylan and, as we begin to see the fruits of the seeds of change sown in the 1960s, his words remain remarkably apt for describing the fast-changing religious landscape of contemporary western life. In recent years, my own particular focus on this changing religious scene has been on forms of spirituality emerging outside of institutional religion. This had led me, in particular, to think about whether popular culture was becoming an increasingly important vehicle for the spiritual aspirations and experiences of a younger generation, increasingly alienated from institutional religion. I reflected on what kind of spirituality might be evident in the writing of Canadian Zeitgeist novelist, Douglas Coupland,[1] and conducted my own field work on whether contemporary club culture could be seen as an important source of moral formation and spiritual experience for some young adults.[2]

So when my editor, Alex Wright, and I first discussed this current project, we imagined that this would be about trying to analyse the nature of the emerging spirituality in a western society in which traditional institutional religion is in serious decline. Responding to Thomas Luckmann's challenge for sociologists to clarify the emerging worldview of an increasingly secularized society,[3] I thought it would be possible to identify a particular set of values and beliefs that were developing in modern society as a replacement for traditional religion. Over the past two years though, whilst researching and writing this book, I have come to realise that such a project is fundamentally flawed – for three main reasons.

Firstly, although there is still widespread discussion of the secularization of the West, it is clear that the United States of America – the dominant nation-state of the West – remains a deeply Christianized culture. In the major American Religious Identification Survey (ARIS) of 2001, 81 per cent of respondents identified themselves with a particular religious group, with 77 per cent of respondents identifying with some form of Christianity.[4] In April 2005, a Gallup poll recorded that 65 per cent of respondents claimed that they were members of a church or synagogue[5] – with the vast majority of these presumably reporting church rather than synagogue membership.[6] Similarly, in recent decades, Gallup polls have consistently shown that between 40–45 per cent of American adults claim that they attend church or synagogue on a regular basis. Even allowing for evidence of some decline in post-war American religiosity[7] and the possibility that these polls may give a slightly over-exaggerated impression of the extent of this religiosity,[8] there is clearly still a significant proportion of the American population that at least feels that it should have strong religious, and more specifically Christian, affiliations.[9] This Christianized culture is certainly not uniformly orthodox in terms of traditional Christian beliefs. High levels of belief in God, the importance of prayer, the Devil, angels and both heaven and hell, are mixed in with high levels of belief in the paranormal and alien visitations to our world. But even given this diversity of beliefs, values and practices, it is the Christian religion that provides the broad framework for most Americans' beliefs and sense of identity. The only detectable signs of secularization are the growing number of younger adults who identify themselves as having no religion,[10] and the declining numbers of young adults in mainstream Christian denominations.[11] But this shift away from traditional religion by some younger adults should be put in the context of the ARIS poll in which 70 per cent of respondents aged 18–34 still identified themselves as religious or somewhat religious in their outlook.

There is no evidence, then, of a dramatic change in the religious culture of America which is leading a substantial part of the population to abandon, or identify themselves against, institutional forms of religion or, more specifically, the Christian Church. When individuals do engage in some form of spiritual search, it is likely that they will conduct this with at least some reference to Christian beliefs or resources – even if these are combined with resources from alternative spiritual traditions. The notion that there is a 'new spirituality' replacing institutional religion in America to any significant degree thus lacks any real supporting evidence.

It is clear that the picture looks very different in other western and English-speaking societies. In the 2003 British Social Attitudes Survey, 43 per cent of respondents said that they had no religion, only slightly less than the 48 per cent who identified themselves as Christian.[12] Church attendance in Britain is much lower than in the United States. The English Church Attendance Survey in 1998 indicated that only 7.9 per cent of the population in England attended church on a regular basis, with church-collated statistics indicating a further decline since then.[13] The demographics of secularization are also much more pronounced in Britain, with around 60 per cent of respondents aged 18–34 consistently reporting having no religion in the British Social Attitudes Survey over the past decade.[14] Evidence of spiritual searching outside of institutional religion is also somewhat clearer in Britain. A MORI poll conducted on behalf of the BBC in 2003 recorded 24 per cent of respondents agreeing with the statement 'I am spiritually inclined but don't really "belong" to an organised religion'.[15]

In summary, the search for a vibrant 'new spirituality' in the West beyond the boundaries of institutional religion may have some validity in some countries – Britain, Canada, Scandinavia, and Australia and New Zealand. But if we include the United States (or indeed many Catholic societies in Western Europe), then the picture becomes much more complicated, and the notion of a significant 'new spirituality' wholly outside institutional religion becomes more problematic. As we will see later in this book, a number of writers are now arguing that there is an upsurge of interest in alternative spiritualities across English-speaking societies that is threatening to outgrow traditional religious beliefs and affiliations. Survey evidence suggests that this is not the case, however. Estimates based on returns from the ARIS poll suggest that there are only 140,000 Pagans in the United States and 134,000 Wiccans, which represents around 0.065 per cent of the general US population for each group. Reported levels in the more recent National Study on Youth and Religion were slightly higher – 0.3 per cent of respondents said that they were Pagan or Wiccan.[16] Whilst this reflects a growing interest in these alternative traditions amongst teenagers, this is still a very small part of the population compared to the 83 per cent of teens in the same study who claimed affiliation with some form of institutional religion. It could be argued that people who identify with alternative religious traditions in these kinds of survey are more likely to be actively involved in their chosen religion than people who have a very nominal attachment to Christianity, but, even so, these figures suggest that these alternative 'occultural' religions involve only a tiny fraction of the American public. There is little evidence to suggest that the picture is any different in Britain, Canada, Australia and New Zealand.

A second reason for challenging my initial assumptions about my project was my growing recognition that there is no evidence that the majority of the population in Britain or America are significantly motivated by religious beliefs or affiliations in their everyday lives. Indeed, when pressed, people in both countries are likely to be somewhat inarticulate and inconsistent about their beliefs. Americans may claim to identify with Christianity, and regard themselves as religious, but this does not mean that this religious identity necessarily exercises a strong influence over their self-understanding or lifestyles. This point has been well illustrated by a recent major survey of teenage religious and spiritual beliefs conducted by the National Study on Youth and Religion based at the University of North Carolina in Chapel Hill.[17] In this study, just over 75 per cent of respondents identified themselves as Christian, and around 7 per cent identified with other forms of institutional religion. In interviews, however, the researchers discovered that their teen research participants were 'incredibly inarticulate about their faith, their religious beliefs and practices, and its meaning or place in their lives'.[18] The exception to this tended to be those teens who were committed members of conservative religious groups, such as Evangelical Christians, who had a much stronger sense of their distinctive religious beliefs and identity. Overall, the researchers found that the most common religious attitude amongst the teens studied was what they describe as 'moralistic therapeutic deism'.[19] This perspective can be summarized as a credo which asserts that there is a God who watches over the Earth, that God wants people to be good to each other (as each world religion teaches), that the point of life is to be happy and to feel good about oneself, that God does not need to be involved in one's life unless one has a problem and that good people go to heaven when they die. This is reminiscent of the working philosophy of everyday life that the British sociologist David Chaney has identified as increasingly widespread in contemporary western culture. Dominant features of this include an emphasis on being able to enjoy life, the valuing of close emotional relationships, a sense of responsibility for being as attractive as possible, the search for the 'stress-free' and the 'natural', and the turn to various forms of therapeutic support when personal well-being is under threat.[20] None of the elements of this practical philosophy of how to live everyday life need be coherently grounded in deeper metaphysical beliefs – and indeed, for many people, they rarely are. It is unclear as to what extent people in English-speaking societies outside North America really operate, as Grace Davie suggests, on the basis of 'vicarious religion' – leaving the practice of religion to the Christian churches, which are then used as spiritual and cultural resources in times of personal or social crisis. But whether or not people are likely to return to the Church in their time of need, Davie is surely right to suggest that a significant majority are generally happy to leave 'religion' as something for others to do.

My initial interest in identifying the emerging spirituality of western society rested on the assumption that people are generally motivated by religious or spiritual beliefs. On closer scrutiny, there is little evidence that this is the case – other than for a relatively small part of the population who have strong commitments to religious groups with strong plausibility structures that reinforce a distinctive set of beliefs and attitudes. I had started by assuming that most people were motivated by some form of 'spirituality', or some kind of search for existential meaning in their lives. Perhaps this is not an uncommon assumption amongst researchers with a Protestant upbringing somewhere in their past. But, increasingly, I doubt it is a useful presupposition to bring to the study of changing forms of religiosity in contemporary culture. It is certainly not uncommon for writers on the new spirituality to make this assumption, though. In fact, it is probably one reason why commentators on the new spirituality tend to overestimate its prevalence in the general population.

A third reason why I have come to call into question my initial research aims was my growing dissatisfaction with the tendency for the study of religion to work on the basis of clear boundaries between particular religious institutions and traditions. Researchers often concentrate their efforts in studying Buddhist, Christian, Hindu, Jewish, Muslim or Sikh groups and traditions – or indeed a myriad of other 'religions'. Even those whose research takes them outside institutional religion still relate their work to specific, identifiable subgroups, whether Pagan, Wiccan, or the rather more amorphous remainder categories of 'new age' and 'alternative spiritualities'. Unthinkingly, I had replicated this same tendency in my own initial thinking about this project. I was to study the 'new spirituality' that was emerging beyond the clearly delineated boundaries of institutional religion. As the project has developed, though, I have come to recognize that this conventional way of dividing up the task of studying religion is unhelpfully restrictive. As Linda Woodhead has observed, in a contemporary context in which people's attitudes towards traditions of all kinds are changing and evolving, it makes less sense to restrict our analyses to specific, boundaried traditions.[21] What happens when people begin to try to merge different traditions together? Or, as I have started to ask through conducting this research, how can we make sense of finding the same cluster of values and beliefs amongst groups across different religious traditions? Limiting my scope to studying spirituality outside of organized religion was to miss the possibility that the real story about the 'new spirituality' is one that is happening across and beyond a number of different religious and spiritual groups and traditions. Indeed it is such 'trans-religious' developments that are as likely to influence the future of religion and spirituality in the West as developments within any of the single religious traditions.

My initial project of searching for the emerging spirituality beyond institutional religion thus ran slowly into the sands. As I trawled through books and websites talking about a 'new spirituality', however, two insights began to crystallize for me. The first was that the study of the new spirituality could be likened to staring into a deep, dark pool. The clearest picture to emerge from such study was often the reflection of the researcher themselves. Writing about the new spirituality functions as a kind of religious and cultural Rorschach test, where what the researcher sees is often a projection of their own values, hopes and concerns. So when David Tacey looks at the new spirituality, he sees a promising upsurge of a open-minded, generous mysticism amongst younger people.[22] When James Herrick looks at the new spirituality, he sees a threat to orthodox, doctrinal Christianity.[23] When Jeremy Carrette and Richard King look at the new spirituality they see an insidious ideological trick of late modern capitalism.[24] And when John Drane looks at the new spirituality, he sees both a challenge and a missiological opportunity for the Christian Church.[25] In one sense, none of these analyses are unhelpful. The notion of the 'new spirituality' provides an important opportunity for talking about what values and beliefs should shape our lives, and what will really promote the flourishing of life. But at the same time, it serves as a warning that when we talk about the new spirituality we are in the realm of telling stories about contemporary culture that may bear varying degrees of resemblance to the world that exists beyond our imaginations. It is always true that religious scholars construct the objects of which they speak. But there can be varying degrees of reality behind those constructions. Serious scholarship on changing patterns in religion and spirituality in the West can only really proceed on the basis of careful reading of cultural products – like books, websites, magazines – as well as the close empirical study of people's attitudes, discourses and actions and the wider organizational and social contexts in which these take place. Not all of the literature purporting to analyse the new spirituality offers this kind of rigour. I hope that I have done enough of this in this current book to be able to see something beyond my own reflection, but I will leave that judgment to my readers.

The second insight that began to dawn on me was that, amongst certain books and websites on the emerging spirituality, I was finding certain recurring ideas. I began to realize that what I was discovering was not so much a mass spiritual movement beyond the orbit of traditional religious institutions, but a new religious ideology that was developing across and beyond a range of religious traditions. In this book I will refer to this as 'progressive spirituality' – for reasons that I will explain more fully in the opening chapter. Progressive spirituality is not a mass movement. It does not encompass all the hopes, fears and meanings that get poured into the term 'the new spirituality'. It is a more specific, and more clearly defined, set of beliefs than the amorphous beliefs and practices that have come to be fitted into the category 'New Age'. And it is a project that has evolved in a particular context – the wider progressive milieu of western religion and spirituality. I doubt that progressive spirituality will become the dominant religious ethos of the coming century to which most people in the West will subscribe. But it does represent an important and viable part of the future of western religion, and one which we need to take seriously.

In a moment, I will offer a brief overview of the structure and content of the book. Before this, though, a brief personal note is needed. I have approached this project as an academic researcher interested in understanding more about progressive spirituality, and the wider progressive milieu out of which it has emerged. I have sought to ground my analysis in a careful reading of progressive spirituality literature, in some initial empirical study of progressive spirituality groups and networks, and through the discussion of a wider sociological literature on contemporary western society and religion. Ultimately, this book should be judged on how adequately it describes and analyses the specific social and cultural phenomena that I am studying.

At the same time I am, to a limited extent, a participant in the phenomena that I am describing as well. I have spoken at progressive religious events, have written for progressive magazines, and in previous books have discussed the limitations of conservative forms of religion and the value of an inclusive mystical spirituality for the contemporary western religious landscape.[26] In many respects, this background has been an asset for me in writing this book. When conducting interviews with people in the progressive milieu, some were already aware of my work and some were not. Either way, my background – and fundamental sympathy for many of the ideas and initiatives I was encountering – was helpful in building open, collaborative research relationships with these participants. I have also, I will confess, been very touched or deeply inspired by some of the books I have read and people I have met whilst conducting this research.

Negotiating one's position as a researcher in such circumstances can be a complex task. Writing about the perils of research into new social movements, Alberto Melucci comments how some researchers can develop a messianic fantasy that they have a key role to play in shaping the identity and consciousness of social movements.[27] I hope to have avoided that kind of grandiosity in this project. At the same time, I recognize that I am no neutral observer of the progressive milieu, either. What I hope to do is to make a wider audience aware of the interesting developments that are taking place within the progressive milieu, but also to offer a mirror up to those involved in the progressive milieu itself to help them reflect on their background and context, and on the challenges that await them in the future. The mirror image I offer could never be a perfect one, and needs to be supplemented by more detailed research in this field in the future. But I hope, at this important moment in the evolution of the progressive milieu, it stimulates some new ideas and questions about the nature and shape of progressive faith at the start of the twenty-first century.

A further brief reflexive comment is needed. I am conscious that writing as a white, male, English-speaking post-Christian hardly counts as an unusual profile within the wider literature on progressive spirituality. At the same time, though, whilst writing this book, I have become conscious of working on a form of spirituality that is significantly shaped by the experiences and innovations of women. The current shape of progressive spirituality in the West owes a great deal to a generation of women who, from the late 1960s onwards, took on traditional, institutionalized forms of religion, and sought to develop new theologies and new forms of religious and spiritual ritual and practice. There is a danger, in this book, that I appropriate the often costly labour of these women, without acknowledging the still-privileged gender position from which I benefit – or perhaps, even worse, failing to recognize the courage that these women showed that made these spiritual innovations possible. I hope I avoid such thoughtless appropriation in this book, but remain open and accountable for criticism if I have not.

Having made these introductory comments, let me now say something briefly about the structure of this book. In Chapter One, I introduce two key concepts on which my account of progressive faith in the West is based. Firstly, I refer to the *progressive milieu* as a diffuse collection of individuals, organizations and networks across and beyond a range of religious traditions that are defined by a liberal or radical approach to religious belief and/or a green or left-of-centre set of political attitudes and commitments. Secondly, I define *progressive spirituality* as a particular form of religious ideology that has been refined over the past thirty or so years by a range of 'organic intellectuals' within the progressive milieu of western religion. Having explained these terms, I then go on to examine the roots of progressive spirituality, arguing that it has emerged out of four key concerns: the desire for an approach to religion and spirituality that is appropriate for modern, liberal societies, the rejection of patriarchal forms of religion and the search for religious forms that are authentic and liberating for women, the move to re-sacralize science (particularly quantum physics and contemporary theories of cosmology), and the search for a nature-based spirituality that will motivate us to try to avert the impending ecological catastrophe.

In the second chapter, I then go on to explain the key elements of progressive spirituality as a religious ideology, illustrating how progressive writers from across and beyond a range of religious traditions exemplify these core values and beliefs. I argue that progressive spirituality is grounded in the belief in the immanent and ineffable divine which is both the intelligence that guides the unfolding cosmos as well as being bound up in the material form and energy of the cosmos. This notion of the divine can take either pantheist or panentheist forms in progressive spirituality – though, in practice, I suggest that there tends to be little difference between these two forms and that progressive spirituality is best summarized as having a pan(en)theist view of the divine. This view of the divine is often held in conjunction with an emphasis on the value of mystical union with this grounding source of life, and it is common for advocates of progressive spirituality to either actively endorse, or be sympathetic to, feminine metaphors for describing the divine. Arising out of this progressive view of divinity, progressive spirituality promotes the sacralization of nature as the site of divine presence and activity in the cosmos – and the sacralization of the self, for the same reasons. The emphasis on the ineffability of this divine presence leads advocates of progressive spirituality to regard all constructive religious traditions as containing insights that can be valuable for encountering the divine. But, at the same time, progressive spirituality is highly critical of aspects of these traditions which are patriarchal and offer a 'top-down' notion of a God, separate from the cosmos, who seeks to order human life in an authoritative way. Religious tradition is therefore valued in so far as it points to the core assumptions of progressive spirituality – and other meaning-systems, such as rational secularism, or even eastern and New Age spiritualities that are also subject to critique where they differ from these core assumptions. Finally, in this chapter, I argue that progressive spirituality may be not so much a symptom of the 'Easternization of the West', as a continuation of particular western cultural traditions: the post-Reformation turn to the self, the Romantic turn to nature, and even the ongoing development of modernism. Furthermore, it is not a wholly new religious innovation, but an extension of a longer project of progressive faith in the West whose roots can be traced back at least into the early part of the nineteenth century.

In Chapter Three, I move on from describing the contours of progressive spirituality as an ideology to analyse the organizations and networks that make up the progressive milieu. I argue that these organizations and networks have four key areas of interest: to provide an environment and resources for the personal and spiritual development of individual religious progressives; to act as advocates for progressive theological, moral and political perspectives in larger religious institutions and traditions; to provide a progressive religious presence in the wider public sphere (including direct action of various kinds); and to build up stronger communication and collaboration within the progressive milieu. I suggest that many organizations within the progressive milieu operate with limited financial and human resources, and as a consequence tend to concentrate on relatively specific priorities. This can make it harder to develop stronger collaborative links between different organizations where these do not fit within the organizations' existing plans and commitments. In the latter part of the chapter I go on to critique the suggestion that the progressive milieu is too diffuse to be regarded as a coherent religious phenomenon, arguing that there is clear evidence of a sense of collective identity emerging within the progressive milieu. Accounts of collective progressive religious identities need to be nuanced, however: there is no simple collective identity to which all religious progressives subscribe, but a range of collective identities which have both an underlying cohesion and local differences. I also go on to critique suggestions that the cohesion within the progressive milieu is such that is in the process of becoming a significant 'religion' in its own right to which the majority of western society will subscribe. In reality, there are a number of factors that limit the collaboration that takes place between the wide spectrum of progressive religious organizations which will not be easily overcome in the very near future.

In the fourth and fifth chapters, I move on to place this discussion of the progressive milieu and progressive spirituality in a wider context. In Chapter Four, I explore how the progressive milieu and progressive spirituality can be understood in relation to a wider literature that attempts to analyse the changing face of religion and spirituality in modern western society. After providing an overview of this wider literature, I argue that progressive spirituality fits well within broader trends within western religion – such as Durkheim's notion of the rise of the cult of the individual, Heelas' concept of the turn to the self in western spirituality, and the 'new mysticism' identified by Simmel and Troeltsch. Indeed the development of the progressive milieu and expansion of progressive spirituality could be seen as a popularization of religious ideas which were more the preserve of a cultural elite at the turn of the twentieth century. Progressive spirituality is therefore well at home in a particular liberal and mystical strand of western religion. It can also be understood as a form of religion that is well-adapted to the cultural conditions of late modernity – offering a structure for the pursuit of a personally meaningful spirituality in the expanded spiritual marketplace of contemporary western society for those motivated enough to pursue it. At the same time, it can also be seen as a form of resistance to a secularized world view generated by the modernization of society, and as an attempt to regain a sacralized basis for modern life. The fact that core beliefs and values of progressive spirituality are shared by people in both mainstream religious institutions and the holistic milieu of alternative spiritualities suggests that the boundaries between them may be somewhat more porous than, say, clear divisions between Christianity and 'occulture' suggest.[28] But, at the same time, the barriers to collaboration discussed in Chapter Three demonstrate that it would be wrong to imagine that progressive spirituality is becoming an identifiable religion in its own right, or that a 'progressive' religious identity has now transcended identities grounded in particular religious traditions and belief systems. The concern with women's spirituality within the progressive milieu also supports the contention of writers such as Linda Woodhead and Callum Brown that the failure of traditional religious institutions to address the changing experiences, roles and concerns of women in late modern society is a significant influence on the contemporary religious landscape.

In the fifth chapter, I explore the progressive milieu and progressive spirituality in the context of the wider debate on the demoralization of western society. I set out four variants of the demoralization thesis which define the causes of the moral decline of the West as the consequence of, respectively, the moral liberalism of the 1960s, the secularization of society, capitalism, and the increasing dominance of a particular form of rationality as a basis of moral reflection and social planning. Given its left-of-centre leanings, it is unsurprising that progressive spirituality hardly adopts – or even engages with – right-wing critiques of 1960s moral liberalism (although there are some exceptions to this). More generally, though, progressive spirituality can be identified with versions of the demoralization thesis that point to secularization, capitalism and the dominance of instrumental rationality as sources of moral decline. More specifically, the perspective on demoralization broadly shared amongst many advocates of progressive spirituality is that moral decline arises out of an instrumental secular world view (or its 'other' – patriarchal religion) which provides the ideological support for a rationalized, capitalist structure that exploits both humanity and the wider natural world. Progressive spirituality's critique of capitalism may benefit from a more nuanced use of social theory. But it could be argued that if we are indeed living in the throes of a cultural crisis in values then progressive spirituality offers a viable world view and ethos that grounds sympathy for liberal values and respect for the natural world in a sacralized sense of wonder at the emerging universe. How progressive spirituality can be successfully disseminated as a means for the re-moralization and re-sacralization of society remains, however, an open and unresolved question.

At the conclusion of the book, I finally offer some brief thoughts on the size of the progressive milieu, its significance, and the future prospects for progressive spirituality. Despite some grandiose predictions about the growing numbers of people involved in the progressive milieu, in practice the numbers of people with any direct contact with progressive religious organizations and media probably form only a small part of the population. I estimate that the proportion of the population with any kind of active engagement in the progressive milieu is probably around 2–3 per cent in the United States and slightly less than that in the United Kingdom. Paradoxically, though, the proportion of people in Britain and America who share the liberal and progressive values of the progressive milieu is much higher – probably in the region of between 30–40 per cent of adults in the USA. This raises the question of whether the progressive milieu will grow numerically and become more culturally and politically influential in the coming years. Whether this happens will depend on how the organizational structures of the progressive milieu develop, whether progressive religious groups become more adept at recruiting and retaining committed members, the effects of changing public consciousness about our relationship with the natural world, and whether religious and spiritual progressives succeed in campaigning effectively with others sympathetic to their social and political aims. The book concludes with some predictions about the future of progressive spirituality and the progressive milieu. Here I suggest essentially that whilst progressive spirituality will remain an integral, and possibly growing, part of the religious landscape in the West, it will not yet form a religion in its own right, nor will there be a sudden reversal in the various factors which limit collaboration amongst progressive religious groups.

There are many people that I need to thank by way of acknowledgments. As ever, I am conscious that my work with this project has benefited tremendously from the support of friends and colleagues. Without their involvement, this work would have been greatly impoverished and any limitations in my final analysis of the progressive milieu are, of course, my responsibility. Firstly, I want to thank those people who have read various drafts of this book and have offered valuable and encouraging feedback: Naomi Goldenberg, Paul Heelas, Eley McAinsh, Diarmuid O'Murchu, Chris Partridge, Stephen Pattison, Leigh Schmidt, Tess Ward and Linda Woodhead. I am also very grateful to other colleagues with whom I have had invaluable conversations about this work – including in particular Martin Stringer and Ian Draper. Two particular conversations were profoundly influential on this project. Werner Ustorf raised questions with me about progressive understandings of God which proved inspirational in guiding me to see the structure of the beliefs and values that make up progressive spirituality. Ben Whelan also pointed me in the direction of a range of important writers in the progressive milieu which helped me to get a much clearer sense of some of the key thinkers and ideological positions within it. A number of people also generously gave up time to allow me to interview them for this book (and allowed me access to relevant events and research resources). My thanks here go to Adrian Alker (and everyone involved in the Centre for Radical Christianity at St Mark's, Broomhill), Jean Boulton, Chris Clarke, Hugh Dawes, Janice Dolley, Eley McAinsh, Ian Mowll, Diarmuid O'Murchu, Sister Marian O'Sullivan, Davie Philp, and Ben Whelan. Completion of this project was made possible through a sabbatical, additional teaching relief and a research travel grant from the School of Historical Studies at the University of Birmingham, and I am grateful to my colleagues there for their support with this work.

It remains to thank two other people. Alex Wright, my editor at I.B.Tauris, commissioned this book and has supported me through its production. Alex has been a valuable supporter of my work at times when my research career appeared to take idiosyncratic and untrodden paths, and I am grateful for his ongoing faith in me.

Finally, my love and thanks go to Duna. Writing a book like this is always a strange mixture of excitement, angst and self-absorption. Duna has been a patient and loving support during all of this, allowing me to test ideas on her, bearing my latest enthusiasms, and acting as proofreader extraordinaire. I'm grateful to her for all of this and for so much more, and it is to her that I dedicate this book.

1 The roots of the new, progressive spirituality

Since the end of the Second World War, one of the defining features of western society has been the growing division between liberal and conservative forms of religion. In his influential study on *The Restructuring of American Religion*, Robert Wuthnow argues that such tensions have been evident before, for example, in the fierce disputes between modernist and fundamentalist forms of Christianity, symbolized by the notorious trial in 1925 of John Scopes for teaching evolution at a high school in Tennessee. But these tensions were not as significant, however, as divisions between Christian denominations or between different religious traditions. In the 1950s, Wuthnow argues, there was even a rapprochement between liberal and conservative forms of religion, with some liberal pastors and theologians admiring the passion and missionary commitment of Evangelical faith.[1] The 1960s, however, saw much clearer divisions begin to emerge between religious liberals and conservatives.[2] The focus of conflict varied from issues of personal morality (particularly relating to sexuality), government intervention on welfare and other progressive social causes, to contentious political issues such as civil rights and the Vietnam War. Energy for this conflict came particularly from a generation of younger adults who were the products of a rapidly expanding higher education system in America, and who tended to espouse more liberal and progressive social and political values. What has been true in the American experience has also been true of many other western societies. Since the 1960s, for example, the polarization between liberal and conservative religious positions within western Christianity has tended to deepen as a result of contentious debates focusing on the ordination of women and, more recently, of people in same-sex relationships.[3] Further fuel has been added to this fire as religious conservatives in the West have begun to build stronger alliances on these contentious issues with co-religionists in the developing world. It is inaccurate to characterize the religious landscape of any western society as neatly divided into monolithic camps of religious liberals and religious conservatives.[4] Many people continue to practise their faith without any particular interest in the focal issues over which liberals and conservatives have fought. But there is no question that this liberal-conservative split has become an increasingly important framework within which people construct their religious identities and express their values and beliefs – across a range of religious traditions. This split is becoming even deeper with the rise of initiatives such as the Anglican Communion Network which is forming a new, conservative sub-network of dioceses and churches in the Episcopalian Church in America.[5] Traditional religious institutions are now starting to fragment into liberal and conservative subgroups, and it may only be a matter of time before we see serious schism along these ideological lines.

The central thesis of this book relates to the current stage of development of this tension between liberal and conservative forms of religion in western society. Its focus is particularly on the liberal side of this division. In recent years, the term 'liberal' has tended to fall somewhat out of favour amongst those to whom this term is often applied. In its place, those on the religious Left now refer to themselves more often as religious progressives. Although the term 'progressive' religion does have deeper historical roots – see, for example, the progressive Quaker meetings of the mid nineteenth century and the rise of progressive Judaism – its more widespread use is a recent innovation. The contemporary use of this term seems to have particular origins in North America, in which the religious and spiritual Left has sought to revitalize its links with 'progressive' politics. Even as recently as five or six years ago, Hugh Dawes, the Chair of the Progressive Christian Network for Britain and Ireland, recalls that religious liberals were still unsure about adopting the term 'progressive' to refer to themselves.[6] Identifying oneself as a religious or spiritual progressive is certainly becoming increasingly widespread in western religion. But the progressive religious identity is also very much a work in progress, nurtured by an emerging ideology and organizational structures which have really only coalesced to any significant degree over the past twenty years.

In its widest sense, the term 'progressive' religion tends to denote at least one of two things. Firstly, it normally indicates a commitment to understanding and practising religion in the light of modern knowledge and cultural norms. The World Union for Progressive Judaism, for example, identifies itself as a movement grounded in the Jewish tradition and Hebrew Scriptures, but seeks to encourage forms of Jewish faith and identity that are consistent with contemporary conscience and consciousness.[7] Similarly, one of the aims of the Progressive Muslim Union of North America is to provide a forum for those who wish to develop liberal, tolerant forms of Islam that are intellectually credible in the light of modern knowledge.[8] Part of this religious accommodation to late modern liberal democracy is a fundamental sympathy to notions of democratic society, gender equality and a welcoming of diversity (including diversity of sexual orientation). A second defining feature of 'progressive' religion is a sympathy with, and often active engagement in, green and left-of-centre political concerns. Spiritual and religious progressives are therefore involved in campaigns on issues varying from debt in the developing world, gay rights, global warming, the abolition of the death penalty, provision of adequate health and social welfare provision for the poor to solidarity with Palestinian interests in the Middle East peace process. Some religious groups who are progressive in this social and political sense do not necessarily share the more liberal religious beliefs of organizations such as the Progressive Muslim Union of North America or the Center for Progressive Christianity.[9] For example, the Sojourners, a radical Evangelical network, place a strong emphasis on the authority of the Bible and do not entirely share the more liberal view of gay sexuality held by other progressive groups.[10] Nevertheless, the Sojourners' left-of-centre social and political commitments, and their ecumenical desire to work with other religious groups that share the same concerns, mean that they retain a sense of themselves as working within a wider progressive religious movement.

Progressive religion, in its widest sense then, is constituted by individuals, groups and networks who tend to be either liberal or radical in theological terms or green and left-of-centre in political terms. Often religious progressives are both. Progressive religion typically defines itself over and against forms of religion that are both theologically and politically conservative, and it is a shared sense of opposition to such religious conservatism that can generate a sense of mutual identity amongst progressives across different religious traditions. This sense of a progressive identity defined in opposition to political conservatism is particularly true in the United States, in which the New Christian Right has a much stronger political profile than any comparable groups on the religious Right in Britain.[11] It is this broader context of liberal and left-leaning forms of religion that I will refer to in this book as the *progressive milieu*.[12] This milieu stretches across and beyond individual religious traditions, and so within it we find progressive Jews, Christians and Muslims, various forms of feminist or holistic spirituality, Pagans, Wiccans, and Quakers, as well as 'Engaged' Buddhists and Hindus.[13]

The central thesis of this book concerns an important development within this *progressive milieu* of western religion. Over the past thirty years we have entered a new phase of progressive religion in the West which has led more recently to the development of new religious identities, groups and networks. Over the course of this book I will argue that an important aspect of these recent developments has been the emergence of a particular ideology, a *progressive spirituality*, which is forming the basis for these new forms of religious identities, communication and collaboration. This spirituality is not simply a diffuse sentiment of tolerance and openness amongst religious liberals but arises out of particular concerns and is organized around a common set of clearly identifiable values and beliefs. Progressive spirituality is a particular way of understanding the world shared by individuals and groups across and beyond a range of religious traditions, who seek to understand their particular tradition and commitments through the lens of progressive spirituality's basic assumptions. It can be seen as a step beyond multi-faith tolerance and collaboration, towards the definition of a spiritual ideology that could unite people across and beyond religious traditions.[14] At its heart, this book is an attempt to define progressive spirituality, to examine some of the ways in which it finds expression in different groups and activities, and to reflect on its significance in the context of wider developments in western religion and society.

It is important to clarify from the outset that the religious ideology that I describe in this book as progressive spirituality is not universally shared within the wider progressive milieu of western religion. Rather, progressive spirituality is a phenomenon that has emerged out of this wider progressive religious milieu, and is supported in varying degrees by participants in that wider milieu. Importantly, though, this ideology offers the potential for a shift within the broader religious Left from a sense of mutual identity based on common social and political concerns or opposition to the religious Right, to a sense of identity based on a shared *theology* (or, as we shall see, *thealogy*). The shared ideology of progressive spirituality makes it possible for people to form stronger identifications with people from other religious traditions (or none) who share its basic assumptions than with people from their own religious tradition. Progressive Christians, Jews, Muslims, Quakers, Pagans and Wiccans et al. may therefore find more in common with each other, based on this shared ideology, than they do with other adherents of their same traditions. Progressive spirituality is therefore likely to play an important role in shaping the new kinds of collaborative networks, sacred rituals and social and political activism that will emerge out of the progressive milieu of the religious Left as this century progresses.

It may be that what I set out to describe here is a symptom of short-term fluctuations in the rapidly evolving forms of modern religion and spirituality in the West. Or it could be that the new, progressive spirituality could prove to be as important in the restructuring of religious identities and affiliations in the West as the Reformation was nearly five hundred years ago, and that we are facing what John Shelby Spong and Matthew Fox have referred to as a 'new Reformation'.[15] My hope is that the following discussion will provide a workable definition of progressive spirituality, and some basis for assessing its significance within the wider context of contemporary western religion and society. Through the course of this book, I will seek to describe the roots and main characteristics of progressive spirituality, to locate it in the context of deeper western cultural traditions, and to describe some of the ways in which it is finding expression in various groups and networks, and different forms of religious and social activism. Later in the book, progressive spirituality will be discussed in the wider context of debates about the changing face of western religion and the demoralization of contemporary society. Through analysing and contextualizing progressive spirituality in this way, it will be possible by the end of the book to begin to offer a clearer assessment of both the potential and the limitations of this progressive spirituality as a source of transformation of western religion and society.

Four imperatives for the development of a new spirituality

Let us begin by trying to understand more about the recent sources of progressive spirituality. As an ideology, progressive spirituality has not appeared out of a vacuum but is the product of a longer religious and cultural history in the West. Some of these influences extend back before the twentieth century, and we will consider these in the next chapter. Progressive spirituality has been particularly shaped, though, by a range of cultural and intellectual movements that have become increasingly influential on western religion since the 1960s. These movements have emerged as a response to four different perceived needs – the need for a credible religion for a modern age; the need for religion which is truly liberating and beneficial for women; the need to reconnect religion with scientific knowledge; and the need for a spirituality that can respond to the impending ecological crisis. In the remainder of this chapter, we will now think about how each of these developments has contributed to the emergence of progressive spirituality.

i)   Progressive spirituality has arisen out of the desire to find new
     ways of religious thinking and new resources for spiritual
     growth and well-being that truly connect with people's beliefs,
     values and experience in modern, liberal societies.

A common observation in books, articles and websites which
advocate progressive spirituality is that something has gone wrong
with traditional forms of religion. In part, this is because traditional,
western monotheistic religion is seen as inherently authoritarian,
exclusivist, patriarchal and overly bound to timeless (i.e. irrelevant)
rules.[16] This is particularly problematic when growing numbers
of people are seen as becoming disillusioned with a spiritually
arid, materialist and instrumental contemporary western culture,
and are actively seeking help in trying to develop lifestyles with
greater spiritual depth. As David Tacey puts it, 'we are caught in a
difficult moment in history, stuck between a secular system we have
outgrown and a religious system we cannot fully embrace'.[17]
     Sometimes this notion is expressed in the complaint that
participating in traditional religious institutions involves an
implicit requirement to stop thinking. 'You don't need brain
surgery to be faithful' proclaims the website of the Australian-based
Progressive Spirituality Network, as it seeks to offer an alternative
to 'lobotomised' religiosity.[18] Or, as one person explained to post-
evangelical writer, Dave Tomlinson, 'I have suffered twenty years
of religious and theological censorship [in the Church] – I have
been warned about this and told to keep away from that. I've had
enough of it. It's time to make up my own mind.'[19] As a consequence,
advocates of progressive spirituality often emphasize the importance
of developing forms of belief that are intellectually credible, and
that do not demand a lower level of open and critical thinking than
one would normally apply in other areas of one's life. Such concerns
arguably reflect the educated, middle-class demographic of those
drawn to progressive religious ideas.[20]
     More generally, though, there is a recurrent accusation that
traditional religious institutions are providing inadequate structures
and resources for the contemporary upsurge in spiritual searching.[21]
A serious stumbling block is the perceived requirement of religious

institutions to fit spiritual beliefs and practices into neatly, pre-formed doctrines and rules, which claim an absolute authority over the personal experience of the individual seeker. Diarmuid O'Murchu illustrates this point with his story of Ian, a young man with deep ethical commitments and nature-based spiritual sensitivities, who was left distraught by a conversation with a clergyman who was uninterested in anything other than whether or not he believed in Jesus Christ.[22] As a counterbalance to this, progressive spiritual groups typically emphasize the importance of the open and ongoing spiritual search over and against simple reliance on religious certainties. The sixth of the eight grounding principles of the US-based Center for Progressive Christianity therefore states that 'by calling ourselves Progressive, we mean that we are Christians who find more grace in the search for understanding than we do in dogmatic certainty – more value in questioning than in absolutes'.[23] A related point is that the insistence on the timeless truth of central religious doctrines is unhelpful when it becomes increasingly difficult to relate traditional beliefs meaningfully to contemporary experience and understandings of the world.[24]

In light of these failings of traditional religion, it is therefore argued that a new spirituality is needed which better addresses the needs, concerns, knowledge and experiences of life at the start of the twenty-first century. As Richard Holloway suggests, this process is analogous to the notion of paradigm shifts in scientific thinking developed by the philosopher Thomas Kuhn.[25] The data of contemporary life no longer fits the paradigm of traditional religion, and this creates pressure for a new spiritual paradigm to be developed which takes better account of contemporary experiences, values and concerns.

From a sociological perspective, it is important to recognize that this perception of an upsurge in spiritual searching – and the failings of traditional religion to address this – functions as an important narrative in the rhetorical world of progressive spirituality. This narrative doubtless gains its vitality from individuals' own struggles with conservative forms of religion,[26] and often finds support in a range of anecdotal evidence. What is neglected, however, is the fact that although the term 'spirituality' has clearly become common currency, there is no consistent empirical evidence of a substantial level of spiritual seeking outside of organized religion. In their recent study of religion and spirituality of the British town of Kendal, Paul Heelas and Linda Woodhead discovered that although the 'holistic milieu' of alternative spiritualities in Kendal had grown rapidly since the 1970s, only 1.6 per cent of the town's population were still actively involved in group activities associated with new, holistic spiritualities. Similarly, whilst the research of Robert Wuthnow and Wade Clark Roof indicates the rise of a spirituality of seeking in an 'expanded religious marketplace' in America since the 1960s, their work also suggests that this spirituality of seeking is just as likely to lead people into conservative forms of religion as other progressive alternatives. Indeed the capacity of traditional religious groups to adapt to this culture of spiritual seeking – famously through the seeker services of the Willow Creek Church, the Alpha Course, and other forms of experimentation with the 'emergent church' – is wholly ignored within this progressive spiritual perspective. The narrative of 'empty churches and crowded [spiritual] pathways'[27] thus provides an important context and rationale for the development of progressive spirituality. But this narrative is as much, if not more, an expression of the cultural and religious imagination of religious and spiritual progressives as an accurate sociological description of contemporary culture.

ii)   Progressive spirituality has arisen out of various initiatives to develop a spirituality that is not bound up with patriarchal beliefs and structures, and which can be a relevant and liberating resource for women.

With the rise of the third wave of feminism in the 1960s and 1970s came a growing critique of traditional Jewish and Christian religion. Growing numbers of feminist writers observed the way in which the patriarchal language of this religion (e.g. God as male ruler) played an ideological role in validating religious and wider social structures in which men were dominant and women were marginalized and even demonized.[28] Such patriarchal symbol systems functioned on the basis of dualities such as soul/body, spirit/flesh, rationality/

emotion, righteousness/sin and divine/nature in which men were typically identified with the more positive pole and women with the negative one.[29] Traditional religion was therefore bound up with cultural ideologies and social structures which limited the possibilities for women's lives, excluded them from power, and perpetuated the sense that to be female was inferior to being male. As Heather Eaton observes, this was religion based on a 'logic of domination' that excluded not only women, but also other social groups vulnerable on account of their ethnicity, class or sexual orientation.[30] Furthermore, because of this patriarchal bias, traditional religion could not properly serve women's needs for religious ritual, symbols and myth that gave adequate expression to their experience or offered a healthy basis for their understanding of themselves, the world or the divine.[31]

Women's experience of the issues at stake here were far from abstract. Feminist writers found confirmation of the patriarchal nature of religious institutions as they began to publish their critiques. Probably one of the best-known cases involved Mary Daly, a pioneer in feminist theology, who found her teaching contract at the Catholic Boston College terminated in 1969 following the publication of her book, *The Church and the Second Sex*.[32] Daly was subsequently reinstated – and given tenure – following a series of campus protests, but the institutional resistance to her ideas had been clearly dramatized. Often less public were many women's struggle for self-esteem and a meaningful spiritual framework for their lives in the face of a religious ideology that gave them little freedom or sense of their inherent value – a process which, for some, was bound up with depression, anxiety and eating disorders.[33]

A significant imperative behind the development of progressive spirituality has therefore been the move to develop forms of spirituality that are relevant to the needs and experiences of women. Indeed some of the most important writers involved in shaping progressive spiritualities have been women forging various forms of feminist spirituality both within and beyond traditional religious institutions. The impetus behind this movement was to develop forms of spirituality that offered women significant alternatives to the 'prefabricated identities'[34] normally offered to them by religious traditions, which challenged the old dualities of patriarchal religion,[35] and which could provide a spiritual framework based on women's authentic experience and full humanity. For many, this work was not an incidental part of the struggle for women's liberation – a side interest for those with particular niche interests in religion – but a central element of that struggle. Mary Daly, for example, has argued for seeing 'women's liberation as spiritual revolution', because greater freedom, power and self-expression for women would require nothing less than a renewed spiritual vision of what it means to be truly and fully human.[36]

The search for new feminist spiritualities has taken a range of different forms. Some writers, for example, Rosemary Radford Ruether and Elizabeth Schussler Fiorenza, have tried to reconstruct a feminist theology from within the Christian tradition. Others, like Carol Christ and Zsuzsanna Budapest, have rejected institutional religion and turned instead to goddess spirituality and feminist Wicca respectively. Although part of this work has involved an academic critique of religious traditions, it has also led to the formation of new groups and networks involved in developing and practising these new spiritualities, such as the Woman-Church movement and Dianic Wiccan covens. Creating new rituals and religious liturgies has also been an important element in this work, as women have sought to find new forms of religious language that can adequately house and express their spiritual experience and aspirations.[37]

One of the leading edges of the search for appropriate language and symbols for feminist religious expression has been the (re)turn to various forms of goddess spirituality, and a move from *theology* to *thealogy*, as the study of the female divine.[38] A number of feminist writers have argued that pre-biblical human societies were matriarchal (or matrifocal),[39] egalitarian and focused around the worship of the Goddess, as the sustaining and nurturing spirit of the earth.[40] In their influential book, *The Great Cosmic Mother*, Monica Sjoo and Barbara Mor argue that paleo-archaeological evidence of religious shrines and devotional statues of the female body indicate that 'the first "God" was female'[41] – a state of affairs that persisted for the first 200,000 years of human life on Earth. It was only with the relatively recent displacement of this Goddess with the male God

– as part of the male-led ideological struggle to replace matriarchal society with a patriarchal, hierarchical and militaristic one – that this idyllic, earth-centred religious cult was lost. Whilst the notion of the recovery of an ancient goddess cult has been important for many feminists, it has also proven to be controversial – not least amongst those feminist anthropologists and archaeologists who have described it as an imagined history with much less corroborative evidence than its advocates suggest.[42] Rosemary Radford Ruether has suggested that the idea of an ancient goddess cult may be helpful not so much as literal history but as a possible grounding myth for feminist spiritualities developed outside institutional religion.[43] Mary Daly has also counselled against replacing the noun 'God' with the noun 'Goddess' – a process she describes as 'a transsexual operation on the patriarchal god', which risks being 'a mere semantic shift... unaccompanied by profound alteration of behaviour or consciousness'.[44] For Daly, the value of developing the religious language of the Goddess can only be demonstrated through its practical effects on women's lives. Advocates of goddess spirituality, however, argue that this is precisely why the language of the divine as goddess can be so valuable. As Starhawk, a leading figure in the development of feminist Wicca, asserts, 'the image of the Goddess inspires women to see ourselves as divine, our bodies as sacred, the changing phases of our lives as holy, our aggression as healthy, our anger as purifying, and our power to nurture and create, but also to limit and destroy when necessary, as the very force that sustains all life. Through the Goddess, we can discover our strength, enlighten our minds, own our bodies, and celebrate our emotions. We can move beyond narrow, constricting roles and become whole.'[45]

The attempt to move beyond patriarchal religion to authentic feminist spiritualities has not been without its tensions. Fierce disagreements have taken place as to whether religious traditions such as Christianity and Judaism can really be rehabilitated through a feminist reconstruction or whether anything other than a completely new spirituality – or a completely archaic return to the pre-biblical goddess cult – means propping up an inherently oppressive religious system. The desire for a spirituality that is true to women's experiences also raises serious questions about what constitutes an 'authentic' experience for women and what feelings and aspirations might still be the product of a false consciousness generated by patriarchal society.[46] The notion of 'women's experience' as a generic category has also come under criticism from those who note that social class, cultural and ethnic identities also produce quite different kinds of experience.[47] Furthermore, the role of magic within feminist spirituality is contested, even amongst those who identify themselves with non-institutional forms of goddess spirituality.[48] Whilst these questions persist, Rosemary Radford Ruether detects a new spirit of ecumenism within feminist spirituality, a more inclusive approach that sees valid feminist spiritualities within and beyond a range of religious traditions.[49] Within such ecumenism lies the potential for a new religious movement that transcends the boundaries of existing religious institutions and traditions – a movement within which progressive spirituality is the underpinning ideology.

iii) Progressive spirituality has arisen out of attempts to reconcile religion with contemporary scientific knowledge, and in particular in attempts to ground spirituality in a contemporary scientific cosmology.

A third imperative that consciously motivates some advocates of progressive spirituality is the need to have a spiritual or religious view of life that is properly related to scientific understandings of the origins and nature of the universe. In his best-selling treatise on theological liberalism, *Honest to God*, Bishop John Robinson began by observing how much the notion of a 'three-decker universe' (heaven, Earth and the waters under the Earth) influenced the language of the biblical writers.[50] The consequence of this, Robinson noted, was a persistent sense in subsequent Christian thinking that even if God was not literally 'up there' in heaven, then He was at least 'out there' somewhere in or beyond the universe. Such a concept, Robinson argued, was no longer tenable in an age of scientific and psychological discovery, in which no home for God could be found in the universe and the suspicion grew that the God 'out there' was as much a projection of the human mind as a metaphysical reality.

What new ways of speaking of God could be found in the midst of this crisis of credibility? How could the 'false dichotomy between spirit and science'[51] that had grown since Darwin published *The Origin of Species* be bridged? With the surprising return of spirituality and the sacred in public discourse in the decades since Robinson wrote *Honest to God*, a parallel concern has also been raised. Can we have a truly humane science if it does not allow for humanity's enduring religious concerns? How can science – 'our most credible modern religion'[52] as Deepak Chopra puts it – contribute to a constructive, progressive spirituality? The quest to reconnect science and religion is therefore not only a search for a faith that is scientifically credible, but also a quest for what David Ray Griffin has called the 're-enchantment of science'.

Since Robinson made these comments in 1963, there have been ongoing attempts to integrate spiritual and scientific understandings of the cosmos. One of the best-known of these attempts is Fritjof Capra's book *The Tao of Physics*, first published in 1975. Capra's ideas were sparked by his long-standing interest in mysticism alongside his work as a physicist, which crystallized in a moment of mystical enlightenment:

> Five years ago, I had a beautiful experience which set me on a road that has led to the writing of this book. I was sitting by the ocean one late summer afternoon, watching the waves rolling in and feeling the rhythm of my breathing, when I suddenly became aware of my whole environment as being engaged in a giant cosmic dance. Being a physicist, I knew that the sand, rocks, water and air around me were made of vibrating molecules and atoms, and that these consisted of particles which interacted with one another by creating and destroying other particles. I knew also that the Earth's atmosphere was continually bombarded by showers of "cosmic rays", particles of high energy undergoing multiple collisions as they penetrated the air. All this was familiar to me from my research... but until that moment I had only experienced it through graphs, diagrams and mathematical theories. As I sat on that beach my former experiences came to life; I "saw" cascades of energy

coming down from outer space, in which particles were created and destroyed in rhythmic pulses; I "saw" the atoms of the elements and those of my body participating in this cosmic dance of energy; I felt its rhythm and I "heard" its sound, and at that moment I *knew* that this was the Dance of Shiva, the Lord of Dancers worshipped by the Hindus.[53]

Capra's book – an extended discussion of analogies between discoveries in quantum physics and concepts from eastern mysticism – found company in the work of other physicists who have made links between their work and mysticism. In 1980, the quantum theorist David Bohm published *Wholeness and the Implicate Order*, in which he argued for the need for a new scientific and cultural world view which emphasized the harmony and interdependence of all reality.[54] Such a world view, Bohm suggested, could emerge out of the recognition of the common ground of reality – a higher-dimensional implicate order which organizes the enfolding and unfolding cosmos – a grounding reality that draws together and sustains all that exists.[55] Since then, the cosmologist Paul Davies, who feels no personal need for religious explanations for the cosmos, has also suggested that mysticism could possibly be a means of directly apprehending the one, interdependent reality towards which contemporary physics points but which no single theory can fully describe.[56]

Attempts to build the bridge between science and spirit have also been pursued by non-scientists.[57] The Catholic eco-theologian, Thomas Berry, has argued that contemporary science is beginning to offer a new story of the universe as an emerging, meaningful, creative process that can serve as the basis of an ecologically oriented moral and spiritual life.[58] With cosmologist Brian Swimme, Berry wrote *The Universe Story*, an attempt to construct a new creation myth based on contemporary scientific knowledge, which can help to make sense of humanity's place within the evolving universe. Through telling this myth, they hope to clarify the perilous choice currently facing humanity between a Technozoic era of self-destructive environmental exploitation for the sake of economic gain or an Ecozoic era based on conscious management of relations within the ecosystem for the benefit of the whole.[59] A similar interest in the importance of the story of the universe, based on contemporary scientific knowledge, has been shown by the leading architect and cultural theorist, Charles Jencks. Jencks' work on postmodern architecture in the late 1970s had played a pioneering role in disseminating 'postmodernism' as a cultural concept.[60] When reviewing the rise of postmodernism some twenty years later, though, Jencks claimed that the postmodern era should not be one in which all meta-narratives collapse, but in which a new meta-narrative – the story of the universe – comes to the fore.[61] This idea has since taken material form in Jencks' landscape gardening project – the 'Garden of Cosmic Speculation' in Scotland – in which the design of the garden is intended to symbolize current scientific understandings of the origins and nature of the universe.[62] Through creating this garden, Jencks hoped to contribute to a much wider task of giving cultural expression to the new truths we are learning in 'the greatest age of discovery' about the cosmos that we inhabit.[63]

Attempts to integrate the spiritual and the scientific have focused on two particular areas of scientific knowledge which address very different scales of phenomena: quantum physics (which attempts to explore reality at a subatomic level) and complexity theories which embrace the whole history of the universe.[64] Developments in quantum physics, for example, have problematized previous assumptions that it is possible to analyse an atom in terms of the properties and processes of its separate constituent parts. Rather than functioning like solid machines, made up of separate identifiable components, atoms operate as complex, interdependent systems whose specific form varies according to their environment.[65] The behaviour of the atom is not the simple effect of prior causes (like billiard balls rebounding off each other),[66] and the form of the atom even changes when it is subjected to external observation. Furthermore, the atom is not a solid entity, as theorists from Democritus to Newton had suggested. Indeed the space between the nucleus of an atom and its orbiting electrons is analogous to a crowd in a football stadium cheering the passage of a marble-sized football. The atom is therefore not solid, but is primarily comprised of space or, more accurately, fields of energy.[67] The study of the smallest components of the cosmos thus reveal that reality is not an elaborate structure built out of the tiny Lego bricks of subatomic particles. Indeed our sense of a stable, material universe made up of distinguishable components is an arbitrary interpretation of reality. As Fritjof Capra states, 'whatever we call a part is merely a pattern that has some stability and therefore captures our attention'.[68] What we perceive as real, stable objects are, to use Capra's phrase, multiple manifestations of the dynamic and unfolding dance of cosmic energy in which forms emerge, disintegrate and then shift into other forms.[69] In place of our conventional sense of a solid universe, quantum physics suggests that reality is made up of dynamic and ever-changing interrelated systems and fields of energy, in which the distinction between the observer and the observed breaks down. We are left, in David Bohm's words, with a vision of 'merging and interpenetrating aspects of one whole reality, which is indivisible and unanalysable'.[70] The fundamental spiritual lesson that writers such as Capra and Bohm draw from this is that we live in an interdependent, cosmic unity. As we shall see in the next chapter, this notion contributes to the particular understanding of God, or the divine unity, that has developed within progressive spirituality.

The second focus for bridging spiritual and scientific understandings of the cosmos relate to theories of complexity, emerging out of attempts to understand the history of the origins and subsequent development of the universe. One possible metaphor for understanding the cosmos is to liken it to an old-fashioned mechanical watch, whose mechanism was wound up with the original events that led to the emergence of the cosmos, but which is now inevitably running down, subject to the laws of entropy. An alternative view is that we live in, what Louise Young has called, an 'unfinished universe',[71] a creative cosmic work in progress that is highly suited to the formation of increasingly complex forms of life and consciousness.[72] The widely accepted account of the origin of the universe – emerging out of an initial event some 13 or 14 billion years ago – can indeed be read in ways that support this more optimistic view. As Paul Davies says, the very existence of life emerging out of this process 'seems to depend on a number of fortuitous coincidences that some scientists and philosophers

have hailed as nothing short of astonishing'.[73] Amongst these
coincidences we could include the fine, and exceedingly improbable,
balancing of forces in the milliseconds after the 'big bang' which
meant that the expanding universe neither blew apart nor collapsed
back into itself.[74] Similarly, the subsequent formation of first- and
then second-generation stars provided both a highly unusual and
uniquely suitable environment for the creation of heavy elements
such as carbon, which subsequently became the basis of organic
life.[75] Beyond this, the cosmos has unfolded on the basis of a set of
laws that provide an orderly context in which life can emerge and
evolve. Paul Davies has commented that, whether or not we believe
in a divine designer – a belief he himself considers unnecessary –
we nevertheless see all the signs of living in a 'designer universe',
organized in ways that encourage the increasing complexity of life.
Rather than a picture of bleak nihilism, in which humanity finds itself
stranded in an arbitrary and meaningless cosmos, this alternative
view places humanity in the context of a meaningful universe story.
Instead of being 'condemned to freedom' in an existential void,
humanity finds itself at a moment in the story of the cosmos in
which the universe has nurtured consciousness and become aware
of itself.[76] How humanity chooses to exercise this consciousness
will determine the extent to which it plays a constructive role in the
ongoing creative process of the unfolding universe. Again, in the
next chapter, we will see how this particular understanding of the
cosmos encourages particular views of God, or the divine energy,
within progressive spirituality. It is worth noting the irony, though,
that science – in the form of quantum physics and complexity
theories of the cosmos – may no longer be a so much of a force for
secularization as an important influence in the re-sacralization of
the universe.

There are, of course, tensions in trying to build such bridges
between scientific theory and discovery and a spiritual understanding
of existence. Linking science with spirituality can be seen by some
scientists as an unwelcome distortion of the scientific task and
methods. There is indeed a danger, as Richard Roberts observes,[77]
that building a set of metaphysical beliefs on the basis of scientific
theory will hinder the open scientific enquiry needed to modify and

perhaps even overthrow that particular theory. When religious or spiritual orthodoxy of any kind hinders open scientific study, bad science is likely to be the result. Some advocates of progressive spirituality are aware of this danger, however. Fritjof Capra has, for example, argued that whilst scientific developments may well lead to renewed understanding of quantum physics, it is highly unlikely that future discoveries will contradict the idea that we live in an interdependent and dynamic universe.[78] Others recognize the provisional nature of any scientific knowledge, yet claim that building a cultural and spiritual awareness on the basis of such knowledge is part of the human condition in which we only ever see through a glass darkly. According to Charles Jencks, we are simply one link in the evolving chain of understanding the universe, and we can only operate on the basis of our current knowledge, knowing that future generations will be able to see more clearly the truths and falsehoods in our current perspectives.[79]

iv) Progressive spirituality has arisen out of moves to develop a spirituality which reflects a healthy understanding of the relationship of humanity to the wider natural order and which motivates constructive action to prevent ecological catastrophe.

A further rationale that drives the development of progressive spirituality is the awareness of impending global catastrophe caused by the harm done to the environment by modern, industrialized societies. The key ecological issues in popular consciousness have changed over the past forty years since Rachel Carson published her warning of ecological apocalypse, *The Silent Spring*, in 1963. Concerns about deforestation, acid rain and the depletion of the ozone layer have shifted more recently to global warming and environmental refugees, and the end of the twentieth century saw fears about an environmental apocalypse displace previous anxieties about a nuclear apocalypse. Issues of religion and spirituality have become deeply implicated in debates about environmental attitudes and ethics. In an influential article published in 1967, Lynn White Jr made the claim that traditional western Christian beliefs about the dominion of humanity over nature were a significant cultural factor behind the contemporary ecological crisis. Through the belief that nature was subservient to human well-being, White argued that the Christian tradition had played an important role in nurturing an instrumental view of the natural world as raw material to be exploited for human benefit. Describing Christianity as 'the most anthropocentric religion the world has seen', White suggested that only a fundamental shift in beliefs about the world could avert environmental catastrophe: 'since the roots of our trouble are so largely religious, the remedy must also be essentially religious.'[80]

White's critique was highly influential in provoking religious scholars from a range of traditions – not just Christian – to examine how their core traditions could be read in ways that supported constructive views of the natural world and encouraged environmental concern. By the mid 1990s, this academic activity became focused around a series of major international conferences organized by the Harvard University Center for the Study of World Religions,[81] in which each conference focused on the ecological aspects of different major religious traditions – a process which Rosemary Radford Ruether refers to as the greening of the world religions.[82] Debates about religion and ecology did not lead simply to 'greener' understandings of traditional religious teaching (for example, an emphasis on Christian stewardship of nature rather than dominion), but to calls to develop wholly new philosophical and spiritual perspectives on the place of humanity within the natural order.[83] One expression of this was the development of 'deep ecology', an ideology inspired initially by the work of the Norwegian philosopher, Arne Naess.[84] In contrast to 'shallow' ecology, an anthropocentric perspective in which environmental action arises out of a primary concern for human well-being, deep ecology is a biocentric approach in which human life is seen as simply one element in the larger ecosystem.[85] Shallow ecology places humanity above or outside nature, and encourages ecological concern out of human self-interest. Deep ecology sees humanity as simply one part of the greater 'web of life' (to use Capra's phrase), which is to be valued as a whole system in its own right. In its more spiritual forms, deep ecology recognizes the importance of mystical states of consciousness in which the individual person achieves a sense of their deeper unity with all that is. It has also found more common ground with eastern religious concepts of the fundamental unity of existence than with traditional western concepts of a transcendent God who stands above and beyond nature.

Another important example of the new spiritual ideology generated out of a response to ecological crisis is Matthew Fox's 'creation spirituality'.[86] Fox's perspective, rooted in Christian mysticism and a regard for nature-centred indigenous religions, emphasizes the idea that spirituality should emerge out of cosmology. In other words, the human story needs to be placed in the wider context of the story of the evolving universe. Within this cosmological story, humans find themselves called to accept both the wonder and suffering of creation, and to live creatively, compassionately and justly. Humanity becomes co-creators in the ongoing divine process of creation in the emerging cosmos. Such a perspective rejects the anthropocentrism of pragmatic environmental concern for a deeper spiritual vision of the fundamentally interconnected nature of all reality and a proper understanding of the human place within this wider story. The divine is no longer placed in a realm above and beyond the natural world, nor located simply in the person of Jesus, but is spread throughout the emerging cosmos. Creation spirituality, then, 'truly honors the soil as a divine locus'.[87]

It is worth noting that such ecological philosophies and spiritualities have not been uncontroversial. Matthew Fox has been unpopular amongst his some of his erstwhile peers in the Catholic Church. His decision to employ Starhawk as a tutor at his Institute in Culture and Creation Spirituality drew criticism from religious conservatives unhappy that a Wiccan should be associated with Fox's teaching programme. Fox's theology was subsequently investigated by the then Cardinal Ratzinger – now Pope Benedict XV – and he was subject to a year's silencing from the Vatican in 1989 before being dismissed from his Dominican Order in 1993. Deep ecology has also been subject to criticism, including criticism from the political left. Ramachandra Guha and Juan Martinez Alier have, for example, argued that deep ecology's emphasis on biocentric well-being rather than human well-being has led to cases

where western ecological groups have insisted on the creation of
environmental zones in developing countries which have displaced
and significantly disadvantaged poor communities living in those
areas. At its worst, Guha suggests, deep ecology represents a
vague mysticism which offers an inadequate analysis of the social
and economic roots of environmental exploitation and whose
idealization of eastern religious thought represents simply another
version of Orientalism.[88] Nevertheless, deep ecology and Fox's
creation spirituality remain important attempts to offer spiritual and
philosophical responses to the contemporary ecological crisis, and
they remain highly influential sources for progressive spirituality.

So far, then, we have identified four different reasons why
advocates of progressive spirituality claim that developing this
new religious ideology is an urgent task. Indeed its advocates claim
that what makes this spirituality *new* is precisely that it represents
a coherent and constructive response to the particular ecological,
social and cultural challenges of our times.[89] Progressive spirituality
rests on the recognition that these challenges demand a radically
different kind of religious response to that of traditional religious
conservatism. Whilst its advocates may adopt differing strategies in
deciding whether, and how, to lay claim to earlier religious traditions
– and indeed which traditions to lay claim to – there is a shared
sense that the imperatives described above demand a new spiritual
perspective. Identifying these imperatives also helps to clarify the
kinds of individuals and groups who are now coalescing around
progressive spirituality: liberal Christians, Muslims and Jews critical
of restrictive, literalist, conservative interpretations of their faith;
spiritual feminists and women seeking a more constructive spiritual
framework for their lives; and people drawn to various forms of
nature religion, including contemporary forms of Paganism and
Wicca.

As our discussion has developed, it has also become clearer that
these imperatives – and the progressive responses to them – are
far from being isolated points of concern. Indeed for most spiritual
progressives, they are significantly interrelated. For example, eco-
feminist theology/thealogy sees a common 'logic of domination'
behind the exclusion of women and other marginalized groups,

together with the instrumental exploitation of the Earth's natural resources.[90] All rest on the assumption of a patriarchal hierarchy which makes use of whatever human or other natural resources that it needs to perpetuate itself with little regard to the effects of this exploitation. Eco-feminists draw on the ground-breaking work of writers like Radford Ruether, Daly, Starhawk and Carol Christ (each of whom have made significant connections between feminist and ecological insights), the new cosmology constructed by writers like David Bohm and Thomas Berry, as well as deep ecology and Fox's creation spirituality, to construct their spiritual responses to our contemporary social situation.[91] These progressive concerns and ideas thus become intertwined. As one teenage Wiccan told Catherine Edwards Sanders, 'After I read the book about love spells, what really began to attract me was that Wicca respects nature, that God is in nature, that it focuses on protecting the environment, and that it empowers women.'[92]

In recent years, a growing awareness of a common agenda of concerns has led to what Radford Ruether has referred to as a new spirit of ecumenism, 'in which all movements that seek a feminist earth-renewal spirituality in various traditions can see one another as partners'.[93] Tensions that have previously hindered such collaboration – such as the dichotomous thinking amongst some feminists of Paganism as inherently good and Christianity as inherently bad – appear to be softening. Radford Ruether thus calls progressive Christians to defend the civil liberties of Pagans and Wiccans because all share a commitment to the same 'life-affirming values'.[94] Judith Plaskow has similarly criticized 'Jewish anti-Paganism' in both the Torah and subsequent Jewish theology.[95] As we shall see in the coming chapters, fresh attempts are also being made to develop closer collaboration amongst those sympathetic to progressive spirituality through initiatives such as Tikkun's Network for Spiritual Progressives. The new, progressive spirituality therefore represents the developing ideology of a new phase of organization of the religious Left in western society, and it is to an overview of this ideology that we will now turn.

2 The ideology of progressive spirituality

In this chapter, I now want to turn to a description of the key ideas, beliefs and values within the ideology of progressive spirituality. A note of caution needs to be sounded before embarking on this, however. To focus on progressive spirituality as a religious ideology carries the risk of equating 'religion' with 'world view'. To assume that religions or spiritualities function as world views is a well-trodden path by many social scientists and religious scholars,[1] but is also a problematic one.[2] Ethnographic and other empirical studies often show that members of religious groups do not necessarily support the espoused religious ideology or world view of their group in straightforward ways. People may participate in religious groups and activities for reasons quite different to those of supporting that group's world view.[3] Indeed 'religions' may be more useful for people as a source of relationships and resources that they can use in different ways, depending upon their particular needs and circumstances. Similarly, people may buy books or other media that promote a particular religious ideology, but not fully 'buy into' the ideology itself.[4] It would therefore be a mistake to assume that the ideology of progressive spirituality is universally shared by everyone who participates in the wider progressive milieu or by everyone who consumes media that promote this spirituality: not least because of the strong emphasis on embracing theological diversity in some progressive groups.[5] What I am introducing here is a cluster of related ideas and values that recur with striking regularity in books, articles and websites that seek to cultivate a progressive or holistic spirituality, but which should not be seen as a monolithic world view to which all those sympathetic to this spirituality necessarily subscribe in every detail. Using the term 'ideology' to describe this cluster of ideas and values points to the fact that it is a way of understanding the world that is actively cultivated by a range of well-known and widely read progressive religious writers and thinkers. These writers form a group of – to borrow Antonio Gramsci's phrase – 'organic intellectuals' whose life and work is embedded within the social structures and relationships of the progressive milieu, and who represent its leading intellectual edge.

My preference, then, is to refer to progressive spirituality as an ideology rather than as a world view. In general, it is more useful to think about religion as a form of 'cultural tool-kit' rather than a world view – a set of conceptual, social and material resources that can be drawn on for different purposes.[6] Or, in Catherine Albanese's terms, it may be more useful to see religions as much as *action* systems as *thought* systems.[7] When thinking about progressive spirituality, it is less useful to see it as the universally held world view of a particular group, and to ask instead what kinds of practices, identities, experiences and relationships the ideology of progressive spirituality makes possible. The value of progressive spirituality for its practitioners lies less in its coherence as a world view or piece of systematic theology, than in its usefulness in shaping meaningful religious identities and rituals, providing a framework for making sense of personal religious experience, and nurturing important relationships and social activism. When reading the following summary of the key tenets of progressive spirituality, it is important not simply to think about these as abstract ideas, but as aspects of a lived ideology that are tied in with different forms of spiritual and cultural practice. Although the key principles of progressive spirituality may be described in abstract, theoretical – and sometimes highly complex – ways by their leading intellectual advocates, it is important still to see these progressive theories in the context of concrete social relations and cultural practices. The core ideas of progressive spirituality do not exist in some abstracted realm of Platonic ideas, but are generated and developed through specific cultural practices such as the publication of books, magazines and websites, and the organization of conferences and workshops. Interest in progressive spirituality is sustained through a range of organizational structures, and finds expression in various forms of related cultural practices such as the creation of new religious rituals, organic agriculture or political activism. How the particular values and beliefs of progressive spirituality relate to particular groups and practices is something that we will begin to explore in more detail in the next chapter.

At one seminar in which I was describing the core elements of the ideology of progressive spirituality, someone asked me how many elements of this ideology a person would have to assent to in order to qualify as a 'spiritual progressive'. Whilst being quite a reasonable question, I think this misunderstands the role of progressive spirituality as a form of religious ideology. By and large, progressive religious groups and networks are not interested in boundary issues of who does and does not properly belong to these groups or who does or does not fall within acceptable boundaries of 'orthodoxy' in progressive faith. Indeed the strong emphasis on tolerance and valuing of diversity amongst progressive groups, means that concerns with tightly maintained boundaries and group orthodoxy tend to be seen as the regressive and unhealthy obsessions of more traditional forms of religion.[8] As we shall also see in the next chapter, progressive religious and spiritual identities are always constructed in a range of different ways, reflecting different local cultural, religious and political contexts. Rather than functioning as a 'statement of faith' to which all religious progressives are expected to sign up, the emerging ideology of progressive spirituality is more of a potential basis for mutual identification, communication and collaboration. Progressive spirituality is important, then, for the shared religious identities, affiliations and practices that it can make possible. The more of the core elements of this ideology that an individual or group assents to, the more it becomes possible for them to utilize this ideology as a basis for mutual identification and collaboration with other like-minded people.

Catherine Albanese has suggested that the three key symbolic centres for religious reflection in western culture have been God, nature and humanity.[9] It is therefore perhaps unsurprising that the following description of key beliefs within progressive spirituality is organized around each of these three centres: a particular understanding of the nature of the divine; the sacralization of nature; and the sacralization of the human self. In addition to these three key themes, a fourth will also be discussed: namely the way in which progressive spirituality understands religious traditions. By the end of this chapter, we will have not only defined key elements of the ideology of progressive spirituality, but will have also started to identify their deeper roots in western culture.

The unity of the ineffable and immanent Divine

A number of different specific conceptions of the divine can be found amongst those who advocate progressive spirituality. Within this range we find the monotheist emphases of Jewish and Muslim progressives, reworkings of Trinitarian theology amongst Christian progressives, various notions of a unitary goddess or range of goddesses in different forms of feminist spirituality, as well as the bi-theism[10] of some forms of Wicca and the polytheism of much contemporary western Paganism. Indeed one of the most striking differences across the different forms of expression of progressive spirituality is that between its monotheist and polytheist versions. Whilst it is often true that monotheistic versions of progressive spirituality tend to be associated with the main Abrahamic faiths, and polytheist versions with contemporary Wicca and Paganism, this generalization does not hold true in every case.[11]

Despite what appears to be quite disparate and unconnected notions of the divine, the emerging ideology of progressive spirituality rests on certain common assumptions about divinity which underpin both its monotheist and polytheist forms. These can be summarized as follows:

The divine is an ineffable unity, and is both the guiding

intelligence behind the evolutionary processes of the universe, and (within) the material form and energy of the universe itself.

Let us unpack this in more detail. Firstly, we have the notion here of the divine as a unity.[12] This represents a basic assumption for those who advocate both monotheist and polytheist versions of progressive spirituality. Amongst the monotheists, it is clearly not controversial to assert the unity of the divine. It is worth noting, though, that amongst progressive Christians this can lead to a stronger emphasis on the oneness of the divine spirit rather than the distinctiveness of the three persons of the Trinity. Jesus thus becomes divine through his participation in the one divine spirit rather than being a distinctive divine figure in his own right. As Adrian Smith puts it, 'Jesus, in his humanity, is one who is transparent to the Divine. God was as fully present and active in Jesus as is possible in human form'.[13] Even within polytheist versions of progressive spirituality, there is still a clear emphasis on the ultimate unity of the divine. For example, from a Wiccan perspective, Vivianne Crowley is critical of the potential for monotheism (particularly focused on a male, patriarchal God) to become exclusivist and intolerant of other ways of conceiving and celebrating the divine.[14] At the same time, however, she notes that beyond the different possible manifestations of the divine lies a single divine reality, 'beyond the distinctions of male and female, beyond polarity and personification'.[15] Progressive spirituality, in its various forms of expression, thus rests on what Neale Donald Walsch refers to as a 'theology of oneness'.[16]

Closely associated with the unity of the divine is an emphasis on the ineffability of the divine – what Thomas Moore refers to as the 'imageless, pure divine spirit'.[17] Carol Christ, whose work has been deeply influential in the development of contemporary goddess spiritualities, has commented that questions about the nature of the divine will probably always remain unanswered. The ineffable mystery of the divine ultimately eludes attempts at definition, though, as she observes, fortunately a clear understanding of the divine is not a pre-condition for encountering it through personal experience or ritual.[18] As we shall see later in this chapter, this emphasis in progressive spirituality on the ineffability of the divine provides an important ideological basis for the progressive view of religions as culturally and historically specific attempts to engage with this single divine mystery.

A second important element in the understanding of divinity within progressive spirituality is that of the divine as the guiding intelligence behind the evolutionary processes of the universe. In the previous chapter, we noted the work of cosmologists such as Louise Young and Paul Davies who have argued that the universe is designed in such a way as to favour the evolution of life and, over time, consciousness itself. Progressive spirituality assumes such a view of the universe of an unfolding, evolutionary project. Within this schema, the divine becomes the intelligence that both sets this project in motion and seeks to guide and sustain it. Deepak Chopra therefore describes God as both the pre-creation state that allows creation to be brought into being and the process of bringing order and development to this evolving cosmos.[19] Within progressive spirituality, therefore, there is a frequent reference to the cosmos as an expression of the divine mind or imagination.[20] The divine underpinning of this cosmic project means that we do not inhabit an empty or meaningless universe, but one which is held together by a divine spirit which offers us the prospect of a constructive future.[21] Such a positive view of the progressive, unfolding universe is tempered, however, by a recognition of the shadow-side of this process. Progressive spirituality is typically sceptical of sanitized, 'fluffy-bunny' new age accounts of this cosmic process, which fail to give proper recognition to the ways in which suffering and death are built into evolution.[22] Instead, progressive spirituality recognizes the often painful cycles of life and death that make this unfolding process possible.[23] As Keith Ward observes, suffering is an inevitable part of human experience, because our frail and open-ended cosmos is, in scientific terms, the only kind of cosmos in which human life could evolve.[24]

This strong emphasis on the unfolding, evolving cosmos within progressive spirituality raises a number of important implications and questions. Given the divine inspiration of this process, it behoves humanity to identify the ways in which the divine spirit is seeking to sustain and guide the ongoing development of the cosmos, and to work in conjunction with this divine impetus. Some advocates of progressive spirituality describe this process in terms of working with the spirit of Gaia[25] or in accordance with the 'universal process of development'.[26] Others talk more in terms of God needing humans to be partners in the process of creation.[27] Underlying this, however, is a shared sense that humans are responsible for acting in ways that support the divine imperative for the unfolding cosmos. The ethics of progressive spirituality – particularly its ecological ethic – is thus grounded in an understanding of the relationship between divinity and cosmic evolution.[28] A further implication of this is that progressive spirituality draws on, and sacralizes, scientific understandings of evolution as an important source for understanding the nature of the unfolding cosmos.[29] Cosmology and evolutionary science therefore form an important source for the ideology of progressive spirituality, and attempts to displace teaching about evolution in schools – or to present creationism as a credible alternative to it – are therefore regarded with considerable concern.[30]

Whilst this shared emphasis on the role of the divine in supporting the unfolding cosmos is a basic characteristic of the emerging ideology of progressive spirituality, it also raises certain unresolved tensions. To what extent is consciousness, and more specifically human consciousness, the pinnacle towards which the evolutionary process has been developing? A range of writers on progressive spirituality celebrate the emergence of human consciousness as the point at which the divine, or the universe, becomes conscious of itself.[31] Such a viewpoint draws criticism from other progressive writers, however, who regard it as too anthropocentric a view of the cosmos – something that deep ecology has been strenuously seeking to avoid.[32] A more modest perspective, proposed by the Jewish progressive Michael Lerner, is that we see humanity as just one example of God becoming self-conscious, in which many different forms of such divine self-consciousness have and will emerge in the history of the cosmos.[33] Lerner adds that such modesty is required, not least because humanity has so far made such a poor job of such consciousness of the divine to date. This is echoed by other writers on progressive spirituality who, whilst recognizing the importance of the evolution of consciousness, acknowledge that humanity is neither the end point of this evolutionary process[34] nor indispensable to the cosmos if we continue to prove unable to live in ecologically sustainable ways.[35]

The notion that humanity is not the final pinnacle of the evolutionary process raises further questions about the directions this process may take in the future. A further tension within progressive spirituality concerns the role of technology in future evolution. The progressive emphasis on the ongoing development of consciousness could be seen as open to ideas about the role of technology in the creation of the 'post-human' cyborg as the next phase in this process. At the same time, however, some writers within progressive spirituality are highly critical of new technologies – what Mary Daly calls 'necrotechnology'[36] – as a source of spiritual evolution. What this tension indicates is that whilst belief in the divinely inspired process of cosmic evolution is a fundamental tenet of progressive spirituality, the exact nature of this evolutionary process and what it means to nurture it, is still contested. In practice, this means that the positive perspective on the evolutionary process in progressive spirituality still allows for a considerable diversity of philosophical and moral views.

In addition to seeing the divine as the mind, imagination or spirit that creates and sustains the unfolding cosmos, progressive spirituality also identifies the divine with (or within) the material form and energy of the universe itself. The divine cannot therefore be separated from material reality. Material reality is therefore a theophany – a manifestation of divinity[37] – and the physical senses become a crucial medium for the personal encounter with the divine.[38] Rather than simply equating the divine with physically observable objects (for example, rocks, trees, animals, people), progressive spirituality often refers to the divine as energy. Drawing on ideas from quantum physics of the cosmos as a field of energy,[39] progressive spirituality identifies the divine as the energy that vitalizes the universe and that is the motivating force behind all that gives life and health.[40] Or, simply stated, in Neale Donald Walsch's words, 'life is God, made manifest'.[41]

The understanding of the divine as both the creative imagination behind the unfolding cosmos, and the life-sustaining presence of the cosmos itself, performs a central function in the ideology of progressive spirituality. One of the fundamental concepts of God that progressive spirituality seeks to overturn is what Neale Donald Walsch refers to as a 'theology of separation'[42] in which God exists as a separate entity or being, removed and distant from us. From a progressive perspective, the notion of a transcendent God has all too often become associated with patriarchal, hierarchical forms of religion, in which men codify religious belief and practice on the basis of fixed, authoritative revelations of the divine will. To use Walsch's phrase, 'we need a new God'; an understanding of the divine which validates embodied human experience, offers non-patriarchal models for social relations and inspires people to face the serious challenges of contemporary global society.

Pantheism/Panentheism

By conceiving of the divine as both the imagination behind the cosmos and the life-sustaining energy of the cosmos, progressive spirituality seeks to replace the image of a transcendent, patriarchal view of God with a pantheist or panentheist notion of the divine.[43] From this perspective, the divine life is bound up with the life of the cosmos. God is no separate entity, far removed from the cosmos, but deeply bound up with its fabric and life. The divine is that in which all things live and move and have their being.[44]

Defining whether progressive spirituality is pantheist or panentheist is somewhat problematic. Different writers on progressive spirituality identify themselves with either position, with Wiccan and Pagan writers tending towards pantheism[45] and members of the Abrahamic faiths (as well as some writers on goddess spirituality such as Carol Christ) preferring panentheism.[46] Other writers on progressive spirituality do not use either term at all. To make matters more complex, some writers identify themselves with one position whilst talking in ways that seem to reflect the other. Vivianne Crowley, for example, equates Wicca with pantheism,[47] but then has also written about the divine as being both transcendent and immanent[48] – the language of panentheism. In practice, the pantheist and panentheist forms of progressive spirituality have much in common.[49] Pantheists often talk about the divine in ways that emphasize its distinctiveness within the cosmos, and panentheists talk in ways that emphasize the immanence of the divine over its transcendence. In practice, technical discussion about the relative merits of pantheism and panentheism is often seen as rather arcane amongst religious progressives. As Diarmuid O'Murchu observes, this debate 'may be of concern to us as humans, but it is unlikely to be of any consequence to the creative life force that impregnates and enlivens our world with prodigious resourcefulness'.[50] The result is a broadly shared discourse amongst religious and spiritual progressives about the divine life being bound up with the unfolding cosmos. For the purposes of describing progressive spirituality, I will reflect the ambiguities of this position by referring to its view of the divine as pan(en)theism.

This pan(en)theist view of the divine is of fundamental importance to progressive spirituality. It subverts patriarchal, transcendent notions of God by asserting that the whole cosmos, including ourselves, participates in the divine life. God is not some holy entity, set apart from us, wholly good in opposition to our inherent badness. Rather, the divine infuses our existence, providing the structure and energy for life itself, and is thus inseparable from the material world and our embodied experiences. God is 'the breath within our breath', as Samina Ali puts it.[51] The divine is thus the source and guarantor of the fundamental goodness of creation. At the same time, however, even pantheist forms of progressive spirituality tend not to equate the divine with everything that is in the cosmos. By not adopting the view that God and the cosmos are one and the same thing, progressive spirituality avoids sacralizing parts of the cosmos that are harmful or degraded. As Rosemary Radford Ruether observes, if we see everything that exists as sacred, then we also make sacred 'great superstructures of dominating power' that oppress humanity and destroy the natural world.[52] By seeing the divine as more than just the physical universe, we can identify it not only as that which sustains the natural cycles and processes of the cosmos, but also as a presence that empowers us to damaging and dehumanizing forces. Or, in Carol Christ's terms, we can understand the Goddess as the

loving persuasion that calls beings to change, as well as being that
which suffers when hurt is caused to the cosmos.[53] As we shall see
later in this chapter, this pan(en)theist view of the divine presence in
the universe, which is both within and beyond us, is of fundamental
significance for the understanding of nature and of the self within
progressive spirituality.

Mysticism and the divine feminine

Before going on to think about progressive views of nature and
the self, two further understandings of the divine in progressive
spirituality need briefly to be addressed. Firstly, progressive
spirituality tends to recognize the importance of mystical union
with the divine.[54] As we have seen, progressive spirituality does
not seclude the divine mystery in some realm far removed from
human experience, but sees it as deeply woven through the fabric
of existence. As a consequence, every person has the potential for
spiritual experience – a sense of connection with this divine energy
and presence.[55] As William Bloom says, 'we are all mystics'.[56] In
part, this mystical experience entails a deeper awareness of one's
authentic self. Through silence and meditation, Deepak Chopra
counsels, it becomes possible to develop a clearer sense of our true
selves as part of the wider divine field of energy.[57] More broadly,
though, such mystical experience can entail a profound sense of
union and merger with the greater divine ground of all existence.

Whilst such mystical experience may take place through
encountering nature, or through periods of silence and meditation,
progressive spirituality also allows for the importance of word,
symbol and ritual as frameworks that allow mystical encounter
with the divine to take place. Mary Daly, for example, has spoken of
the mysticism of words being tied to the mysticism of creation,[58] and
her later writings took increasingly poetic form as invocations to the
divine mystery she has come to refer to as 'quintessence'. In recent
decades, ritual in Pagan and Wiccan contexts has also tended to shift
away from a more traditional focus on fertility rituals to a wider
sense of personal encounter with the divine.[59] As Doreen Valiente
has commented, 'what witches seek for in celebrating these seasonal
festivals is a sense of oneness with Nature, and the exhilaration

which comes from contact with the One Universal Life'.[60]

Progressive spirituality is therefore closely associated with the modern notion of mysticism as a form of universal experience of union with the divine which is found across all human societies, and recognizes the value of particular spiritual and ritual practices in creating the opportunity for such mystical encounters. Again, however, there is considerable diversity amongst religious progressives about the kinds of symbols and ritual practices that people find helpful in this regard. Even within particular religious traditions, there can be strongly contested disputes about appropriate symbolic and ritual forms – such as disputes about the importance of the presence of both men and women at Wiccan ritual.[61] One of the possible effects of progressive spirituality as a religious ideology, though, is that it can generate a sense of shared identity amongst groups who engage in quite different kinds of spiritual and ritual practice. Whilst this shared ideology may not make combined rituals across religious traditions any easier to achieve, it may at least contribute to a spirit of ecumenism amongst religious progressives that recognizes the common ground which they share.

A second, and final, point to be made here relates to this issue of the way in which the divine is symbolized in progressive spirituality. Whilst there is considerable diversity in the way in which religious progressives characterize the divine, from a monist deity to a polytheist pantheon of divine beings, there is one common element to the symbolization of the divine in progressive spirituality. This is, at the very least an openness to, if not an active use of, feminine symbols to express the divine mystery. Feminist theology/thealogy has been deeply influential on the development of progressive spirituality over the past thirty years. As we noted in the previous chapter, the feminist move away from patriarchal religion was in many cases accompanied by a turn to the Goddess – or to many goddesses – as an alternative way of understanding the divine. For many women – who form the largest single constituency of religious progressives groups and networks[62] – approaching the divine as a goddess has proven valuable in developing forms of spirituality that value their experience (including their sexuality), generate constructive self-identities and provide role models for full and authentic lives.[63]

What is striking, however, is how the use of goddess imagery has spread beyond women to be used by male religious progressives as well. Philip Shallcrass writes warmly about his Pagan spirituality which is grounded in reverence for the goddess.[64] From a progressive Catholic perspective, Diarmuid O'Murchu not only commends such language, but argues for the importance of pre-biblical traditions of the worship of the Goddess in guiding contemporary spirituality.[65] Even male writers, who do not make use of goddess language themselves, recognize that it can have an important and necessary place in contemporary progressive spirituality. Michael Lerner declares his personal preference for understanding YHVH as a gender neutral term, 'the unpronounced name that indicates a movement towards the future – the transformation of that which is toward that which can be'.[66] Yet, at the same time, he recognizes the positive role that conceiving the divine in female terms can have for nurturing healthy female spirituality. He asks if God really has no gender and, if 'Hebrew always seems to construe reality in male or female language, why not render God in female language for a few thousand years to make up for the past few thousand years of male language?'[67] Although liberal and progressive religious groups may not always necessarily have been supportive of such feminization of the divine,[68] progressive spirituality as an ideology welcomes the feminine symbolization of the divine as an important part of the shift away from patriarchal religion.

In certain respects, the understanding of the divine within progressive spirituality may not be that surprising to some readers – and hopefully will be easily recognisable to those already familiar with progressive spirituality literature. Certainly for readers who are already aware of wider developments in academic theology, such as process theology, the pan(en)theist view of the divine in progressive spirituality is hardly novel. What is more remarkable, however, is how widely these ideas have spread across and beyond religious traditions. Amongst the writers cited in this section are Jews, Christians, Muslims, Wiccans, Pagans and others associated with holistic spirituality but with no formal religious affiliations. What is emerging here is a common conception of the divine – one which is broad enough to allow for different religious and spiritual practices, but which is also specific enough to provide a shared language for communication and collaboration between religious and spiritual progressives. How this understanding of the divine informs particular views about the self, the world and the nature of religion is where we will turn our attention for the remainder of the chapter.

The sacralization of nature

In his recent book, *Pagan Theology*, Michael York argues that there are two distinctively different types of religion.[69] One type has an instinctively negative view of the material world, and sees salvation in terms of some form of flight from the material into the realm of the spiritual. This type of religion, York suggests, includes many eastern religions, much of western Christianity, as well as other esoteric traditions such as Gnosticism and more recent forms of esoteric New Age thought. The other type of religion affirms the material world and sees the spiritual as deeply embedded within the material. Such religion does not seek salvation or escape from the material, but instead seeks to celebrate and revere the spiritual within the experience of the material universe. Paganism, Wicca and other nature-based religions and spiritualities make up this latter type.

Within York's schema, progressive spirituality clearly falls within the latter of these two types. Nature, within progressive spirituality, is typically seen as sacred, a site of divine life and activity. Given its pan(en)theist view of the divine, progressive spirituality regards the existence of the natural order as only possible through the inspiration of the divine imagination and the enlivening of the divine energy. In Deepak Chopra's words, 'all of creation... is the result of the unmanifest transforming itself into the manifest'.[70] Or, as Vivianne Crowley suggests, 'nature itself is sacred and holy, a manifestation of the Divine Life Force'.[71]

Like other elements of the ideology of progressive spirituality, this emphasis on the sacralization of nature still allows room for a range of different perspectives. At its strongest, the sacralization of nature in progressive spirituality becomes the divinization of nature. In this view, nature is the physical manifestation of the divine spirit and as such is to be treated with the reverence due to the divine. A weaker form of the sacralization of nature makes a clearer separation between the divine and the natural order, whilst still seeing nature as sacred by virtue of it being a site of divine life and activity. Writing from a progressive Christian perspective, Marcus Borg rejects the idea of the universe existing as a separate entity from God and argues instead for seeing God ('as the nonmaterial "ground" of all that is'[72]) continually bringing the universe into existence. Such a view still retains a sense of nature as being sacred – by virtue of it being an ongoing expression of the work of the divine spirit – but does not go as far as to see nature as itself participating in divinity.

These differences between the stronger and weaker forms of the sacralization of nature in progressive spirituality can have significant implications for religious symbolism and ritual practice. Does one construct symbols and rituals that address and revere the divine *in* nature or the divine *behind* nature? In terms of ecological ethics, though, the differences between these stronger and weaker versions of the sacralization of nature have less importance. In regarding nature as sacred, both positions place a strong emphasis on the importance of acting in ways that respect nature and avert the threat of ecological catastrophe. Indeed both forms recognize that the re-sacralization of the natural world is an urgent spiritual task if humanity is to find the necessary moral and cultural resources to turn from its current progress towards ecological ruin and to build sustainable societies. If, as Mircea Eliade suggested,[73] the industrialization of modern societies has left us with a disenchanted world, progressive spirituality sees our only hope in a re-enchantment of the world, a renewed vision of the divine presence within the natural order that can generate new respect for nature and new ways of harmonious living within the natural order.[74] This is not simply a theoretical stance. The emphasis on the sacralization of nature in progressive spirituality finds concrete expression in various forms of environmental activism. These include religious progressives' involvement in direct action against environmental pollution and global warming, experiments in organic farming and permaculture, and the performance of sacred rites for the healing of the Earth.[75] The pan(en)theist vision of the divine in progressive spirituality, bound up with its sacralization of nature, is therefore deeply implicated in the forms of social and political activism in which religious and spiritual progressives engage.

Again it is worth noting that the pan(en)theism of progressive spirituality does not entail the sacralization of everything that exists. The 'nature' that is being sacralized here is typically the natural order that exists outside of the sphere of human cultural activity.[76] Whilst William Bloom claims that everything that exists is sacred, his illustrative list of sacred phenomena – 'every rock, wave, cloud, petal, flame, breeze, animal, mountain, tree, planet, star, galaxy'[77] – is clearly free of human activity or products. Similarly, when advising people on how to sense the presence of the divine spirit in urban environments, Vivianne Crowley suggests that we try to sense the divine presence in the natural world *beneath* the concrete of city streets.[78] The sacred natural order, therefore, is primarily the non-human natural order. It is the spirit of Gaia, the universal movement towards self-regulating and increasingly complex ecological systems, with which humans can either co-operate or resist against.

The sacralization of the self

In the same way that the pan(en)theism of progressive spirituality leads to a positive view of the natural order, so it also leads to a positive understanding of the individual self. In contrast to religious views of the self as inherently flawed or sinful, progressive spirituality sees the self as another manifestation of the divine intelligence and energy. The embodied experience of the self is therefore seen as a more valid source of revelation about the divine than external teachings from scriptures or prophets, and the ongoing development of the self is seen as part of the wider divinely inspired unfolding of the cosmos. Again, let us take time to unpack these ideas in more detail.

Firstly, then, progressive spirituality typically understands the self as an aspect of the divine life. In the same way that progressive spirituality endorses a sacralization of nature, so it also supports the sacralization of the self. Within progressive spirituality, the self is seen as another manifestation of the divine life in the cosmos. The energy and matter from which we are constituted was present at the very moment of creation, and so the very fabric of our individual being is part of the unfolding of the wider cosmos.[79] Human consciousness derives from the greater divine supra-consciousness which holds the evolving cosmos together.[80] Our existence as living beings rests on the ongoing divine life, and every part of who we are is attuned to this divine presence. Progressive spirituality uses a range of images to describe this relationship between the self and the divine. Each person can be seen as carrying a spark of the divine essence,[81] or as containing her own 'inner goddess'.[82] Alternatively, as John O'Donohue suggests, we can understand the human soul as the divine ground in which we both share in the divine spirit and encounter the movement of this spirit in the universe.[83] An important source of connection between the self and the divine emphasized by many writers on progressive spirituality is that of sexuality and the erotic. The erotic energy of the self (understood in a broad rather than just specifically sexual sense)[84] draws from the wider divine, erotic energy of the cosmos. Our erotic energy is thus an expression of the wider divine life,[85] and constructive erotic experience has the potential to draw us into a deeper awareness of the spiritual nature of the universe.[86] This positive view of the erotic in progressive spirituality has an inclusive emphasis. Gay sexuality is thus welcomed as being as much a source of encounter with the divine as heterosexuality.

As with the sacralization of nature in progressive spirituality, the sacralization of the self can stated in strong or weak versions. At its strongest, the self becomes divine. In weaker forms, the self is an expression of divine activity in the cosmos and a sacred site in which the divine can be encountered.[87] Again, as in the case of progressive spirituality's understanding of nature, the differences between the strong and weak versions of the sacralization of the self are arguably less important than their fundamental assertion of the sacredness of the self. The implication of this is that embodied human existence is inherently good, something to be celebrated and enjoyed. Notions of a fundamental alienation from the self and the divine – of being irrevocably cast out from Eden – are rejected in favour of the notion that the divine is 'completely here, close with us'.[88] There is, therefore, no need for us to pursue the divine through special esoteric knowledge or dramatic religious conversions. The divine is already here with us in the very fabric of our beings as human selves. The spiritual journey of the self is therefore not one of trying to cross the chasm between the self and a distant God, but of recognizing the depth of the presence already in our very being. As John O'Donohue remarks, if there is such a thing as a spiritual journey for the self, it 'would be only a quarter-inch long, though many miles deep'.[89]

One important implication of the sacred ground of the self is that embodied experience can be trusted as a revelation of divine truth.[90] This basic concept is expressed in different ways by writers on progressive spirituality. One of the chapters in Carol Christ's seminal work, *Rebirth of the Goddess*, is titled 'Thealogy begins in experience'.[91] Dianne Neu describes 'women's bodies and nature as holy vehicles of divine revelation'.[92] John O'Donohue writes that 'your soul knows the geography of your destiny'.[93] Neale Donald Walsch declares that 'every human being is both the Messenger and the Message'.[94] Emma Restall Orr comments that the Pagan world view in which she shares is characterized by the 'lack of a divine command', and by an emphasis on the importance of 'personal reality in a web of connectivity'.[95] Donna Freitas approvingly cites Elaine Pagels' notion of authority arising out of the experience of human authors: 'we need to remember that we're the authors of our own authority… you can give yourself authority'.[96]

Personal experience thus becomes the authoritative source on which people should build their understandings of divine truth. As Starhawk observes, if the divine is truly ineffable, then direct personal experience of the divine becomes its own authority. No external source can dictate how a particular religious experience should be interpreted.[97] She also affirms the value of constructing religious practices and rituals that are true to our own experience. Rather than relying on fixed traditions – symbols and rituals from the past – we should value our own creative capacity to create new religious forms.[98] Personal experience should also form the basis on which we decide whether a particular set of religious symbols, rituals and practices is helpful and healthy for us or not.[99]

This emphasis on the authority of personal experience raises the problem of whether progressive spirituality risks becoming a purely privatized and atomized religious phenomenon which is unable to sustain forms of collective religious practice. One response to this is to recognize the value of communal traditions and rituals as a framework for deepening and reflecting on personal experience. For example, writing about Paganism, Prudence Jones comments that whilst personal experience is given the greatest authority, Paganism holds together as a form of communal practice through shared rituals which participants are then able to use as a source of individual spiritual experience.[100] Progressive spirituality does not therefore advocate abandoning all communal religious practice in favour of purely personalized rituals or devotions, but recognizes that communal religious practice has a valuable role to play in nurturing individual experience of the divine.

Given the identification of the divine with the evolutionary unfolding of the cosmos in progressive spirituality, a further understanding of the self relates to the moral and spiritual importance of ongoing personal development.[101] Indeed the continued development of one's self is seen, within progressive spirituality, as an integral part of cooperating with the divine evolutionary impetus. One's spiritual development is therefore underwritten by the same divine energy and dynamic that underwrites the emerging complexity of the cosmos.[102]

This evolutionary development of the self is often described within progressive spirituality in terms of the pursuit of the authentic self which is both deeply connected to the divine and is conscious of the implications of this connection. Using language that Paul Heelas has suggested is typical of the wider New Age milieu,[103] writers on progressive spirituality often refer to the 'ego' as the superficial, socialized or false self which overlays the authentic self (which is sometimes referred to as the 'soul').[104] Spiritual development consists of a movement beyond this false ego towards one's true self. Unlike forms of New Age thought which describe this process in terms of a flight from the material to a higher 'spiritual' self, however, progressive spirituality understands this process more in terms of an authentic integration of the self which is conscious of the divine presence within the complexities of embodied experience. As Vivianne Crowley and Joanne Pearson separately state, Wicca does not seek the creation of a perfect life for its adherents, but an integration of one's self with one's shadow.[105] The search of authentic selfhood does not, then, mean an escape into disembodied bliss but a recognition of the depth and complexity of human experience. As Donna Freitas asserts, the spiritual search of the self is ultimately 'about discovering the messier side of the divine: a god/dess that feels, cares, yearns, grieves, and knows when life calls for laughter... one who is alive in all of us'.[106] Through coming to see our full, true humanity, and the ways in which this humanity is interwoven with the divine, we develop a proper perspective on ourselves. Through this process it also becomes possible to have a clearer understanding of our unique place within the cosmos, and the particular kind of service that we can give to others.[107] The move towards authentic selfhood can be helped by particular therapeutic and spiritual resources – including regular self-reflection[108] and constructive religious ritual.[109] But ultimately the move towards authenticity is not so much a striving towards a state as yet unachieved, as it is a process of learning to recognize the true spiritual condition in which we are already living.[110]

The sacralization of the self in progressive spirituality therefore involves the recognition of the sacred ground of our selfhood, a strong emphasis on the authority of personal experience and encouragement to seek authentic selfhood. As with the sacralization of nature, though, the pan(en)theism of progressive spirituality provides an important context for understanding the sacralization of the self. In the same way that material reality and the divine are not simply seen as one and the same thing, so in progressive spirituality there is generally a recognition that the divine is more than just an aspect of the human self. There is something about the divine that is genuinely beyond human being and consciousness. As Deepak Chopra suggests, the power of divine grace in the cosmos is supra-personal, a reality that cannot be reduced to the will or consciousness of the human self.[111] This point is important not only because it assures us that our own personal being is held in a divine ground, or fabric, of being that is greater than all human life, but because it also provides an ongoing challenge to false notions of the self. If the divine is truly ineffable, truly ultimate, then it always challenges us not to become complacent in our limited goals, perceptions and structures.[112] The divine ground of being affirms human existence as good, enlivening our very breath and substance, but it also calls us to humility in the face of the divine reality that is greater than any of our individual beliefs or projects. It challenges us to avoid becoming overly preoccupied with our own concerns and self-development, but to understand our 'big self', as Warwick Fox puts it[113] – the self deeply conscious that is but one part of the wider, interconnected and unfolding cosmos.

Understandings of religion

So far, then, we have seen that progressive spirituality affirms the ineffable divine as both the guiding intelligence and enlivening energy of the cosmos, to be found in the sacred sites of nature and of the self. This fundamental understanding of the relationship between the divine, the cosmos and the self has particular implications for the way in which progressive spirituality perceives religious traditions and positions itself in relation to religious 'others'.

Firstly, the emphasis on the ineffable nature of the divine in progressive spirituality leads to the recognition that all concepts of God, and all systems of religion, are historically and culturally bound attempts to approach the mystery of the divine presence – a mystery which ultimately defies definition.[114] Particular concepts of God are therefore mental representations of the infinite divine, rather than absolute and fixed truths about the nature of divinity.[115] As such, all religious symbols and traditions are seen as partial but potentially helpful ways of conceiving of the divine, and it is not unusual to find writers on progressive spirituality talking about 'drawing wisdom' from these traditions. No single tradition can claim to be the final, authoritative revelation of the divine, however, as all traditions are but incomplete renditions of ultimate truth. Religious symbols are therefore more likely to be treated as metaphorical ways of conceiving the divine, than literal and direct representations of the truth.[116] Neale Donald Walsh offers a clear summary of this view of religion when we writes that 'God and life are One... everything in life is part of a unified whole. Our different religions are merely wonderfully divergent paths to the same destination – a destination the soul does not need to strain to reach, because it is already there in the everlasting embrace of God.'[117]

It is important to note, however, that progressive spirituality does not represent an uncritical welcoming of all religious beliefs and traditions. It is not the superficial tolerance of religious diversity born out of polite, liberal society. Rather, progressive spirituality values religious traditions in so far as they support its core assumptions about the divine, nature and the self. William Bloom, for example, comments that holistic spirituality 'deepens the essence of all religious traditions'[118] – a perspective that Paul Heelas has referred to as 'perennialism'.[119] This notion of the 'essence' of truth within all religious traditions rests on the assumption that religious traditions are meaningful and truthful precisely to the extent that they confirm the basic assumptions of progressive spirituality.

An apparent contradiction could be seen here between the valuing of diverse traditions and perspectives in progressive spirituality and the belief that the core assumptions of progressive spirituality are correct. This is not so much a contradiction, however, as an indication of the way in which progressive spirituality functions as an ideology. What I have described so far in this chapter as the core assumptions of progressive spirituality represent a baseline of common ideas and values that recur throughout the progressive spirituality literature. If one actually reads Starhawk, Marcus Borg, Michael Lerner, Vivianne Crowley, Carol Christ or Neale Donald Walsch, however, one rarely finds these assumptions stated in the abstract terms that I have used here. This is because each of these writers operates within the context of particular religious traditions and symbol systems, whether Christian, Jewish, Wiccan, Pagan or goddess spirituality. Within their work, then, readers will find the core assumptions of progressive spirituality articulated through a range of different religious idioms. The valuing of religious diversity in progressive spirituality comes from the recognition that different religious traditions can be used to articulate the core assumptions within progressive spirituality about the divine, nature and the self. Different traditions might give different emphasis or different inflections to the core ideas and values of progressive spirituality,[120] but this is welcomed in progressive spirituality precisely because humanity is diverse and needs diverse frameworks for its religious and spiritual life. This dual recognition of the core truths of progressive spirituality and the diverse religious paths to these truths is precisely what makes progressive spirituality useful as an ideological basis for mutual identification, communication and collaboration between different religious groups. By offering a set of basic assumptions about the nature of the divine in the cosmos, progressive spirituality provides a common ideological framework within which progressive monotheists, bitheists and polytheists can all find a common home. In doing so, religious progressives acknowledge that their monotheism or polytheism, Christian or Wiccan sensibilities, are second-order expressions of the more fundamental truths towards which progressive spirituality points. The identification, both of common assumptions and the valuing of diverse religious expressions of these basic assumptions, is therefore at the heart of how progressive spirituality as an ideology has the potential to encourage a growing spirit of ecumenism amongst religious and spiritual progressives.

An important implication of this is that writers on progressive spirituality therefore interpret their particular religious and spiritual traditions in ways that support the core assumptions of progressive spirituality. This is arguably not so difficult for writers operating within Wiccan or Pagan contexts, as a belief in the divine presence in the cosmos, and reverence for nature and for the self, have been central emphases in late twentieth-century reconstructions of these traditions.[121] For writers in the main Abrahamic faiths, however, there is a more obvious need to work at developing readings of these traditions that support the core beliefs of progressive spirituality. Sometimes this work will be conceived of in terms of revising religious traditions in line with these contemporary insights. Book titles such as *Why Christianity Must Change or Die* and *Tomorrow's Faith: A New Framework of Christian Belief* reflect this revisionist tone. Others describe this work more in terms of a recovery of ancient religious truths that had been lost through unhelpful accretions of subsequent religious teaching. Marcus Borg's *Meeting Jesus Again for the First Time* and *The God We Never Knew* adopt this tone of recovery, as does Diarmuid O'Murchu's *Reclaiming Spirituality*.

In addition to seeking to revise or to recover the lost essence of religious traditions, progressive spirituality also distinguishes itself very clearly from certain other forms of religion and cultural ideology. Defining these opposing religious and ideological viewpoints plays an important role in giving shape and content to the identity of religious and spiritual progressives.

The form of religion that is most commonly rejected by progressive spirituality is, as we have already noted, hierarchical religion grounded in a belief in a personal God who is removed from the cosmos. William Bloom refers to such forms of religion as being based on the idea of God as 'General in Command' or 'Chief Executive Officer'.[122] Such religion, it is argued, is authoritarian – dictating what kinds of beliefs and lifestyles its adherents should follow. It is patriarchal – using its power structures to reinforce certain assumptions about who should hold power and what kinds of gender and ethnic identities, or sexual orientation, are more inherently valuable than others. It is rigid and inflexible – asserting timeless doctrines and moral codes without asking whether these are meaningful or constructive in a modern context. It inserts the need for religious authorities and institutions for mediating the divine rather than allowing people to pursue their spiritual search on their own terms. It devalues embodied experience and makes us suspicious and guilty about sexuality. It removes the sacred from the cosmos, and in doing so leaves a desacralized world ripe for capitalist, industrialist exploitation. It places salvation in a life and context above and beyond this one, rather than seeing the cosmos as the only real context in which issues of life and death, salvation and grace are worked out. Because of this, it is argued, traditional hierarchical religion has little to offer by way of a framework for an authentic spiritual search or to inspire constructive responses to contemporary problems. Again it is worth remembering that this depiction of hierarchical religion is a construct of the ideology of progressive spirituality. That is not to say that it has no external validity. In many respects it is a construct that can be mapped well on to traditional western religious institutions.[123] But it does not necessarily acknowledge the inventive and more complex forms that neo-traditionalist types of religion, such as Evangelical Christianity, can take as they negotiate the social and cultural challenges of late modernity.

Patriarchal religion is not the only 'other' identified by advocates of progressive spirituality. Of equal concern to them is a secular, instrumental view of the world which sees it as devoid of any sacred significance.[124] Such a philosophy, progressives argue, has depicted nature as a resource to be exploited in pursuit of profit and economic growth. It equates what is valuable with what is measurable. It reduces the body to a machine, requiring only periodic medical attention in the same way that a car requires regular servicing. And it rejects concerns with the religious or spiritual dimension of life as flaky, out of date or as a fringe issue, important only for those with the time and inclination to be interested in it. Such a secular viewpoint, religious progressives argue, suffers from the same fundamental problem of authoritarian, theistic religion, namely, that it banishes the sacred from the cosmos and from the realm of everyday human experience. Even progressive politics – when allied to an arid secularism – can fail to address the deeper spiritual needs of people for a sense of meaning and purpose in the larger story of the cosmos.[125]

A further – and perhaps more surprising – differentiation is also drawn between progressive spirituality and eastern religious traditions. The openness to eastern religious symbols and teaching in the wider progressive milieu of western religion would seem to make such a distinction unlikely. But, drawing on Michael York's schema again, progressive spirituality identifies itself as an earth-based religious outlook that sees the divine within the cosmos as opposed to esoteric traditions which value the spiritual over the material and see salvation in terms of a flight from the material world. On this basis, religious traditions such as Hinduism and Buddhism can be identified more within the esoteric than earth-based categories.[126] As Starhawk comments, there is a profound difference between eastern concepts of the material world as *maya*, an illusion, and the belief in the goddess who is immanent in the cosmos, whose presence affirms the vital importance of what happens in the material world.[127] Eastern religious traditions thus become an 'other' to progressive spirituality when they fail to affirm the presence of the divine in the cosmos and the inherent goodness of nature and the authentic self. This tension is less evident, though, with forms of eastern religion such as Engaged Buddhism and Engaged Hinduism, which are much closer to the broad ethos and political leanings of progressive spirituality. A similar point can be made about 'New Age' spirituality. Some advocates of progressive spirituality are highly critical of what they see as the narcissism, apolitical detachment and implicit patriarchy of New Age thought.[128] New Age beliefs and practices are only consonant with progressive spirituality when they involve a recognition of the sacred nature of material existence, understand the divine as something greater than an aspect of human consciousness, and engage in various forms of activism in support of the divine tendency towards health, justice, sustainability and complexity.[129]

The deeper cultural roots of progressive spirituality

Having offered this review of the key tenets of progressive spirituality, let me say more about its deeper cultural context and sources. Certain generalizations abound about the wider culture of contemporary spiritualities in which progressive spirituality finds its place. One is the idea of spirituality as a pick'n'mix phenomenon, a superficial raiding of religious traditions to suit the needs and tastes of the contemporary consumer in the spiritual marketplace. Often the term 'postmodern' is attached to this type of consumer spirituality, reflecting the personalized construction of meaning in a culture characterized by Lyotard's concept of the 'death of meta-narratives'. Contemporary spirituality – from this critical perspective – is typically incoherent, narcissistic, relativistic, disconnected from wider community and cultural traditions, and an uncritical expression of the cultural assumptions of late capitalism. Another generalization – which we shall consider in a bit more depth in Chapter Four – is the claim of the 'easternization' of the religious landscape of western societies, in which eastern religious beliefs and practices (from reincarnation to yoga) are displacing more traditional forms of western religion.

Neither of these generalizations are particularly helpful for understanding progressive spirituality. To label progressive spirituality as a variant of pick'n'mix spirituality is to miss its underlying coherence, in which belief in the ineffable and immanent divine unity leads both to the sacralization of nature and the self and a recognition of the potential and limitations of all religious traditions. To describe contemporary 'spirituality' as an uncritical expression of late capitalism – as Richard King and Jeremy Carrette do[130] – misses the obvious point that advocates of progressive spirituality are often at the forefront of critiquing the economic injustice and environmental harm caused by capitalism. To see progressive spirituality as the product of some kind of easternization of western religion is also problematic, if pushed too far. Whilst there is clear sympathy with forms of eastern religion within the progressive milieu, progressive spirituality is not the straightforward product of the rise of eastern religion in western societies. As we noted earlier, advocates of progressive spirituality are critical of eastern religions when they are patriarchal or world-denying. But importantly, progressive spirituality is also the expression of longer western cultural and religious traditions.[131]

The western cultural roots of progressive spirituality are varied. Its emphasis on the sacralization of the self, and the authority of personal experience, can be traced back to the Reformation's assertion of personal authority and conscience in the reading of Scripture. As Colin Campbell has argued, the anxious self-scrutiny of seventeenth-century Calvinists led to a more diffuse and secular movement in the eighteenth century – the cult of sensibility.[132] This newer cultural shift towards sensibility emphasized the importance of a rich interior life for the individual – a state which the middle classes sought to cultivate through the recent media innovation of the mass-circulation printed novel. The cult of sensibility also heralded the emergence of the Romantic movement in the nineteenth century, in which an authentic personal life became celebrated as a good in its own right. Each of these developments can be seen as the longer cultural sources that fund progressive spirituality's notion that the interior life of personal experience should be the ultimate arbiter of spiritual authority. Beliefs associated with the Romantic movement can also be seen elsewhere in progressive spirituality. The Romantic notion of the sublime forms a precedent for progressive spirituality's notion of the ineffable divine spirit, manifest in nature. Indeed the turn to the idea of nature as a source of truth following the Enlightenment can be seen as a fundamental cultural concept on which progressive spirituality builds.[133] The Romantic emphasis on intuitive, expressive engagements with nature – both external nature and one's own inner nature – can be seen in progressive spirituality's cultivation of the relationship with nature and one's self.

Progressive spirituality can also be understood as a product of what Charles Taylor has described as the long cultural march in western modernity towards a new sense of moral order based on the rights, freedom and inherent value of the individual.[134] It celebrates the importance of the individual not only through its emphasis on the importance of personal experience as a guide for the spiritual life, but in its welcoming of religious diversity within which individuals can make choices about religious beliefs and affiliations that are personally meaningful to them. The social causes supported by religious and spiritual progressives reflect an underlying belief in the importance of individual rights and freedom as a basis for moral order. Their support for issues of gender equality, gay rights, and their campaigns against poverty and the death penalty, all reflect an underlying assumption in the inherent rights, value and equality of every human person.

Progressive spirituality can even be seen as a descendent of western modernism.

Modernism – as many contemporary religious commentators incorrectly imply – was never simply about the celebration of Enlightenment rationality, and the pursuit of truth through science or overarching ideologies.[135] Modernism has always been a more complex and conflicted movement than this. One element within the various intellectual and cultural expressions of modernism was a concern with ultimate truth.[136] But not all forms of modernism claimed that this truth could be grasped through cold, objective rationality. In the abstract paintings of Kandinsky, Mondrian and the American abstract expressionists – or the music of John Cage – we can see an aesthetic and mystical pursuit of a truth that eludes rational analysis.[137] The same aesthetic and mystical pursuit of the ineffable divine characterizes progressive spirituality. It is no coincidence that modernism has left us with sites for progressive religion such as the Rothko Chapel in Houston or the Unitarian chapels designed by Frank Lloyd Wright. Another defining feature of modernism was the willingness to face honestly the modern human condition, to seek liberation from the dead hand of empty and oppressive tradition, and to find new ways of living and thinking that encouraged human flourishing. Again, progressive spirituality has this same quality – seeking to embrace the challenges of modern life and to generate new spiritual resources for our times. It has become an ever popular cliché to describe contemporary forms of spirituality as 'postmodern'. Progressive spirituality does resemble postmodernism in its celebration of different religious styles and traditions, rather than the pursuit of a unitary style that characterized some forms of modernism, but in reality, progressive spirituality is much closer to modernism. Underlying the range of religious traditions that it welcomes, progressive spirituality sees a common essence of truth – the spiritual equivalent of Clive Bell's aesthetic concept of 'significant form'.[138] Progressive spirituality is not so much postmodern, as a particular form of modernism – a softer modernism – a spiritual way of living for the modern age. It may be less optimistic about social and cultural progress than some earlier forms of modernism – but progress it seeks, nevertheless, towards a more spiritually grounded, sustainable and just society. Indeed progressive spirituality could be seen as a viable form of the modernist project – one that does not make the mistake of celebrating the shock of the new for its own sake, and that connects a progressive social and cultural outlook to a sense of deeper spiritual roots.[139]

Progressive spirituality has not emerged simply out of broader movements in western culture, but out of a more specific western religious tradition – religious liberalism. As Leigh Schmidt argues, in his excellent book *Restless Souls*, the phenomenon of contemporary western spirituality owes much to this older liberal religious movement. With its North American roots in the nineteenth-century writings of Ralph Waldo Emerson and Walt Whitman, religious liberalism typically valued individual spiritual and mystical experience, emphasized the immanence of the divine in nature and the self, recognized the potentially valuable resources offered by religious traditions, supported progressive social causes, and encouraged the individual spiritual quest.[140] The similarity between these emphases and those of contemporary progressive spirituality are obvious.[141] Indeed, far from being a wholly new phenomenon, progressive spirituality is better understood as the latest phase of expression of this longer progressive religious tradition. The creation spirituality of Matthew Fox is anticipated in the natural mysticism of Emerson and Whitman. Feminist progressive spirituality finds its ancestors in first-wave feminists and religious progressives such as Margaret Fuller and Elizabeth Cady Stanton. Deepak Chopra's spiritual teaching is anticipated from the 1890s onwards in the work of the Vedanta Society and the inspirational writings of Ralph Waldo Trine. And the fruits of Neale Donald Walsch's conversations with God bear a strong similarity to late nineteenth-century ideas in the New Thought movement. Even the term 'new spirituality' is not new – Carl Bjerregard, for example, can be cited as having used it in a lecture on mysticism back in 1896.[142] To make these connections is not necessarily to suggest unoriginality on the part of contemporary writers, but is merely to make the point that progressive spirituality draws on a deeper pool of religious and spiritual teaching whose modern roots date back into the early part of the nineteenth century.

Understanding contemporary progressive spirituality in light of this longer tradition of religious liberalism in the West is important. Since Emerson began publishing his essays on nature, the self and transcendentalism, there have always been progressive religious ideas in circulation that have provided a basis for communication and collaboration between religious progressives. Contemporary progressive spirituality is not a wholly new phenomenon, but the latest phase of an unfolding liberal religious ideology in modern western society. It is somewhat different from earlier forms of progressive religion. Contemporary progressive spirituality is distinguished by its stronger roots in feminist spirituality, and the turn to goddess spirituality. It is grounded in sacralized understandings of quantum physics, as well as evolutionary and complexity theories, whereas nineteenth-century progressive religion tended to distinguish itself from the secularized science of its day.[143] And the contemporary awareness of impending ecological catastrophe makes environmental concern a much stronger feature of contemporary progressive spirituality than its earlier manifestations. Modern day advocates of progressive spirituality would be unlikely to agree with the anthropocentrism implied in Emerson's assertion that 'nature is thoroughly mediate. It is made to serve. It receives the dominion of man as meekly as the ass on which the Saviour rode.'[144] By contrast, the interest in spiritualism – prevalent in nineteenth-century progressive religious circles – is far less evident in contemporary forms of progressive spirituality. But the core values and beliefs of progressive religion – valuing mysticism, searching for a universal spirituality across and beyond all religions, emphasizing the immanence of the divine, and supporting progressive social causes – are common to this longer tradition.

Recognizing the longer historical and cultural antecedents for today's progressive spirituality makes it harder to imagine that progressive spirituality is a flash in the pan – an epiphenomenon of late twentieth-century political correctness. Progressive spirituality has deeper roots in western cultural and religious traditions which suggests it will continue to be with us in varying forms for the foreseeable future. As Leigh Schmidt observes, understanding the historical roots of progressive spirituality can also be helpful in giving religious progressives a greater sense of historical identity, as well as examples of previous experiments in progressive religion from which advocates of progressive spirituality can learn.[145] Progressive spirituality, then, is not a completely new religious phenomenon. Drawing from deeper roots in western culture, it is merely the latest expression of a longer history of progressive religious thought and practice. It is also a broadly coherent form of religious ideology, which has distinctive elements and emphases compared to previous forms of progressive religion in the West. How progressive spirituality functions within the wider organizational context of the progressive milieu is the issue to which we shall now turn.

3 Progressive spirituality and the new generation of religious progressive organizations

So far, in this book, we have explored the idea of the progressive milieu and examined the rise of progressive spirituality as an ideology within this milieu in recent decades. In this chapter, I will now try to flesh out how the concerns and ideologies that we have explored so far relate to actual progressive religious organizations and activities. It is worth saying at the very outset that this is work in its very earliest stages of development. There have been valuable empirical studies of different groups and traditions within the wider progressive milieu – such as Cynthia Eller's work on feminist spirituality in North America, Kathleen Rountree's work on feminist Wicca in New Zealand, and Daren Kemp's study of 'Christaquarians' in Britain. But, so far, little scholarly work has been done in trying to map the wider progressive milieu as a whole. In this chapter, I want to offer one of the first attempts at such a map, describing the kinds of organizations and networks that constitute the progressive milieu and the kinds of activities that these organizations and networks engage in. Inevitably such early attempts at mapping a territory have their shortcomings, and my hope is that in offering such a map I am helping to give greater clarity to a particular field of study whilst giving an open invitation to discussion about how this map can be improved upon.

One of the important questions that goes beyond the scope of this chapter is the extent to which progressive spirituality, as defined in the previous chapter, is a widely shared ideology within the progressive milieu. To answer this would have required a large-scale piece of survey research that is beyond the resources that were available to me in producing this particular study. It is reasonable to suggest, looking at the books and conference talks produced by the organic intellectuals of the progressive milieu, that the core ideas of progressive spirituality are circulating widely within this milieu. But without more knowledge of how people consume or make use of such resources, it is difficult to say much at this stage about the wider impact of progressive spirituality. My more modest aims here, in this chapter, are to say more about how the progressive milieu is constituted and to give some illustrations of how the ideology of progressive spirituality finds expression in certain forms of social and cultural activity within it. By the end of the chapter, though, I will explain why progressive spirituality is likely to play an important role in the development of collective identity amongst those involved in the progressive milieu.

Organizational structures within the progressive milieu

Firstly, then, let me turn to the task of mapping out the progressive milieu, and in particular the new generation of religious and spiritual progressive organizations. It is worth saying, at the outset, that not all of those people who might identify as religious or spiritual progressives – or who are involved in some form of progressive religious belief or practice – necessarily have much involvement with such organizations. Rather, their progressive faith is expressed through more individually constructed religious identities and practices, developed through the consumption of various media (e.g., magazines, books or websites). A recent poll of Wiccans and Pagans conducted by the Covenant of the Goddess, for example, indicated that 62 per cent of respondents practised their spirituality in isolation from covens or other groups structures,[1] a phenomenon made possible by the upsurge in books and websites aimed at helping the solitary Wiccan and Pagan practitioner. Nevertheless, the organizational base of the progressive milieu has a decisive effect on the kind of religious media that is made available to such progressive individuals, and the nature of these organizational structures will inevitably shape the future content and significance of progressive spirituality and the progressive milieu more generally.

Structurally, the progressive milieu is made up of individuals, organizations, and sub-networks which seek to maintain progressive religious identities and beliefs and to act on progressive religious and political concerns. This milieu is partly made up of primary religious institutions such as individual congregations and religious denominations. Historically, certain congregations have come to be strongly identified with progressive religious and political beliefs. Examples of these would include St James', Piccadilly in London,[2] the Riverside Church in New York,[3] and a range of San Francisco Bay Area congregations including the Glide Memorial Church,[4] the Church for the Fellowship of All Peoples[5] and the Beyt Tikkun synagogue.[6] Particular religious denominations have also become integral parts of this progressive milieu, notably the Religious Society of Friends,[7] the Unitarian Church (in the UK)[8] or Unitarian Universalist Association (in the US),[9] and the Metropolitan Community Church.[10] Umbrella organizations for the Pagan and Wiccan traditions – for example, the Pagan Federation[11] in the United Kingdom and the Covenant of the Goddess[12] in the United States – also represent important 'denominational' structures within the wider progressive milieu.

Perhaps even more important to the progressive milieu than these primary institutions are a range of 'secondary' institutions: independent organizations, NGOs, retreat and study centres, and networks which provide a range of services and means of activism for religious and spiritual progressives.[13] Indeed many religious and spiritual progressives may only have tenuous connections (or indeed no connection at all) with local congregations, and may instead develop their personal spirituality through taking part in a range of different retreats, workshops, conferences or local meditation or activist meetings. This is often not the bricolage spirituality, constructed from different religious traditions, that some have suggested is symptomatic of a 'postmodern' culture. Rather, people tend to engage with a range of activities within the same broad religious tradition (for example, remaining within progressive Christian groups and networks).

Some of these secondary organizations have a longer history, such as Quaker study centres like Woodbrooke College[14] and Pendle Hill,[15] the Iona Community,[16] the Scargill House community and retreat centre,[17] the Sojourners[18] and the Student Christian Movement.[19] But many of the key organizations that make up the contemporary progressive milieu have emerged in the past fifteen years. An illustrative list of some of these new organizations is included in the table in Appendix 1.

This new generation of progressive religious and spiritual organizations engage with a range of overlapping concerns. Some focus on exploring what it means to have an authentic and progressive faith in the context of contemporary society. Others focus more on a broad range of social justice campaigns. Some groups focus on single issues – such as gay rights. Some see their primary role in terms of fighting against the cultural and political influence of the religious Right. Others seek to develop earth-centred spiritualities and lifestyles. As we noted in Chapter One, though, such concerns are not mutually exclusive. Whilst religious and spiritual progressives might choose to focus their limited individual or organizational resources on one or two of these emphases, in practice they tend to be sympathetic to all of them.

Another kind of organization and network that religious and spiritual progressives are often involved in are various interfaith initiatives. As Leigh Schmidt has argued, the progressive milieu in western religion has historically not only been characterized by theological liberalism and political radicalism, but also by an interest in exploring spiritual wisdom across religious traditions.[20] This interest in interfaith communication, and the search for elements of a common spirituality, are still pursued today through major events and organizations such as the Parliament of the World's Religions[21] and the Interfaith Alliance,[22] as well as through local grassroots, interfaith meetings.[23] Such interfaith organizations and networks provide another important context for the pursuit of progressive religious interests and concerns, and any complete map of the progressive milieu will need to explore how such interfaith groups relate to the other kinds of organizations and networks that I have described earlier. For the purposes of this chapter, though, I want to note this as an issue for future discussion, and instead turn my attention more specifically to the new generation of organizations and networks which are explicitly seeking to build up the life and work of the progressive milieu of western religion.

The activities of the new religious and spiritual progressives

These new organizations that I am referring to engage in four different types of activity:

i)   providing resources that help the personal and spiritual development of progressive spiritual seekers

The progressive milieu is perpetuated by organizations that offer a range of resources and structures to help individuals maintain a progressive religious identity and lifestyle. These resources and structures take a variety of forms, but can be summarized as *social support, ideological support* and *outlets for progressive religious values and aspirations*. Partly, then, these organizations offer social and emotional support for individuals as they pursue their own spiritual quest. The Christians Awakening to a New Awareness website states, for example, that this network seeks to offer people 'nurture and companionship in their process of [spiritual] awakening'.[24] Similarly, the SnowStar Institute describes itself as 'neutral territory, a safe haven, where seekers and followers of all faith traditions can come together to respectfully and courageously examine... historical and progressive theologies'.[25] In organizational terms, such social support can be provided through a range of means: national events and workshops, local grassroots groups linked to larger organizations (e.g., Tikkun, Greenspirit, PCN Britain), or informal communication through email lists and online discussion boards. This social and emotional support is partly offered in recognition that progressive spiritual searching can be an isolating experience. Social networking and support does not take place simply around issues of personal spiritual formation, however. Some groups offer wider opportunities for social interaction through organized holidays and other social events, and a 'Friendster'-style online chat and dating service has even been created for religious progressives.[26]

Many of these new organizations also seek to provide what can be described as ideological support for religious progressives, intended to help them maintain and develop their personal religious identities and beliefs. This consists of publications (websites, books, pamphlets, magazines, newsletters) that articulate progressive religious values and beliefs,[27] as well conferences, talks and workshops that provide people with the opportunity to hear progressive speakers and to discuss issues of spiritual, social and political concern. Some of this material has an experiential emphasis (for example, stories of individuals' spiritual journeys). Some of it is more abstract and conceptual, exploring progressive perspectives on particular religious questions and traditions. An important concern here is often that of connecting the spiritual formation of religious progressives with insights from contemporary scholarship.[28] Whilst this ideological support can take the form of one-off workshops and conferences, it can also include more sustained educational opportunities such short courses like 'Living the Questions'[29] or 'The Quest',[30] or, even more substantially, advanced programmes of study at specialist educational institutions such as Wisdom University or Integral University.[31] The strong emphasis on educational formation underlying these various activities is again, arguably, symptomatic of the predominantly middle-class membership of these organizations. However, ideological support for religious progressives does not simply take place through more explicitly educational activities. Amongst the new generation of progressive religious and spiritual organizations are attempts to develop new sacred rituals that provide powerful experiential opportunities for connecting one's spiritual experience with a progressive religious outlook.[32]

In practice, social and ideological support are often closely bound together. Religious progressives who are still involved in mainstream religious institutions can often feel isolated, unable to articulate their questions and beliefs in local congregations which are more traditional or conservative. This sense of isolation and alienation within traditional religious institutions can be compounded when religious leaders criticize emerging forms of spirituality as flaky, superficial and narcissistic. The act of attending a conference or workshop focused on progressive religious ideas can therefore be experienced as helpful, both in confirming the validity of these ideas and in helping individuals to feel part of a larger movement. Feedback from participants at such events can refer to them as affirming, an experience of 'home-coming' and providing an important reassurance that there are other people 'on a similar journey'.[33] Trying out progressive theological ideas in small group discussions, or experimenting with new sacred rituals with an established and trusted group of people, can also allow people to nurture a progressive religious identity in an emotionally safe environment. Such social and ideological support is not only provided through face-to-face meetings. Online communication through websites, email lists and internet discussion boards can also be an important supplement to (and sometimes even substitute for) face-to-face interaction. Reading books on progressive approaches to religion and spirituality can also represent a form of both social and ideological support. When reading such books, individuals not only have an opportunity to confirm and develop their progressive religious thinking, but can also experience themselves as part of a wider imagined audience addressed by the writer.[34] This act of reading is also not an atomized activity in the sense that it depends on wider social networks of authors, publishers and progressive religious booksellers.[35]

In addition to this social and ideological support, progressive religious organizations also enable individuals to maintain and develop their sense of identity as religious progressives by providing them with concrete means of embodying and enacting their particular values and beliefs. It is through taking part in workshops, conferences, sacred rituals or various forms of social and political activism that individuals can rehearse their self-identity as a religious or spiritual progressive. A specific example of this can be seen in the progressive spirituality ritual of the 'Cosmic Walk', which has been practised at some Greenspirit meetings.[36] The Cosmic Walk is a walking meditation, conducted in some natural setting, in which each metre of the walk represents 10,000 years of the history of the cosmos. The total length of the walk – a little more than three kilometres – represents a physical walking along the timeline of cosmic history. At different stages during the walk, the facilitator talks participants through a brief summary of key evolutionary events that were unfolding at the particular point in the history of the cosmos. Through this walking meditation, participants are able to engage physically with a central tenet of progressive spirituality – the story of the universe – in a way that maintains this evolutionary notion of cosmic history, whilst embedding participants' sense of their bodies and their personal life-stories in the context of this broader story. The Cosmic Walk therefore provides the opportunity for a shared experience in which people structure their imaginations and embodied experience in line with central tenets of progressive spirituality. It offers a concrete means by which personal identity, physical experience and religious ideology can be fused together.

ii)   articulating progressive perspectives and pursuing progressive campaigns within religious institutions

In addition to generating resources to support individual religious and spiritual progressives, this new generation of progressive religious organizations also seek to influence the wider religious traditions and denominations within which they function. This work is partly about ensuring that religious progressives have a clear public presence in wider religious institutions. The Progressive Muslim Union of North America for example seeks to give a clear voice to progressive perspectives in the wider context of western Islam. It is also partly about developing teaching, liturgical and pastoral resources that support the development of progressive religious congregations.[37] Furthermore, this work is partly focused on conflict over claims of authentic religious identity and the interpretation of religious texts and traditions. The website of the Christian Alliance for Progress contains the headline caption: 'I feel embarrassed and angry that Christianity has been used to divide our country and to promote bigotry and war. I joined this movement to stand up for compassion and justice.'[38] This reflects the sense of many progressive religious organizations being involved in conflicts with religious conservatives over what constitutes an authentic interpretation and performance of a religious tradition. Many progressive religious organizations see themselves as being concerned with reclaiming religious texts and religious symbols from religious and political conservatives who have used them to their own ends. Finally, progressive religious engagement with wider religious institutions involves campaigning for change in those institutions' theological, moral and social teachings and practices. Following in the wake of bitter disputes over the ordination of people in same sex relationships in the Anglican Communion, organizations such as Changing Attitude and InclusiveChurch.net have been formed in the United Kingdom to campaign for more tolerant attitudes towards gay sexuality within the Church.[39] In the case of InclusiveChurch.net, this has extended to a campaign to get its supporters elected to the General Synod of the Church of England in order to increase their influence within that institution.

iii) developing a clear presence for progressive religion in the public sphere and engaging in direct forms of social and political activism

For many progressive religious organizations, particularly in the United States, raising the public profile of progressive religion is perceived to be an urgent task. In a North American context in which the religious Right has largely monopolized the religious contribution to public policy and debate in recent years, religious progressives are keen to regain the initiative. They have, to some extent, sought to do this though events designed to raise their public and media profile. One example of this is CrossWalk America, a 2,500 mile march by progressive Christians in 2006 from Arizona to Washington, DC. This march was intended to stimulate public attention on core progressive Christian beliefs and concerns – partly by nailing a declaration of these progressive beliefs on the doors of the head offices of each major Christian denomination in the country.[40] Another recent initiative has been the 'State of Our Values' events organized by the Sojourners which were designed to try to secure media coverage of progressive religious responses to President George Bush's State of the Union address in January 2006.[41] In Britain, the Holism Network is seeking to raise the profile of progressive forms of spirituality by campaigning for holistic spirituality to be included as an option in answer to the question on religious identity in the 2011 National Census. The Holism Network is also seeking to put pressure on policy-makers to get supporters of holistic spirituality the same degree of recognition on public bodies as representatives of more traditional faith communities.[42] Specific campaigns such as these may therefore be aimed at raising the public profile of religious and spiritual progressives. But events such as the publication of books by leading progressive writers can also be a focus for raising public awareness. When Michael Lerner's book, *The Left Hand of God*, was published in February 2006, it was supported not only by publicity from his publishers – HarperCollins San Francisco – but by regular emails from the Tikkun community urging those on its mailing list to go out and buy the book in its first two weeks of release to ensure that it stayed on the main display tables at the front of bookstores such as Borders and Barnes & Noble.

Such attempts to raise the profile of spiritual and religious progressives are designed not only to communicate core progressive values and beliefs, but also to challenge public perceptions of religion as irrelevant, judgmental and out of touch with contemporary social realities. Speaking of the work of the Progressive Christian Network for Britain and Ireland, its chair, Hugh Dawes, describes this in terms of 'making the public face of Christianity more acceptable'.[43]

More sustained influence on public policy is sought through the development of progressive religious think tanks such as the Tikkun Institute.[44] Conferences continue to be organized to bring together leading thinkers and activists from the religious Left such as the Progressive Christian Leadership Summit held by CrossLeft in San Francisco in February 2006, the Spiritual Activism Conference organized in Washington, DC by Tikkun in May 2006, Pentecost 2006: Building a New Covenant with America organized (again in Washington, DC) by the Sojourners, as well as the events organized within the Faith and Progressive Policy initiative developed by the Center for American Progress.[45] There is a sense in which the religious

Left is trying to learn from the past successes of the religious Right, and is trying to build resources and structures that will enable to it develop long-term social and political influence. Whilst these efforts certainly pre-date the Presidential election of 2004, there is also no doubt that the re-election of George Bush has focused the determination of many religious progressives to develop a stronger political movement in the United States.

In addition to broader think-tank and policy development work, religious progressive organizations are also involved in direct forms of social and political activism. In some instances, progressive organizations create 'one-click' electronic campaigns, in which supporters can use online resources to send prepared letters and emails to elected representatives. Faithful America, for example, has organized such electronic campaigns on issues ranging from low pay, torture, climate change, genocide and peace in the Middle East.[46] The Sojourners similarly have provided online petitions and pre-written campaign letters on issues ranging from welfare support in the wake of Hurricane Katrina, demands for a full inquiry into the decision to engage in the war with Iraq in 2003, and calls for the closure of an American military base implicated in training people involved in human rights abuses in Latin America.[47] In addition to such online campaigns, religious progressives have also been involved in other forms of off-line direct action. The Jubilee Debt Campaign has enjoyed considerable success in attracting attention to issues of debt relief for the developing world through organizing major demonstrations around international events such as G8 summit meetings.[48] At a more local level, CLUELA, an interfaith organization in Los Angeles county concerned with issues of economic justice, have run campaigns against low-paying employers and held public meetings in support of low-paid workers protesting at their conditions.[49]

Direct action does not only take the form of political campaigns against political authorities or large corporations. Organizations associated with progressive spirituality are also engaged in forms of action designed to encourage sustainable and ecologically sensitive lifestyles. The Cultivate Centre in Dublin, for example, runs talks and workshops, and holds a range of resources on different aspects of sustainable living, including the development of alternative energy sources, alternative healthcare and eco-building. Beyond this, though, it also seeks to organize a wider range of events that offer a sustainable alternative to a mass, homogenized culture that encourages passivity rather than autonomy and creativity.[50] In addition to this, Cultivate also offers training courses in permaculture, designed to help people engage in more sustainable ways with their natural environment. Female religious orders have also been particularly important in taking the lead in linking progressive spirituality with sustainable approaches to agriculture. One of the pioneering initiatives in this regard has been the Genesis Farm, originally set up by a group of Dominican Sisters in New Jersey in 1980.[51] Grounded in the belief in the Earth as a 'primary revelation of the divine', this project is both a working farm and an ongoing experiment in sustainable agriculture, as well as a training centre for events on sustainable living and an accredited Masters' programme in Earth Literacy. This initiative has also subsequently inspired similar projects elsewhere around the world, such as the An Tairseach Dominican Farm and Ecology Centre in County Wicklow, Ireland.[52] Direct action by religious and spiritual progressives thus involves campaigning for social, economic and political change, as well as trying to develop new sustainable ways of living and managing human societies.

iv) building up the infrastructure of the progressive milieu of western religion

A final category of activity undertaken by the new generation of progressive religious and spiritual organizations is that of trying to strengthen the social links and structures that make up the progressive milieu. Both the Tikkun Community and CrossLeft have, for example, developed initiatives to try and improve communication and collaboration between religious and spiritual progressives. In the case of the former, this has led to the development of the Network for Spiritual Progressives, based around online discussion lists.[53] In the case of the latter, CrossLeft has sought to strengthen communication links between progressive Christians by offering a clearing house for information and resources on relevant events and organizations.[54] In Britain, another similar initiative, the Meta-Net roundtable forum, has sought to bring progressive Christian groups together for an annual face-to-face meeting to discuss issues of common concern.[55] The University for Spirit Forum, also based in Britain, similarly seeks to bring together spiritual progressives beyond the boundaries of mainstream religious institutions who have a particular interest in spiritual education.[56] Other organizations seek to provide umbrella structures around within which local initiatives can be developed. Christians Awakening to a New Awareness, for example, seeks to provide a forum in which locally run groups with an interest in ongoing spiritual searching can find a larger structure for sharing ideas and resources. Groups such as the Progressive Christian Network for Great Britain and Ireland, and the Progressive Spirituality Network, also seek to be a focus for communication and resource-exchange amongst progressive Christians. Within the progressive milieu, therefore, a number of groups are trying to develop what is often a loose constellation of individuals and groups into a more clearly structured network in which the possibilities for communication, collective action, and sharing resources are significantly improved. This kind of activity may be focused primarily around developing the organizational and communication infrastructure of the progressive milieu, but it can also have useful, if more informal, benefits. Those employed as workers within progressive religious and spiritual organizations can benefit from such networking when it provides peer support from other workers, providing opportunities for sharing ideas and experiences.

These four different types of progressive collective activity can be understood along a continuum from those with a primarily *internal* focus within the progressive milieu to those with a primarily *external* focus into wider social and political contexts.[57] Examples of the former include activities that seek to deepen the personal spirituality of individual spiritual and religious progressives, or which seek to strengthen communication and collaboration between individuals and groups within the progressive milieu. Examples of activity with an external focus include attempts to raise the public and media profile of religious progressives and various forms of campaigning and direct action designed to create specific social or economic changes. Attempts to transform religious institutions in line with progressive values and beliefs could be seen as falling midway along this continuum. Thinking in terms of this continuum of internal and external activities may be useful in analysing the work of specific progressive organizations. Some are clearly involved primarily in internal activities designed to nurture and build up the progressive milieu (for example, the Living Spirituality Network, Meta-Net, or the Centre for Progressive Christianity). Others are predominately focused on external activities within the wider public sphere (for example, the Christian Alliance for Progress, or Faithful America). The decision to focus primarily on internal or external activities within such organizations is often shaped by their current social context, as well as the specific history behind the development of particular organizations. Organizations with limited financial or staffing resources are also likely to concentrate their activities either within or beyond the progressive milieu because they have to make strategic choices about how best to utilize their limited resources. Some organizations which are somewhat better resourced, like the Tikkun Community, are better placed to engage in activities that seek to build up the progressive milieu as well as engaging in wider public campaigning. Similarly, some organizations explicitly see their mission in terms of reconciling personal spiritual development with sustainable living and constructive social and political action. As a recent publicity tag line for the Cultivate Centre in Dublin states: 'Cultivate yourself, your community, your world'. But the fact that many of the new progressive organizations have to adopt a specific focus for their activities because of their limited resources sets up potential structural problems for collaboration between such groups. For if there is little overlap between the established priorities of such groups and networks, it becomes harder to establish the shared agenda for collective action that would help to shape the progressive milieu into a more clearly structured social movement. We will return to this issue in more depth, though, later in the chapter.

Towards a collective identity in the progressive milieu

The picture of the progressive milieu drawn so far in this chapter is of a cluster of networks and organizations with a range of different foci and priorities and varying degrees of connection and collaboration. In constructing this account of the progressive milieu I hope to avoid two opposing, but equally wrong, judgments about progressive faith in the West. The first of these judgments is that progressive religion in the West is too diffuse and inchoate a phenomenon to have any defining features or for religious progressives to have any sense of mutual identification. The other judgment, by contrast, is that the progressive milieu represents the leading edge of the new spirituality for the majority of western society and that the new generation of progressive organizations will together form an increasingly cohesive religious movement.[58] Such judgments respectively underestimate and overestimate the potential significance of the progressive milieu, and in the rest of this chapter I want to explain more why such judgments are wrong. I will do this, first, by saying more about the kinds of collective identity that are formed in the progressive milieu, before going on to talk about the various factors that still hinder collaboration between progressive religious groups.

Firstly, then, it is important to recognize the degree of cohesion that already exists within the progressive milieu. Unlike the so-called 'New Age movement', which in practice lacks any shared programme, forms of collective action, or even a strong sense of identification with the term 'New Age',[59] religious progressives are showing signs of forming into a somewhat more cohesive movement. Progressive religious groups work together on specific social programmes or political campaigns,[60] and there is clear evidence of individuals and groups wanting to identify themselves as religious or spiritual progressives. The term 'progressive', in this context, is also providing a framework for new, cross-faith collaborative initiatives such as Tikkun's Network for Spiritual Progressives.

An important part of the cohesion of the progressive milieu is provided by the sense of collective identity generated within it. Indeed, the progressive milieu can be understood as a 'new social movement' for which the production of a shared identity is an important part of its work. Writers associated with 'new social movement' theory have argued that such movements, which have grown since the 1960s, are less involved in class-based conflicts focused on economic and political control at the level of the nation state and more concerned with wider issues of cultural identity and lifestyle – or so-called 'post-materialist' values.[61] Examples of such 'new' social movements include the women's movement, the environmental movement, the civil rights movement and the gay rights/queer identities movement. Some obvious connections can be made between the progressive milieu and such 'new' social movements. The progressive milieu clearly shares many of the same concerns as these new movements – regarding gender, ecology, sexuality, freedom and social justice – indeed the progressive milieu could precisely be seen as the context in which these wider concerns engage with questions of religious and spiritual identity.

Understanding more about the production and role of collective identity in 'new social movements' like the progressive milieu can be helpful in understanding more about how it functions as a social network.[62] Collective identity can be seen as important for such social movements for three reasons. Firstly, as Manuel Castells has suggested, social movements are an important source of identity for individuals in a fragmented society, in which defining one's identity is a pressing and complex task.[63] The progressive milieu, for example, functions as an important source of identity for individuals with liberal or left-leaning values, in a way that other sources of social identity such as religious conservatism/fundamentalism or nationalism obviously cannot.[64] Secondly, collective identity is important for social movements because it is this shared sense of a common bond that makes being part of a movement a meaningful experience for its members, and provides the emotional and moral energy required for sustained commitment to a particular cause. Thirdly, and perhaps less obviously, the production of collective identity can be seen as one of the particular goals of contemporary social movements. Alberto Melucci has argued, for example, that in economically developed societies, contemporary social movements are less concerned with conflicts over access to material resources than with issues of cultural meaning and identity. Key battles are therefore not simply fought over crude economic and political goals as much as with the frameworks one uses to interpret life, and the identities and behaviours that such frameworks validate or disqualify.[65] Contemporary social movements may therefore be as concerned with providing resources for developing particular kinds of human identity, as well as with more tangible social and political goals.[66] A good example of this could be seen in the gay rights movement, which is concerned not only with countering specific problems of violence, prejudice and discrimination, but which also seeks to validate alternative sexual identities to the dominant heterosexual norm. Gay pride marches, then, are as much about the development and validation of particular cultural identities as about more specific political goals.

If collective identity is so deeply bound up with the needs of both individuals and social movements, how can we define collective identity and explain how it is produced? Taylor and Whittier suggest that collective identity within social movements consists of three key elements.[67] The first of these is a sense of mutual identification, of belonging, of identifying with others in the movement as a 'we'. Such identification may focus partly around the 'brand name' of a particular social movement – such as being a religious or spiritual 'progressive'. But even in the absence of a readily used brand name, such mutual identification is still evident whenever people experience themselves as part of a meaningful movement or network with a particular ethos and concerns. Related to this, secondly, is a shared consciousness in which people share an overlapping cluster of ideas, beliefs, values and ways of interpreting their particular social and cultural situation. Thirdly, collective identity within social movements is usually characterized by a sense of opposition to a dominant order. Those involved in social movements therefore experience themselves as engaged in some kind of collective, oppositional activity to a mainstream or more politically influential set of ideas and structures (whether that be, for example, the neo-liberal economics of the Washington consensus, secular liberal humanism, or patriarchy). As Melucci suggests, this perception of being engaged in conflict with opposing groups and ideas can perform important functions in sharpening collective identity within social movements, as well as generating the emotional resources that sustains individuals' commitment to a cause and reduces their sense of ambivalence whilst engaging in social conflict.[68]

There is ample evidence of such a sense of collective identity amongst religious progressives. This runs more deeply than simply the use of the 'progressive' brand name. Whether familiar with the term 'progressive' or not, religious and spiritual progressives generally perceive themselves to be part of a wider body of people with similar values and concerns. Everyone in the various progressive organizations that I approached to interview for this book was able to identify other individuals and organizations whom they recognized as sharing a similar ethos and pursuing similar aims.[69] It is not uncommon to find that members of one progressive organization are also members of another. There is frequent cross-advertising of events within clusters of organizations in the progressive milieu, and each of these clusters engages with the work of organic intellectuals within the progressive milieu. Events are also organized within the progressive milieu – such as the Wrekin Trust's Emerging Spirituality Conference in London in November 2006 – with the specific intention of deepening a sense of collective identity amongst religious and spiritual progressives.[70] None of the progressive organizations that I have located on the internet present themselves as isolated entities, but each has connections, of varying degrees of formality, with other progressive organizations and projects. New initiatives within the progressive milieu are often influenced by other existing projects and organizations. The development of the Centre for Radical Christianity, at St Mark's Church in Sheffield, was, for example, heavily influenced by ideas and materials produced by the Jesus Seminar based at the Westar Institute.[71] Similarly, the An Tairseach ecological farm in Wicklow was directly influenced by the Genesis Farm in New Jersey, with all of the Dominican sisters at An Tairseach having spent some time at the Genesis Farm, and Miriam MacGillis from the Genesis Farm was also involved in developing An Tairseach's first five-year plan.[72] Such relations of influence can even reflect wider patterns of social migration. For example, several people involved in running the Cultivate Centre in Dublin were part of the last generational cohort to leave Ireland during the economic depression of the 1980s and early 1990s, only to return during the subsequent economic rise of the 'celtic tiger'. On their return they brought back, from their travels, experiences of engaging with alternative spiritual and cultural networks – most notably the Burning Man festival – which subsequently influenced their approach to setting up Cultivate.[73] The progressive milieu is not a collection of isolated individuals and organizations, but a complex web of relationships, in which people generally perceive themselves as being part of a larger collective.

Following Taylor and Whittier's framework, the substance of being a religious progressive can also be defined more sharply through a sense of opposition to particular groups or ideologies. This process is perhaps more marked amongst religious progressives in North America, who have a stronger sense of opposition to the political and religious Right. This is less true of religious progressives in the UK, who do not face such a clear political threat from religious conservatives – though opposition to the influence of conservative theology on the Church has been an important source for mobilizing groups such as Changing Attitude and Inclusive Church.net who seek to promote more positive church policies on issues of gay sexuality. Although complex, and taking many different localized forms, there is nevertheless clear evidence of religious progressives experiencing themselves as a 'we', sharing common concerns, against (in some cases) identifiable opponents.

Recognizing the various localized forms that this progressive collective identity can take is also important for a nuanced understanding of the progressive milieu. Whilst the use of broad terms such as 'the feminist movement', 'the ecological movement', or the 'anti-capitalist movement' may suggest relatively unified social groups with stable collective identities,[74] it is more useful to see the collective identity of social movements as a complex work in progress. Alberto Melucci has been influential in arguing that collective identity within such movements is socially constructed, focused around overlapping and sometimes contradictory accounts of both the movement's goals and methods, and the social and cultural environment in which it operates.[75] This process of ongoing negotiation occurs not simply through explicit conversations about the movement's identity, activities and context, but also takes place through the movement's developing practices and rituals, and the way in which it produces and uses cultural artefacts.[76] It is also a process that is embedded in a range of social relationships – from friendships, activities within particular organizations and networks, attendance at festivals, conferences and marches, to the more virtual or imagined relationships created by the consumption of a range of media from books and magazines, to films, websites and email lists. As we noted in this chapter, many of these activities are an integral part of the ongoing life of the progressive milieu, and the development of a collective progressive religious identity is an intended or unintended consequence of such relationships and activities. Collective identity within a social movement, then, is far from being stable or unified, but an ongoing project evolving within its relationships, activities, conversations and media. Whilst there is evidence of the rise of collective progressive religious identities, such identities are therefore still under negotiation in different ways within different contexts.

Let me give a brief example of this. At one progressive Christian event that I attended, I took part in a small discussion group focused on the event's particular theme. Within that group it was clear that the discussion – at times explicitly and at times more implicitly – was concerned with establishing what it meant to be a progressive Christian, and how this influenced the group members' perceptions of the Church and of wider society. The positions staked out by people within that group fell within a field of possibilities created by a range of (sometimes contrasting) symbols, beliefs and values. These included an emphasis on maintaining a rational approach to life, a desire to find meaning in life, a willingness (and even pride) in rejecting Christian doctrines that were perceived to be unhelpful or obsolete, a sense of flux and uncertainty about cultural sources of authority, and a desire to retain some kind of Christian identity and connection to the Christian tradition. It was within this field of beliefs and aspirations that members of the group sought to negotiate what it meant to be a progressive Christian. Clearly, given the complex nature of this field, it is possible to construct identities around different emphases within it. But it would not have been possible to have worked within the ethos of this group and to have organized one's identity around, for example, a belief in the Bible as the inerrant Word of God or a belief in the inherently evil nature of the Christian tradition. The ongoing construction of (in this case) a progressive Christian identity, thus operated within a field of possibilities shaped by the particular religious, cultural and political context in which that discussion took place. And the field of possibilities that operated in the context of this Christian group would be somewhat different to those in, say, a progressive Quaker, Wiccan or Jewish group. Accounts of the emerging collective identities amongst religious progressives in the West therefore need to hold in tension the underlying cohesion of these identities together with the various local forms that these identities can take.

Without further research, it remains an open question as to the extent to which collective identity in the progressive milieu is organized around the central ideas of progressive spirituality. Certain generalizations can be avoided. It is clear that people can still feel a sense of identification with the wider progressive milieu, whilst not necessarily subscribing to the ideology of progressive spirituality. Members of the Sojourners, as well as other radical Evangelical groups, would share social and political concerns with other religious and spiritual progressives, but would not necessarily sign up to pan(en)theist views of the divine, or the sacralization of nature and the self. Collective identity within the progressive milieu does not rest simply on a shared consensus around the core tenets of progressive spirituality, but on a wider range of potential foci for agreement and mutual identification which include political concerns as well as religious ideology.

At the same time, however, progressive spirituality is becoming an important focus for mutual identification within the progressive milieu. As we have seen, collective action can generate a sense of collective identity. So when religious and spiritual progressives organize together on issues of social and political concern, it becomes possible for them to build a collective identity around a common political agenda. Earlier in this chapter, we described this as collective action with an *external* focus. Increasingly, though, collective action in the progressive milieu with an *internal* focus is organized around the ideology of progressive spirituality. Many of the leading organic intellectuals of the progressive milieu advocate some form of progressive spirituality, including Marcus Borg, Michael Lerner, Starhawk, John Spong, Judith Plaskow, Matthew Fox, Rosemary Radford Ruether, Carol Christ, Diarmuid O'Murchu, William Bloom or Ken Wilber. This means that when progressive organizations focus their activities on discussing what it means to be a religious or spiritual progressive, or on how to develop a progressive theology for understanding life, it is to writers advocating progressive spirituality that they often turn. Those who construct new liturgies or rituals are often shaped by their exposure to this literature. Religious and spiritual educational resources developed in the progressive milieu often make reference to this literature. Progressive spirituality may not, therefore, be the only possible focus for mutual identification or source of shared consciousness in the progressive milieu. But it is becoming a theological lingua franca within this milieu, and those who wish to find collective identity at the level of a common religious or spiritual ethos are likely to try to find a common home within it. Progressive spirituality offers a field of symbols, beliefs and values that allow for the construction of a progressive religious identity that is not simply organized around social and political concerns. If the progressive milieu is indeed in the process of developing into a somewhat more cohesive social movement with a deeper sense of mutual religious identification, then it seems inevitable that progressive spirituality will play an important ideological role in this process. Progressive spirituality cannot be taken in any simplistic way to be *the* theology of the progressive milieu. But it does represent an ideological resource that will play an important role in the ways in which many people in the progressive milieu construct their sense of shared identity.

Boundaries and the limits to collaboration within the progressive milieu

When I first engaged in the literature review for writing this book, I was surprised at the degree of consensus amongst progressive writers from within and beyond a range of religious traditions around the core tenets of progressive spirituality. This consensus was such, I assumed, that it must be leading to greater collaboration on the ground amongst progressive individuals and organizations across a range of different religious affiliations.

As I developed the empirical part of this project, though, looking at websites, attending events, and interviewing individuals with leading roles in organizations within the progressive milieu, it became clear that the degree of collaboration across and beyond religious traditions was actually much less than I had anticipated. Although the ideology of progressive spirituality is shared by groups across a range of traditions, this has not yet generally translated either into substantial collaborative activity between them or the emergence of an umbrella organization or network which effectively includes the broad spectrum of religious progressives.

If there is clear evidence of a sense of collective identity amongst religious progressives – and progressive spirituality is offering an ideological structure for a shared consciousness across and beyond religious traditions – why is there so little collaboration amongst religious and spiritual progressives across the whole spectrum of traditions which they represent? Now, there is certainly evidence of collaboration that cuts across some religious boundaries. The Declaration of Interdependence, a response to social inequalities highlighted in the wake of Hurricane Katrina, drew together Christian, Jewish and Unitarian groups. There has also been close collaboration between the Tikkun Community and the Sojourners. But it is much harder to find evidence of collaboration between the traditional Abrahamic faiths and alternative traditions such as Pagans, Wiccans or those involved in developing non-affiliated forms of holistic spirituality, though such collaboration is not entirely unknown. We have previously noted the work done by both Matthew Fox and Starhawk in the former Institute for Culture and Creation Spirituality – typical of Fox's ecumenical approach in trying to employ faculty members from a range of religious traditions. Some members of broadly Christian ecological groups are also members of Pagan groups. Some individuals participate in both Christian rituals and Pagan or Wiccan ceremonies. But such crossing of the boundaries between mainstream religious institutions and alternative spiritualities is still relatively uncommon at an organizational level in the progressive milieu. Whilst Matthew Fox may speak of the turn towards a deep ecumenism amongst religious and spiritual progressives, such ecumenism seems more evident at the level of individuals rather than at the level of organizational collaboration. Given that so many of these individuals and groups appear sympathetic to the progressive principles of the pan(en)theist divine, and the sacralization of nature and the self, why do these boundaries still persist?

There are a number of reasons for this. Firstly, as we noted earlier in this chapter, many progressive religious and spiritual organizations operate with very limited financial and human resources, and historically may have developed a focus on a specific area of concern and activity. Within such organizations there may well be people who are interested in developing greater collaborative links with groups from a range of traditions, but lack the time or resources to develop such initiatives in addition to their existing commitments.[77] Secondly, many people within progressive religious organizations will mainly have contact with religious progressives from the same tradition unless they are involved in some other kind of interfaith organization or initiative. This means, in practice, that religious and spiritual progressives may simply not have the informal social contacts that would help them to builder up wider collaborative relations beyond their particular faith community or spiritual network. With Tikkun's Network for Spiritual Progressives only in its very early infancy as I write this, there are very few institutional structures within the progressive milieu that would serve as a forum for progressives across the divide between traditional mainstream religious institutions and alternative spiritualities.

A third reason for this lack of collaboration is that organizations within the progressive milieu have a range of different priorities. Earlier in the chapter we examined the range of different activities that such progressive organizations are engaged in. In Britain, at the moment, many progressive Christian groups are primarily concerned with activities that relate to their profile and influence within the Christian Church. In the face of the growing influence of conservative Evangelicalism, such groups are keen to try to influence church teaching and policies in more progressive and inclusive directions. Understandably, whilst such reform of the Church may be viewed sympathetically by religious and spiritual progressives from other traditions, it is simply not a priority for them to engage in this particular work as well. Progressive Christian groups, for example, can therefore have quite different priorities to progressive Pagan or Wiccan groups, and as a consequence it can be hard to find a common agenda that could serve as the basis for collaborative action.[78]

A fourth, and related reason, is that some people involved in the progressive milieu may perceive 'deep ecumenical' collaboration not only to be irrelevant, but a potential threat to their primary organizational goals. Writing in the magazine *CrossCurrents*, the Wiccan priestess, Grove Harris, notes how Pagans and Wiccans are still marginalized in some interfaith groups or progressive religious activism because they are seen as a potential liability to the fragile consensus that may have been struck between progressives and more conservatively inclined religious groups.[79] She notes one particular case in which an interfaith event organizer tried to include both Pagans and more conservative religious groups by having them meet in adjoining rooms with the door open so that conversation between them was still notionally possible. Religious progressives in mainstream religious institutions may often rely on links with more conservative or middle-of-the-road co-religionists to achieve certain aims, but these links can be put under pressure if progressives try to build closer relations with alternative spiritual traditions. For example, the Greenbelt Christian Arts Festival in Britain relies on support not only from progressive Christians but also moderate Anglicans and Evangelicals. When a practising Wiccan was invited to speak about her faith at the festival, this was greeted with praying protestors outside the seminar and problems with the festival's perceived image amongst some of its more conservative supporters. If progressives within a particular religious tradition are primarily concerned with developing a progressive identity within that tradition, or with the reform of their institution, then developing links with alternative spiritual groups are likely to be seen as a potential distraction. Such collaboration would add little to these primary goals, and could actively hinder them if it alienated some people who might otherwise join in with this particular kind of progressive project.

A fifth reason is that within the progressive milieu it is possible to detect negative attitudes between some of those people involved in mainstream traditional religious institutions and some involved in the holistic milieu of alternative spiritualities. Diarmuid O'Murchu has commented to me that within the progressive milieu in the 1990s there was, if anything, a deepening of the retrenchment between those involved in traditional religious institutions and those involved in alternative spirituality groups and networks. From my initial empirical work, I would suggest that, for some still involved in mainstream religious institutions, the holistic milieu of alternative spiritualities can appear to be an insecure organizational framework and a limited structural base from which to develop an ongoing religious and social project. By comparison, mainstream religious institutions, however flawed, are seen by them as a better-resourced base from which to develop a progressive religious project with a broad social appeal and impact. At the same time, for some people involved in alternative spiritualities, mainstream religious institutions can still appear to be too bound up with patriarchy, and rigid approaches to ritual and doctrine, to offer an attractive framework for ongoing spiritual development and open spiritual exploration. For people in the holistic milieu of alternative spiritualities who have had their own personal negative experiences of more traditional forms of religion, there can be little incentive to re-engage with these traditional religious structures. These negative attitudes are not so much, then, about one side demonizing the other, but reflect different judgments about what represents a better context for the development of a progressive religious project.

Finally, a sixth factor that potentially hinders collaboration is that progressive organizations in an early stage of development are often reluctant to engage in forms of collaboration that might seem to threaten their emerging sense of identity. Members of progressive Christian groups that I spoke to commented that, as many of these groups were still in the early stages of formation, it was hard for them to contemplate collaboration beyond relatively limited boundaries. In a similar vein, Janice Dolley commented that the Wrekin Trust's creation of the University for Spirit Forum in 2000 would not have been possible twenty years before, as too many of the Forum's associates were in the very early stages of clarifying their identity and mission.[80] Organizational collaboration may therefore only be possible as individual organizations and groups become better established.

Given this range of factors stacked against broad organizational collaboration within the progressive milieu, it is clear that such collaboration is only like to take place if there are sufficiently compelling reasons to try to overcome these structural and attitudinal barriers. Such compelling reasons for deep ecumenical collaboration in the progressive milieu are hard to find at present. Indeed I would suggest that it is difficult to envisage significant levels of collaboration between organizations across the spectrum of traditions represented in the progressive milieu for some years to come. Broad collaboration across the progressive milieu may well require progressives in different traditions and alternative networks to develop more established identities before the risks associated with such collaboration can be embarked upon. Where such collaboration does take place, I would predict that this is more likely to take place in particular contexts – such as the feminist spirituality movement, in which there may be a desire to overcome some of the tensions between institutional religion and goddess spirituality/feminist Wicca that emerged in the 1970s. Earth-centred rituals or activism are likely to be another possible such context. As Janice Dolley of the Wrekin Trust suggested to me, deeper forms of collaboration within the progressive milieu would only become a reality if people experience a strong sense of inner connection with people from other traditions, groups and institutions.[81] Such inner connection may be more likely to be nurtured in the context of shared ritual space and practices. Once again, it may be initiatives within feminist and eco-spirituality that lead to the next stage of the restructuring of progressive religious identities and relationships.

The shape of progressive faith in the twenty-first century: A recapitulation

As the first half of this book draws to a close, I want to summarize briefly five key proposals that have emerged out of the discussion so far:

i)   Although progressive faith in the West has a longer history, clearly dating back to the early part of the nineteenth century, the restructuring of western religion since the 1960s has led to the emergence of a more clearly defined progressive milieu.

ii)   Individuals, organizations and networks can be defined as belonging to the progressive milieu if, in addition to claiming some kind of religious or spiritual identity, they are a) sympathetic to core values of liberal democracy (for example, tolerance, autonomy, diversity), b) have green or left-wing political attitudes (for example, are concerned with environmentalism, social justice, civil rights), or c) hold liberal or radical theological views (for example, are willing to revise religious tradition in the light of contemporary knowledge, are sympathetic to feminist critiques of organized religion, and/or believe that there is a truth inherent in all religious traditions). Individuals and groups within the progressive milieu normally demonstrate at least two of these three traits, and often demonstrate all three.

iii) Since the late 1960s, organic intellectuals within the progressive milieu have generated a particular religious ideology – progressive spirituality – which is advocated by writers across and beyond a wide range of religious traditions. This ideology is characterized by four key elements: a belief in the immanent divine unity which nurtures and sustains the unfolding cosmos; the sacralization of nature; the sacralization of the self; and a belief that these spiritual truths can be discerned within and beyond different religious traditions. The development of progressive spirituality has emerged out of a desire for forms of religious belief that embrace modern values and knowledge, for non-patriarchal forms of religion, for a faith grounded in the sacralization of contemporary science (for example, the new physics), and for a religious faith that reflects an ecological awareness. Progressive spirituality, as a religious ideology, does not represent a monolithic world view of those individuals and groups that make up the progressive milieu. But progressive spirituality does offer the possibility for a sense of shared consciousness based on common religious beliefs for people within the progressive milieu.

iv) Over the past twenty years, the progressive milieu has seen the emergence of a new generation of progressive religious and spiritual organizations. These organizations are engaged in a range of activities varying from those which focus on the internal life of the progressive milieu (e.g. providing support and resources for the spiritual development of individuals, building up the infrastructure of the progressive milieu) to activities which are focused beyond the progressive milieu (e.g. seeking to influence wider religious institutions and to shape debates and policies in the public sphere). Activities which have a stronger internal focus on the life of individuals and groups within the progressive milieu (e.g. conferences, rituals, or religious and spiritual educational programmes) are particularly likely to be influenced by the work of writers and thinkers who advocate the core tenets of progressive spirituality.

v) Whilst there is clear evidence of a sense of collective identity within the progressive milieu – sometimes explicitly constructed around the 'progressive' brand name – the exact content of individuals' and groups' sense of collective identity will vary according to their particular religious, social and political context. Whilst progressive spirituality offers the potential for the construction of a progressive religious and spiritual identity that transcends the boundaries of mainstream religious institutions and traditions, in practice there is still only limited collaboration across certain religious boundaries. This lack of collaboration is particularly noticeable between members of the Abrahamic faiths – Christianity, Islam, Judaism – and those involved in Paganism, Wicca and other forms of holistic spirituality. There is a range of structural and attitudinal factors that discourage such collaboration and, for the time being at least, it is difficult to foresee such barriers being overcome to any significant degree at an organizational level.

Having set out these central ideas about the nature and shape of progressive faith at the start of the twenty-first century, in the remainder of the book I want to turn to thinking about the progressive milieu and progressive spirituality in a wider social and cultural context. In Chapter Five, we will explore how progressive faith engages with broader debates about the moral decline of contemporary society. But before this, we shall explore how the progressive milieu and progressive spirituality fits within wider discussions about the changing face of religion in the modern world.

4 Progressive spirituality and modern religion in the West

During the course of the book, I have made some initial observations about the concerns and cultural traditions that have fostered the development of progressive spirituality. In this chapter, I want to place progressive spirituality in a wider context by thinking about it in relation to theories about the emerging forms of religion in modern western society.

A common assumption in the theories that we will explore in this chapter is that western religion has been transformed by the modernization of society. Modernization can be understood as a process of social change involving the rise of industrial and post-industrial economies, the increasing importance of public, secular and democratic institutions, the expansion of mass media, growing affluence for large sections of society, and greater flexibility in people's physical and social mobility.

Whilst some sociologists have described the religious effects of the rise of modern, liberal, bureaucratic and capitalist societies primarily in terms of secularization and the decline of traditional forms of religion,[1] others have talked about these social changes leading to new forms of religious belief and practice in the West. A complicating factor in such discussions is that, where as writers often talk generally about the effects of 'modernization' and 'modernity' on religion, it is increasingly obvious that modernization involves different kinds of social and cultural change, and has different effects on religion, depending on which part of the world is being discussed. As sociologists like Peter Berger, David Martin and Grace Davie have observed, the effects of modernization on religion in Europe has been very different to its effects on religion in North America, Latin America, Africa or Asia.[2] Recognizing these regional variations is very important in avoiding overly simplistic views of social change in the modern world. But it is also reasonable to suggest that there is enough similarity in the experience of modernity in Britain and North America for it to be possible to develop more general theories about emerging forms of religiosity in these two different contexts. In this chapter, we will examine ideas that are potentially relevant to the changing religious landscape on both sides of the Atlantic. During the course of this discussion we will look at theories of the emergence of a spiritual marketplace, and the subjective turn in contemporary religion, together with ideas about the rise of the 'cultic milieu' and the nature of secular society. Before this, though, we will begin by thinking about the work of three pioneers in theorizing about modern forms of religion – Durkheim, Troeltsch and Simmel.

Three theoretical pioneers

One of the first, and arguably most important, analyses of the new form of religion in modern society was developed by the French sociologist Emile Durkheim, whose main work was written in the latter nineteenth and early twentieth centuries.[3] Durkheim argued that one of the key changes that modernization had brought to western culture was the rise in the social importance of the individual.[4] Writing in his classic study, *Suicide*, Durkheim commented:

> Originally, society is everything, the individual nothing... man [sic] is considered only an instrument in its hands... But gradually things change. As societies... increase in complexity, work is divided, individual differences multiply, and the moment approaches when the only remaining bond among the members of a single human group will be that they are all

men. Under such conditions the body of collective sentiments inevitably attaches itself with all its strength to its single remaining object... Since human personality is the only thing that appeals unanimously to all hearts, since its enhancement is the only aim that can be collectively pursued, it inevitably acquires exceptional value in the eyes of all. It thus rises far above all human aims, assuming a religious nature.[5]

Durkheim recognized that the increasing emphasis on individualism in modern society had a negative side to it. He saw the unrestrained desires and changing interests of the individual as a destabilizing force in society, and argued that the new freedoms of the individual came at the price of a sense of loss of meaning and structure in life – a condition for which he coined the term 'anomie'.[6] Yet, at the same time, Durkheim argued that regard for the individual could become a new form of collective religion – not in the sense of valuing everyone's changing desires or whims, but of valuing the ideal of the free, rational and happy person.[7] This new collective conscience would be based on the recognition of the inherent value and dignity of the individual person, and would seek to create the social and cultural conditions in which all individuals could have the chance to flourish. Describing this new humanist religion in his book, *The Division of Labour*, Durkheim commented:

[The cult of the individual] does not make us servants of ideal powers of a nature other than our own, which follow their directions without occupying themselves with the interests of men. It only asks that we be thoughtful of our fellows and that we be just, that we fulfil our duty, that we work at the function we can best execute, and receive the just reward for our services. The rules which constitute it do not have a constraining force which snuffs out free thought; but because they are... made for us, and in a certain sense, by us, we are free. We wish to understand them; we do not fear to change them.[8]

To this end, Durkheim argued for the importance of social structures that would support individual life, including the nation state,[9] the legal system,[10] as well as other intermediate organizations that could enthuse people in the 'cult of the individual' in more direct ways than more abstract legal and political systems.[11] Indeed Durkheim believed that this new secular religion of the individual would inevitably displace all older religious traditions, which would not survive the passage into modernity.[12] Unlike these dying religions, Durkheim claimed that the growing cult of the individual was the only possible form of collective religion that could serve as a rational basis for modern life,[13] whilst, at the same time, stimulating powerful moral sentiments.[14] Nevertheless, writing at the start of the twentieth century, Durkheim still had the sense of living in a transitional period between the death of the old religions, and the full emergence of the new cult of the individual. Writing towards the end of his life, in 1914, Durkheim commented that 'the old ideals and divinities which incarnate them are dying because they no longer respond sufficiently to the new aspirations of our day; and the new ideals which are necessary to orient our life are not yet born'.[15] He found himself looking forward in anticipation for the new forms of collective ritual that would celebrate this new, emerging religiosity.[16] Despite developing most of these ideas more than a century ago, Durkheim, it seems, was very prescient in anticipating some of the significant religious developments of our time.

Other pioneering writers in early twentieth-century sociology, Georg Simmel and Ernst Troeltsch, saw in modernity the rise of new mystical forms of religion. This new mysticism emphasized the importance of personal, inner spiritual experience and had no more than a very loose attachment to traditional Christian doctrine – either interpreting this doctrine as a symbolic expression of inner spiritual truths or moving away from it altogether. Both Troeltsch and Simmel saw this new form of mysticism as an expression of dissatisfaction with the traditional teachings and structures of the Church, which seemed ill-suited to describing contemporary religious experience, dealing with new scientific ways of understanding the world or facing the challenges of pluralist and democratic societies.[17] Troeltsch saw this mystical and spiritual form of religion as becoming increasingly popular with the 'cultured classes' of artists and intellectuals who no longer found the Church an adequate spiritual or intellectual home.

Troeltsch's comments, made in 1911 in his magisterial study of *The Social Teaching of the Christian Churches*, were certainly borne out by wider cultural developments. By the end of that decade, artists such as Kandinsky and Mondrian had developed new abstract forms of painting which they saw as means of direct mystical engagement with spiritual truth – a process which proved highly influential in the emergence of 'spiritual' art beyond the boundaries of the Church.[18]

For Simmel, this emergent mysticism entailed a new understanding of life. Although many people found themselves alienated from traditional Christian beliefs and symbols, their religious impulses persisted. Lacking any external belief-system to which such impulses could be attached, Simmel argued that these impulses instead became focused on the subjective experience of life. Or, in his words, in this new mysticism, religion becomes 'a way of living life itself', without any reference to an external God.[19] As a consequence the whole of life becomes sacred. The religious, or mystical, life is no longer the pursuit of God, but the pursuit of a particular quality of life characterized by a sense of depth and wholeness.

Both Troeltsch and Simmel were critical of this new form of mysticism. Simmel commented that 'nowhere amongst [these new adherents of mysticism], except in isolated individual cases, can I discern any genuinely viable belief providing an adequate and precise expression of the religious life'.[20] He questioned whether the 'turn to life' in this new mysticism could ever be more than 'a formless energy which can confer upon the ups and downs of life only a certain colouring and grandeur'.[21] Could this post-Christian mysticism ever reach beyond a somewhat banal spiritualizing of everyday life to achieve the transforming potential of deeper forms of religion? Simmel doubted that it could. Troeltsch similarly expressed concern that the individualistic emphasis of this new mysticism tended only to generate small and short-lived networks of like-minded individuals rather than social institutions that could have a more significant and longer-lasting effect on society.[22] As a consequence, Troeltsch could only see this new mysticism as a short-lived phenomenon – simply 'a foreshadowing of coming developments' emerging out of more traditional forms of religion[23] – incapable of 'influencing the masses or effecting any kind of

organization of life on a large scale'.[24] Simmel also speculated
whether this new form of mysticism was anything more than a
temporary phenomenon – a transitional stage between the rejection
of one system of religious dogma and the discovery of a new one.[25]
Arguably, though, Troeltsch and Simmel proved to be wrong on this
point. If anything, the subsequent decades of the twentieth century
saw the spread of this new mysticism from an educated elite to
wider society, in much the same way that Daniel Bell saw, in the
twentieth century, the popularization of the elite, modernist notion
of the individual life as an artistic project.[26]

The next generation

Attempts to define the new, emerging religiosity of the West
continued through the middle decades of the twentieth century. In
his major (and now largely neglected) study on *Social and Cultural
Dynamics*, the Russian social theorist, Pitirim Sorokin, described
western society as having become an 'over-ripe sensate culture',[27]
in which the glories of a culture grounded in the scientific study
and economic management of observable reality were descending
into crass materialism and hedonism. Writing in 1957, Sorokin
saw western culture as standing at the edge of an uncertain time
of transition – 'the light is fading, and in the deepening shadows
it becomes more and more difficult to see clearly and to orient
ourselves safely in the confusions of the twilight'.[28] He predicted
that the near future for western society was bleak – to be marked
by a loss of shared public values, greater exploitation within the
capitalist system, diminishing freedom, the rise of mediocrity over
genuine creativity and growing levels of anxiety and depression.[29]
Unlike demoralization theorists who might see these simply as
symptoms of a culture in decline, Sorokin saw these more as birth
pangs of a new 'ideational' (that is, spiritual) culture, shaped by
a shared commitment to 'eternal, lasting, universal and absolute
values'.[30] Sorokin thus saw the future of the West in terms of the
dawning of a new spiritual era which built on the advances of the
previous scientific, sensate age to forge a new golden age of spiritual
truth and wisdom. He was unable to describe in more specific terms
what this coming golden age would look like – the twilight of the

present was too dark to see what lay ahead in any detail – but his conviction remained that the West was on the verge of some form of spiritual renaissance.

Other attempts to define new, emerging forms of religiosity continued through the twentieth century. Writing in 1963, the German sociologist, Thomas Luckmann, noted the secularizing effects of modern societies and observed that traditional, institutional religion (that is, the Christian Church) was facing a long-term decline.[31] In its place, though, he argued that a new social form of religion was growing which focused on personal autonomy and self-expression.[32] This new form of religion was not based in traditional religious institutions, but was a wider cultural ethos supported by a range of 'secondary' institutions including the media, workshops and training courses, and different forms of health and leisure activities.[33] Luckmann was one of the first sociologists to refer to this new religious landscape in terms of a consumer marketplace, in which individuals make choices about which groups, resources and practices will be most useful for developing their lives.[34] In this consumer environment, there is a continual pressure for the providers of spiritual services to offer resources that are useful for consumers, and the continual risk that such providers become irrelevant or unhelpful to consumers' concerns. The relatively stable picture of traditional religious beliefs supported by long-lasting religious institutions is thus replaced by a more diffuse religious concern with personal meaning and self-development supported by fluid networks of short-lived groups, publications and workshops.

A similar picture of an unstable modern religious landscape was painted by Luckmann's colleague, Peter Berger. Like Luckmann, Berger wrote about the emergence of a new religious marketplace in which people are 'faced with the necessity to choose between gods'.[35] What caused the emergence of this new religious marketplace, he argued, was the growing pluralism of modern society. By pluralism, Berger meant not only an increased awareness of different religious and cultural traditions brought about by immigration and the shrinking of the world through travel, mass media and new communication technologies, but also the growing range of choice at the level of everyday life. Indeed, he argued that the expansion of choice in different areas of life was *the* defining feature of modernity.[36] As one example of this, he noted the relatively recent rise of new birth-control technologies which allow couples much greater choice over when, or indeed whether, to have a child.[37] Such social changes, in which people have much greater choice about how to live – from their choice of fashion, leisure tastes, careers, sexual relationships and beliefs – has created a society in which 'lifestyle' becomes an ongoing source of interest and concern.[38] Within this kind of lifestyle culture, people are inevitably cast into the role of consumers who face a 'smooth continuity between consumer choices in different areas of life'[39] and who are forced to choose between various options on the lifestyle menu.

Berger suggested that the rise of the modern lifestyle culture had had profound effects on religion. In a society in which an open religious marketplace has replaced any traditional religious consensus, people are forced to make their own religious choices about what beliefs and lifestyles are meaningful and useful. Such choices encourage a process of 'subjectivization', in which people become much more self-conscious about their thoughts, feelings, needs and aspirations. For if there is no received wisdom that people can turn to in wider society to guide their religious choices, where else can they turn to but their own subjective sense of what seems helpful or true?[40] Berger also suggested that the expanding menu of religious beliefs and practices did not simply turn people into religious consumers, but also had the effect of weakening their ability to maintain any religious belief at all. It is hard to maintain the belief that one's own religious views are absolutely and uniquely true in a society in which people hold very diverse religious beliefs with apparent integrity. Such depth of conviction is even harder to maintain without the support of strong religious institutions which provide plausibility structures that reinforce those religious beliefs. But, again, the open religious marketplace is precisely one that weakens the influence of individual religious institutions as they are forced to try to protect their territory in an increasingly competitive environment.[41] Berger therefore initially suggested that the greater choice of the open religious marketplace actually led to secularization, as people struggled to maintain any clear religious beliefs or identity in the confusing mix of pluralist society. He later changed his view on this – writing in 1999 that, far from being secularized, the world 'is as furiously religious as it ever was'.[42] Berger suggested that the uncertainty of the modern world might have quite the opposite effect to his earlier suggestion that it would undermine any and all religious belief – indeed this uncertainty might actually be an important stimulus for people to seek for some kind of meaning and comfort in religion.[43] Nevertheless, whether people in modern society espoused some form of religious belief or not, he observed that only the most deluded could fool themselves that underlying their religious stance was some form of personal choice.[44]

From the 1970s onwards, sociological theories about the changing nature of religion in modern western societies emerged out of three (often overlapping) areas of study. These three lines of study focused on the emergence of new religious movements, the nature of the changing patterns of religiosity in the post-war 'baby boomer' generation and the nature of religion in an increasingly secularized society, and we will now consider some of the ideas emerging from these different areas of study.

New religious trends and movements:
The rise of the cultic milieu and occulture

Firstly, then, the rise of new religious movements (often popularly referred to as 'cults') attracted the interest of sociologists in Britain and America in the 1970s and 1980s.[45] The fact that new religious groups could develop – even though numerically small in relation to society as a whole – meant that modern society was not turning out to be universally secular. In attempting to understand these groups, and the wider religious trends that lay behind their popularity, sociologists made some important observations about the changing religious environment in the West. Writing in 1972, Colin Campbell suggested that a network of loosely organized and transitory new religious groups were emerging out of a 'cultic milieu', a cultural underground of 'unorthodox science, alien and heretical religion [and] deviant medicine'.[46] Whilst the particular beliefs and practices of these groups ranged widely across nature religions, UFO cults, esotericism and eastern religions, Campbell argued that there were more general features that were characteristic of this emerging spiritual milieu. He suggested that these included a tendency to be 'ecumenical, … syncretistic and tolerant in outlook', a shared network of media and communication structures that tended to support and cross-publicize the activities and resources of different groups and a common ideology of spiritual 'seekership' in which individuals were looking for satisfying systems of religious meaning beyond the boundaries of traditional religion.[47] Campbell argued that the growing strength of this 'cultic milieu' was made possible precisely because the social standing of the Church had been weakened through the secularization of society. With the diminishing authority of the Church in wider society came greater cultural freedom for people to explore other spiritual alternatives. Thus 'what has been traditionally treated as categorically deviant and subject to… ecclesiastical wrath is gradually becoming merely variant'.[48] As Campbell observed, perhaps the most remarkable sign of this was that witchcraft – so often the focus of Christianized repression in the past – was showing signs of becoming more culturally acceptable as an alternative spiritual practice.

Taking up Campbell's thesis, Chris Partridge has recently argued that the decades following the 1970s have seen the continued rise of this 'cultic milieu' into the cultural mainstream.[49] Nursing manuals now include sections on alternative healthcare practices, top-rating TV shows (from *Buffy* to the *X-Files*) contain references to witchcraft and esoteric religion, and major bookstores such as Borders and Waterstones now carry extensive 'mind-body-spirit' sections. Partridge describes this process as the rise of 'occulture' into the cultural mainstream of society. He prefers the term 'occulture' to 'cultic milieu' because he believes the latter has become too closely associated with mystical forms of religion – and, in his view, mysticism is not a sufficiently accurate umbrella term to describe this alternative spiritual scene.[50] The term occulture is also helpful in reminding us that this alternative spiritual milieu is a form of culture. People engage with occulture, then, through a range of cultural activities – not just obviously 'spiritual' activities like meditating – but through everyday activities like listening to certain popular music, playing certain video games or watching particular films and TV programmes. The increasing pervasiveness of this occultural milieu across society suggests that it is beginning to displace institutional Christianity as the dominant religious culture. Thus, although society is showing clear signs of secularization in terms of the decline of institutional Christianity, Partridge argues that there are clear signs of a re-enchantment of the West if we pay attention to the rising influence of occultural beliefs and practices.

In a similar vein, Colin Campbell has also more recently argued that we are currently witnessing the 'Easternization of the West', in which a traditional Judaeo-Christian culture is finding itself increasingly replaced by an easternized one.[51] Through this process, traditional western assumptions, such as the belief in an external and personal God, the separation of humankind from nature, and an emphasis on the importance of reason and science for cultural progress, fall into disuse. In their place arise an emphasis on the fundamental unity of all existence, the importance of harmony with nature and on meditation as a means to enlightenment and unity with the greater ground of being. Even traditional western beliefs about the nature of the afterlife, such as the reality of eternal punishment in Hell, become less popular, whilst belief in reincarnation increases. Steve Bruce has even suggested, tongue somewhat in cheek, that this process of easternization has reached the point where people in Britain are now 'Buddhist by default'.[52]

The shape of post-war baby-boomer religion

By the 1980s and 1990s, a growing literature had developed on the religion of the post-war baby-boomer generation (that is, those born between 1945 and 1960). Important contributions to this research have been made by leading American sociologists of religion such as Wade Clark Roof and Robert Wuthnow.[53] Roof has argued that since the baby boomers started coming to adulthood in the 1960s, there has been a significant shift in the American religiosity towards what he describes as a spiritual-quest culture characterized by individuals' search for a meaningful spirituality.[54] In this context, terms such as the 'soul', 'sacred', and 'spiritual' have particular resonance and metaphors of spiritual growth and spiritual journeys have become common currency. Roof recognizes that the search for authentic, personalized religion is hardly a new phenomenon in America – indeed the emphasis on the freedom to pursue one's own religion lies at the foundations of the modern American nation. But what is distinctive about this new culture of spiritual searching is how widespread it has become, its emphasis on the importance of self-awareness and self-development in an uncertain world, and the way in which it has evolved beyond immature self-absorption to a deeper interest in self-transformation and the transformation of society.[55] Reflecting this increased emphasis on a personally meaningful engagement with religion, Roof observes that the religious landscape in America has radically changed into an 'expanded spiritual marketplace'. In this market setting, religion becomes far more fluid, as forces of supply and demand shape the rise of fall of particular groups and traditions, and loyalties to particular religious groups weaken as people perceive themselves more as spiritual consumers and less as life-long members.[56]

A similar account of post-1945 religion is given by Robert Wuthnow.[57] Wuthnow describes the 1960s as a critical decade which transformed not only the religiosity of the baby-boomer generation, but also the generations of their parents as well as their children ('Generation X' or the 'baby-busters'). He argues that American religiosity changed from 'spirituality of dwelling' in the 1950s, characterized by a relatively uncritical sense of security in established religious traditions and institutions, to a 'spirituality of seeking' by the end of the 1960s.[58] Wuthnow identifies a range of factors in the 1960s that weakened traditional religious bonds and gave rise to this sense of spiritual searching, if not full-blown spiritual homelessness. These range from greater social mobility that weakened family and local community ties,[59] the increased choices of the new consumer society, the increasing numbers of young people receiving college education,[60] and new forms of contraception which lengthened the period that young adults had for experimenting with different lifestyles before having children.[61] To this list, he adds the challenges to well-entrenched thinking about race and gender raised by the civil rights and women's liberation movements, the intellectual criticism of traditional religious ideas encouraged both outside and within the Church,[62] and the rising interest in eastern religions.[63] As a consequence of these changes, the social, intellectual and emotional ties that connected people to established religious communities weakened. Not only this, but the baby boomers found themselves entering adulthood in a culture which encouraged freedom of thought and self-expression and in which a greater range of lifestyle choices and spiritualities were open to them. In this context, it is unsurprising that fewer baby boomers chose to give their own children traditional religious upbringings, which in turn led to a further weakening of assumed religious loyalties in the younger generations.[64]

The accounts of post-war religion offered by Roof and Wuthnow contain substantial similarities. Both suggest that the relatively stable and unchallenged religious environment of 1950s America began to fragment with the major social changes of the 1960s, which in turn led to a more open and uncertain religious environment. In this new context, people are less likely to stay with the same local church or synagogue for the whole of their lives and are more likely instead to engage with different groups as their needs, interests and indeed physical locations change at different points in their lives. This new spiritual marketplace was a highly diversified one, with new religious movements and alternative spiritual practices flourishing as well as highly conservative groups. The most significant change underlying all of these developments, though, was that religion became increasingly a matter of personal interest and concern and, at times, sheer hard work. Robert Wuthnow's notion of this new approach to religion being a *negotiated* one, captures some sense of the ongoing process of individuals trying to find spiritual resources that match their experiences, values and needs. As he puts it, this process of negotiation involves people searching for 'sacred moments that reinforce their conviction that the divine exists, but these moments are fleeting; rather than knowing the territory, people explore new spiritual vistas, and they may have to negotiate among complex and confusing meanings of spirituality'.[65] How different this culture of spiritual searching is from the experiences of previous generations in which religion may have served more as an assumed backdrop for the drama of everyday life.

The new shape of religion in 'secular' society

One of the dominant debates in the sociology of religion over the past century has focused on whether (and why) western society is becoming increasingly secularized. Whilst this debate remains fiercely contested, it has become clear that significant numbers of people in the West do not conform to a pattern of church-attending Christians who believe all the basic elements of orthodox Christian doctrine (though this still remains true of a greater part of the US population than it is of Britons). In the face of such evidence, an ongoing debate has opened up as to the nature of religiosity beyond the boundaries of traditional religious institutions.

Many writers have argued that belief beyond the boundaries of religion is now essentially secular – devoid of any semblance of traditional religious belief. Bryan Wilson, for example, observes that few people in the West today hope for some kind of salvation beyond this world, or expect some spiritual or divine force to provide healing and salvation in this world or the next. Instead, people are more likely to seek salvation in this world and this lifetime in terms of their own personal well-being, and to turn to sources under human control (for example, education, medicine, psychotherapy, or welfare provision) as the means to achieve this.[66] Wilson regarded this shift with some dismay. Writing from the cloisters of All Souls College, Oxford, he deplored the hedonistic values of consumer society ('indulgence, luxury, extravagance')[67] and saw the decline in manners in contemporary culture as a symptom of a wider moral decline. Other writers have taken a more positive view of the rise of secular beliefs in the West.[68] Richard Fenn, for example, sees secular society as an opportunity to move beyond religious cultures which have tended to demand unnecessary sacrifices of people that have served only to 'create individuals with a faulty sense of their own being'.[69] Fenn regards an open form of secular faith as a promising existential approach to the uncertainties and vulnerabilities of human existence.[70] Such a faith would represent a true openness to the Sacred, unlike institutional religion which tends to replace the unknowable Sacred with tangible symbols, doctrines and rituals. Furthermore, by rejecting religious fantasies about a temporal order above and beyond our own lives (such as eternal life), we may come to a more honest recognition of our condition, even if this means being deprived of 'the narcissistic satisfaction of knowing that one's earthly sacrifices really matter'.[71]

An alternative view of the nature of religiosity in a post-Christian society is provided by David Martin. Martin has been a long-standing critic of the ideas that modern societies inevitably become more secular,[72] and that secularization is an irreversible process.[73] Instead, he argues that for much of the past two millennia western society has oscillated between Christianized and de-Christianized forms of culture, and that we currently find ourselves at a more secular point in this recurrent cycle in which an explicit Christian culture is, for a time, receding.[74] Martin suggests that cultural shifts away from Christianity tend to involve a shift towards some kind of emphasis on 'nature'. In our current situation, he argues that this involves both the residue of Protestant concern with individual belief and experience (what he calls 'evangelical heartwork')[75] combined with a Romantic belief in the sacredness of nature. This mixture leads to a view of life that regards nature as essentially good, rejects the need for salvation from any supernatural source mediated through religious ritual, and encourages the pursuit of authentic and natural lives. This emerging world view is not universally held throughout western society. Martin notes, for example, how Evangelical Christianity has been relatively successful in remaining in tune with the contemporary emphasis of personal experience and quality of personal life, whilst at the same time emphasizing the importance of faith and obedience before God. Furthermore, whilst the current 'turn to nature' may appear more Pagan than Christian, he argues that it unconsciously draws on Jewish and Christian assumptions about the goodness of creation. In summary, the rising religiosity of contemporary post-Christian society is not pure secularism, but a form of Christian Romanticism which values the natural over the supernatural. The capacity of Christianity to infuse society with 'contrary imaginations',[76] however, means that this current turn to nature may well be replaced by some other new form of religiosity which gives more weight to transcendence and the call of a higher spiritual authority.

The extent to which new forms of religiosity in the West continue to be dependent on some form of Christian roots remains controversial. For example, Grace Davie has suggested that British society remains infused with a nominal Protestantism,[77] and argues that religiosity beyond the institutional Church falls on a spectrum from nominal Christianity to an eclectic mix of spiritual beliefs and superstitions.[78] She has also described contemporary religiosity in Europe as 'vicarious religion', in which 'a significant proportion of Europeans delegate to their churches... what they no longer consider doing themselves'.[79] In other words, a substantial part of the population in modern European societies do not maintain much by way of an active religious life, but are happy for mainstream churches to continue to act as religious resources that they might turn to in times of need or uncertainty.[80] This pattern of 'vicarious religion' may be more common to Europe, with its tradition of established state churches, than in America, where religious involvement has always been a matter of individual choice. Nevertheless, Davie emphasizes that such vicarious religiosity does not represent a significant shift in the content of religious beliefs in Europe – it is simply a different way of being religious. Vicarious religion is still broadly Christian in terms of its content.[81]

Davie's views are certainly not universally accepted. There is, for example, a striking difference between her analysis of the current religious milieu of the West, and Chris Partridge's claims about the rise of 'occulture'. Where Davie sees a mix of nominal Christianity and eclectic spiritual beliefs and superstitions, Partridge sees the emergence of a cultural reservoir of spiritual beliefs and practices that are primarily influenced by eastern thought or reconstructed forms of western nature religions. 'Occulture' is, at best, indifferent to Christianity, but more often actively hostile to it and attempts to define itself over and against Christian institutions and traditions. Similarly, David Tacey suggests that, whilst emerging trends in youth spirituality are not necessarily anti-Christian, young people tend to be more sympathetic to personalized, nature-based, mystical spiritualities which they do not normally associate with traditional religious institutions. Their preference, claims Tacey, is for an 'immanentist' belief in the presence of the spirit within this world, rather than a 'transcendent' theology of an external God who commands love and obedience.[82]

As this brief discussion indicates, there is a consensus amongst these writers that a significant shift is taking place in religiosity in the West but little consensus as to what new forms and patterns of religiosity are emerging. Is belief beyond the boundaries of formal institutions like the Church still broadly Christian? Or is it secular, Romantic, Pagan, occultural or mystical? It is within this ongoing debate that Paul Heelas and Linda Woodhead have recently argued that we are experiencing a particular form of spiritual revolution – and it is to their work that we shall now turn.

The spiritual revolution: The importance of subjectivity and the rise of spiritualities of life

Heelas and Woodhead's book, *The Spiritual Revolution: Why Religion is Giving Way to Spirituality*, represents one of the most important recent interventions in the debate about the nature of new forms of religiosity in contemporary western society. *The Spiritual Revolution* summarises findings from a two-year study of changing patterns in religion and spirituality in the town of Kendal in the north of England. This study sought to examine what Heelas and Woodhead describe as their 'subjectivization thesis'.[83] This thesis begins from the assertion that modern western culture has undergone a 'massive subjective turn', in which individual life has become increasingly valued, greater authority is given to personal experience, and concerns about personal health, relationships and meaning have become more important.[84] Unlike Peter Berger who, as we noted earlier, saw this process of subjectivization as essentially a by-product of a modern culture in which people are forced to make more choices about their lives, Heelas and Woodhead see subjectivization as the driving force behind cultural change in the West. In this regard, Heelas explicitly acknowledges his debt to earlier sociologists such as Durkheim and Simmel who initially described the emerging cult of the individual and the turn to life in modern society.[85] As a consequence of this subjective turn, Heelas and Woodhead's 'subjectivization thesis' suggests that forms of spirituality which emphasize individual freedom and autonomy, value personal experience and address issues of personal concern are more likely to flourish. At the same time, traditional forms of religion which emphasize divine authority over personal experience, place religious duty before personal freedom and self-expression, and 'subsume'[86] the self within the rules and traditions of a particular religious community are likely to be in decline.

The kind of religiosity that Heelas and Woodhead suggest is most likely to flourish in this subjectivized culture are what they refer to as 'spiritualities of life' or 'subjective-life spiritualities'.[87] Such spiritualities focus on the importance of personal health and well-being in this lifetime, rather than seeing this world as a stage towards a more important, and eternal, life beyond this one. They also involve a rejection of the notion of an external God who is to be loved and obeyed, but instead see the spiritual dimension of life as one part of human experience. The divine is therefore not to be found in religious scriptures and laws, but in personal experience and the natural world. Indeed Heelas has argued that one of the defining features of New Age spiritualities is that God is seen not as an external being but as a higher part of the self.[88] The rising forms of religiosity do not necessarily even refer to 'God' or the divine at all, however. Indeed spiritualities of life which use religious language drawn from nature religions, mysticisms, eastern religion or other esoteric traditions, are only part of a wider growth of what Heelas calls 'humanistic expressivism'.[89] This broader movement is humanist in the sense of valuing personal experience, individual freedom and self-expression and is again analogous to Durkheim's 'cult of the individual' and Luckmann's 'new social form of religion'. Broader than Campbell's notion of the 'cultic milieu' or Partridge's concept of 'occulture', it embraces not only specialized groups and networks concerned with New Age or alternative spiritualities, but also the increasing movement towards personal development and holistic well-being in healthcare, leisure industries, business and education.[90]

Whilst Heelas and Woodhead's subjectivization thesis explains the growth of spiritualities of life and the wider cultural concern with subjective life, it also suggests which forms of religion may be better suited to this new cultural environment. Conservative forms of religion which simply emphasize obedience to divine authority, or old-style liberal religion which emphasizes the importance of adhering to basic values but has little to say about the challenges of contemporary lifestyle culture, are ill-suited to the subjective turn. By contrast, forms of religion that maintain a sense of divine authority, but focus on the relevance of divine truth for practical concerns of personal life or which approach God as a force for personal healing and growth are better placed, because they demonstrate the relevance of religion to subjective life.[91] Thus whilst mainline liberal churches continue to decline, many Evangelical and Charismatic congregations fare much better as they provide more substantial religious resources for dealing with lifestyle issues, structures for experiencing divine healing, and small groups that provide spaces to reflect in a religious context on personal experiences and concerns.[92]

In summary, then, Heelas and Woodhead's subjectivization thesis suggests that modern western culture has been characterized by a turn to the self and a turn away from the importance of salvation in the next life to well-being in this one. Those forms of religion and spirituality that address the concerns of subjective life, and provide resources for well-being in the here and now, are therefore more likely to survive and grow than those which do not.

The empirical evidence from their study in Kendal supports this thesis.[93] Heelas and Woodhead found that there was a clear divide amongst those people in the town engaged in some form of explicitly religious or spiritual activity. Those who held traditional religious beliefs about the importance of obedience to an external God were almost entirely based in church congregations. By contrast, those who demonstrated attitudes associated with spiritualities of life or subjective-life spiritualities were based in what Heelas and Woodhead describe as a 'holistic milieu' of alternative healthcare and spirituality groups. Since the 1960s, the church congregations in Kendal had experienced significant decline. Although the raw numbers of people attending Kendal's churches had actually remained relatively static since the 1960s, the growth of the total population of Kendal meant that as a proportion of that population, the total number of church-goers had actually halved over that period. By contrast, participation in the 'holistic milieu' had increased dramatically from virtually nothing in the early 1970s to more than forty different groups by 1999. In the 1990s alone, the numbers of people taking part in this holistic milieu increased by roughly 300 per cent at a time when the population growth of the town as a whole was 11.4 per cent. Again, as predicted by the subjectivization thesis, those church congregations which gave greater emphasis to subjective concerns tended to fare better than those which did not. The New Life Community Church in Kendal, an independent Charismatic Evangelical congregation, had not experienced the same levels of decline as several old-style liberal congregations in the town – but even the growing numbers of people attending the New Life church failed to match the population growth of the town as a whole. Interestingly, though, Heelas and Woodhead discovered that the total numbers of people taking part in church services still exceeded the numbers of those taking part in the range of groups and activities in the holistic milieu. A headcount of all those taking part in church services in Kendal on a given Sunday in November 2000 gave a total of 2,207 adults and children, whilst only around 600 people were participating in the holistic milieu on a weekly basis during the same period. They note, however, that if church congregations continue to decline at their current rate, and the holistic milieu continues to grow at its current rate, then the numbers participating in the holistic milieu in Kendal would exceed those attending church within the next thirty years. It could also be added that those involved in the 'expressive spirituality' of the holistic milieu in Kendal are simply one part of the wider rise of 'humanistic expressivism' in contemporary culture and that, far from being an imminent possibility, the spiritual revolution has already happened.

Rather than being simply demonstrated in this single case study, Heelas and Woodhead argue that their subjectivization thesis is also demonstrated by a much broader range of empirical evidence from Britain and the United States. The pattern of congregational decline in Kendal is matched by national measures of falling church attendances in Britain, and the growth of the holistic milieu there is similarly matched by national measures of the rising numbers of practitioners of complementary and alternative medicine. Although the percentage of the US population attending church on a regular basis is probably at least three times greater than the British figure of 7.9 per cent, American church attendances have still seen a significant fall since the 1950s. Heelas and Woodhead estimate that around 25 per cent of the US population attend church on a regular basis, and that the percentage of Americans participating regularly in the holistic milieu could be between 2.5–8 per cent. The lack of hard statistical data for the holistic milieu in particular, however, makes it difficult both to judge accurately its size and its rate of growth.

Two further brief points should be made about Heelas and Woodhead's work. Firstly, Linda Woodhead – unlike any of the previous writers we have discussed so far in this chapter – argues that gender plays a significant role in shaping new forms of religion and spirituality in the West.[94] In particular, she has analysed the division between traditional forms of religion and new emerging forms of spirituality in terms of how they help or hinder women's ability to manage their aspirations and roles in modern society. Woodhead notes that male sociologists of religion have often overlooked how modernization in the West has changed women's roles and opportunities. At first, modernity in the West involved a clearer separation of the domestic and public arenas of social life, with women largely constrained to functioning within the domestic sphere.[95] At the same time, religious institutions found their role in the public sphere weakening, and a closer association developed between religion and domestic life, with religion serving as a buttress for domestic morality and domestic hierarchies. Over time, though, the forces that have prevented women from playing full roles in the public sphere of work and politics have weakened, giving women greater access to education, careers and political power. Traditional forms of religion, however, have struggled to adapt to this change and have tended to see the woman's proper social role remaining in the home. Such assumptions about gender roles can be subtly reinforced, for example, by such commonly used metaphors as the 'Church as family'.[96] This is not necessarily a problem for women who do not seek to enter the public sphere, and for them religious institutions can still be an important source of support

– and sometimes even a structure in which they can find their own forms of influence and opportunities for self-expression.[97] But for women who seek to develop their own careers or other public roles, the traditional gender roles assumed within mainstream religious institutions can be problematic and unsupportive of their attempts to participate on equal terms with men in public and professional settings. As a consequence, at least a proportion of women who seek to develop careers may find traditional religious institutions a less supportive environment and may seek spiritual support elsewhere.[98] In this context, it is striking that 80 per cent of those active in the holistic milieu in Kendal are women – though Woodhead speculates that this figure could reflect the fact that women are socialized into relational attitudes more than men, and so the relational emphasis of many of the activities in the holistic milieu might appeal more to women than men.[99] Woodhead's analysis of religion and gender does, then, raise the possibility that women's engagement with modernity may itself be a significant influence in shaping which forms of religion and spirituality grow and which decline.[100]

Secondly, Heelas and Woodhead are not neutral observers of the spiritual revolution, but for different reasons see it as a potentially constructive development. Heelas describes himself as 'an optimistic humanist because my own experience of life makes it much harder for me to believe in atheism than to hope that life really is as mysterious and supra-empirical as it appears'.[101] He thus sympathizes with the 'turn to life' described by Simmel, and sees the cult of the individual identified by Durkheim as an important and hopeful moral resource for the future of western culture.[102] Woodhead, as we have just seen, sees the rise of spiritualities of life as potentially empowering for women who are offered only a restricted sense of their gender role and identity by more traditional forms of religion. Both Heelas and Woodhead are also keen to challenge the idea that the emerging subjective-life spiritualities that they are describing are simply shallow, narcissistic expressions of late modern consumer culture. They have commented that a significant proportion of those participating in the holistic milieu in Kendal were involved in various caring professions.[103] They also note that the phenomenon of 'Sheila-ism', the personalized religion of one Sheila Larson interviewed by Robert Bellah and his associates for their *Habits of the Heart* study, is not in fact the shallow, individualistic spirituality that subsequent commentators have often taken it to be. Indeed Sheila Larson's personalized faith – 'just my own little voice' – was founded on the core principle of 'love yourself and be gentle with yourself. You know… take care of each other. I think [God] would want us to take care of each other'.[104] Far from leading her to live a life of shallow self-indulgence, Heelas and Woodhead remind us that Larson was in fact a nurse, whose life was focused on helping the sick and dying.[105] Far from being 'atomistic or selfish', they comment, 'subjective-life spirituality is holistic, involving self-in-relation rather than a self-in-isolation'.[106] Just as Durkheim saw the emerging cult of the individual as a viable moral resource for modern western society, so Heelas and Woodhead see the fruits of the spiritual revolution with a degree of optimism.

Progressive spirituality as a modern form of religion

So how can we understand progressive spirituality in light of these theories about the changing shape of religion in modern western society? Four points stand out in answer to this question.

Firstly, progressive spirituality reflects emerging trends in western beliefs and values towards the sacralization of nature, the self and everyday life. Its emphasis on the inherent worth of the individual, the importance of subjective life, and the authority of personal experience, makes it a clear example of Durkheim's cult of the individual and Heelas' humanistic expressivism. Its emphasis on direct personal spiritual experience, and its search for a spirituality beyond traditional theism, is the same as that detected in the 'new mysticism' of the early twentieth century by Simmel and Troeltsch.[107] And its combination of a nature-based religious sensitivity, together with concern for the interior spiritual life, clearly reflects the 'Christian Romanticism' that David Martin has suggested is the growing spiritual ethos of our day. Progressive spirituality is not the only example of these religious and cultural movements. The cult of the individual and humanistic expressivism are also clearly demonstrated, for example, in the burgeoning movement of secular counselling and psychotherapy over the past fifty years.

But progressive spirituality is one expression of the broader turn in western culture away from theistic notions of God, and towards an emphasis on the value of nature and the self that so many of the sociologists discussed in this chapter have described.

The fact that progressive spirituality forms part of these cultural trends once again indicates the deep western roots of this religious ideology. Progressive spirituality often draws on, or shows an affinity for, eastern religious ideas and practice. It clearly reflects the changing religious emphases that Campbell associates with the 'Easternization of the West' – such as the belief in the unity of all existence, valuing harmony with nature and encouraging meditation as a spiritual practice. But whilst eastern religious ideas have doubtless been attractive to many people associated with progressive spirituality, and have been important in helping them to find forms of spirituality not grounded in traditional theistic concepts of God, progressive spirituality remains fundamentally rooted in western cultural traditions. Progressive spirituality is a reflection of key post-Reformation trends such as the declining significance of theistic concepts of God, the fascination with the interior life of the self, and the turn to nature as a source of meaning and beauty – trends which find expression in the cult of the individual, humanistic expressivism, new mysticism and the 'Christian Romanticism'. Progressive spirituality certainly draws on religious traditions from the East, but it remains fundamentally a western cultural project, reflecting western religious trends and underscored by particular western cultural traditions.

As I have suggested earlier in the book, the deeper cultural roots of progressive spirituality make it unlikely to be a purely transitory phenomenon. If they were alive today, Simmel and Troeltsch would presumably be surprised to see that the 'new mysticism' of their day continues to flourish, albeit in newer, somewhat different forms. Indeed, if anything, it has spread out beyond the cultural elite with which Troeltsch associated it – as people turn to meditation classes, the underground rave scene and even surfing and snowboarding as sources of direct spiritual experience. In one sense, Simmel and Troeltsch were right to see a certain transience within this progressive religious milieu. Contemporary progressive spirituality has certainly developed in some respects compared to the new mysticism of their day, and it is unlikely that many of the progressive religious groups and networks that are flourishing today will still be with us in twenty or thirty years' time. But whilst progressive religious ideas develop, and progressive religious groups form and dissolve, the longer tradition of progressive religion in the West has proven remarkably resilient over the past two hundred years. The precarious institutional basis of progressive spirituality should not obscure the fact that because it draws on deeper cultural roots it has a longevity that extends beyond the life of individual progressive groups and networks. As Paul Heelas has rightly observed, movements such as progressive spirituality are not a symptom of the de-traditionalization of western society, but of the maintenance and evolution of particular western traditions. And, for this reason, progressive spirituality, in varying forms, is likely to be with us for many years to come. I don't make this observation out of some kind of regard for the magical, self-preserving capacities of western cultural traditions, but because the positive valuation of nature and the self are now so embedded into so many different areas of contemporary life. From the celebration of the importance of subjective life in film and popular music to the turn to 'natural', organic food, so much of everyday life in contemporary western society serves to reinforce the idea that well-being consists of a rich personal life, in close relation with loved ones, in the wider context of a healthy lifestyle and environment. It is in the context of such cultural values that progressive spirituality will continue to appeal to some people as a sacralized version of this celebration of life. Bearing in mind my observation back in the Introduction to this book that most people in contemporary western society are not motivated by clear religious beliefs or personalized spiritualities, progressive spirituality may still only attract a relatively small minority.

A second point to be made about understanding progressive spirituality in this wider context is that it is an example of religion adapting itself to the social and cultural conditions of modernity. Progressive spirituality provides an ideological framework, and networks, resources and practices, for the contemporary spiritual seeker. Its emphasis on the value of diverse religious traditions as resources for contemporary spirituality fits the ethos of the post-1960s spiritual marketplace. By emphasizing the authority of personal experience, progressive spirituality gives its stamp of approval to the process of subjectivization that Peter Berger suggested was an inevitable aspect of the age of religious consumerism. It perpetuates itself through secondary institutions which, although often short-lived, provide suitable contexts for nurturing and disseminating its liberal and democratic ethos. Progressive spirituality seeks to reinforce the benefits of the emergence of the free, modern individual, whilst at the same time offering a potential haven from the anomie and loneliness of the atomized individual by seeing life as lived within the larger story of a meaningful cosmos. It is a form of religion that has successfully adapted to the social and cultural conditions of late western modernity by offering sufficient flexibility for the modern spiritual seeker, but also enough coherence to address personal and social concerns in meaningful ways. Its sympathizers will also see in progressive spirituality an example of Wade Clark Roof's notion of more mature and socially responsible forms of the personal spiritual quest.

Progressive spirituality can therefore be seen as an example of how religion can adapt to modernity. Indeed progressive spirituality can be seen as an active attempt to resist the modern pressures of secularization. Thomas Luckmann argued that one of the most significant causes and symptoms of secularization in the West was the privatization of religion – the drift towards religion being a matter of personal concern for the individual but with little wider social significance. Progressive spirituality addresses the challenge of the privatization of religion, in part, by embracing it. It welcomes the shift towards the personalizing of faith – the emergence of personally authentic spirituality – and seeks to encourage forms of faith that are deeply meaningful for individuals. At the same time, progressive spirituality endorses forms of faith which are outward-looking, positioning the self as a responsible actor in an unfolding cosmic drama and inspiring people to engage in various forms of social activism. Progressive spirituality sees in secularization a dangerous process of the disenchantment of the world, which leaves it more vulnerable to economic and environmental exploitation. It seeks to resist the secularizing pressure for religion to become more marginalized in modern society by asserting that only by developing a constructive spiritual vision will humanity have a viable and sustainable future. Modernization need not necessarily lead to the kind of secularized world view of which Bryan Wilson despaired.

Progressive spirituality can therefore be seen as a form of religion that is at home in late modern, liberal democratic society. If Ernest Gellner and Anthony Giddens, amongst others, are right, though, religion does not necessarily need to embrace modern, liberal society in order to thrive in today's world.[108] Religious fundamentalism, they would argue, draws its strength from its very refusal of the liberal culture of diversity, freedom and choice. But if Heelas and Woodhead's subjectivization thesis is correct, then forms of religion which endorse the value of subjective life and provide resources for people's personal emotional, practical and spiritual concerns are more likely to enjoy the support of larger sections of contemporary western society. Progressive spirituality is one model of religion that has adapted to the culture of the subjective turn. Heelas and Woodhead's 'experiential religions of difference' – Pentecostalism, Evangelical Christianity, forms of Judaism and Islam which openly address issues of contemporary lifestyle concern – are another such model. The example of progressive spirituality suggests that the process of modernization does not necessarily lead to a largely secularized society, but that religion can adapt to the social conditions of modernity and continue to offer possibilities for religious and spiritually oriented lifestyles in the West as we embark on the twenty-first century.

A third point about progressive spirituality in relation to these theories of religion and modern society relates to notions of the rise of the 'cultic milieu' and occulture. As we noted earlier, both Colin Campbell and Chris Partridge have argued that alternative religious beliefs and traditions have become increasingly acceptable and mainstream since the 1960s. Their notions of the cultic milieu and occulture suggest a reservoir of alternative spiritual beliefs and practices, rising up against the crumbling structures of institutionalized Christianity. Whilst Campbell and Partridge suggest that these alternative spiritualities are at best indifferent to, but more often actively hostile towards, Christianity, the phenomenon of progressive spirituality indicates that the reality may be somewhat more complex. It is doubtless true that there is hostility towards Christianity in this alternative spiritual milieu.[109] Many of the bookshops that support this milieu contain texts from most of the world religions apart from Christianity. And for many people in this milieu, Christianity is still equated with hierarchical, oppressive, outdated 'religion', as opposed to egalitarian, creative and authentic 'spirituality'. But the ideology of progressive spirituality suggests that the boundaries between the cultic milieu or occulture and more mainstream religious traditions is potentially more porous than Campbell and Partridge appear to acknowledge. The sacralization of nature and the self may indeed be common characteristics in this alternative spiritual milieu[110] but, as our discussion of progressive spirituality has shown, these emphases can also be found in progressive Christian, Jewish and Islamic thought as well. As an ideology, progressive spirituality crosses the boundaries of the cultic milieu and mainstream, institutional religion. Now it may well be that religious progressives in the main Abrahamic faiths often work on the margins of their religious institutions, and that these religious institutions still generally have a conflictual relationship with the cultic milieu. As we have noted in the previous chapter, there are also a range of structural and attitudinal factors that limit collaboration between progressives in mainstream religious institutions and those involved in the cultic milieu. But the shared ideology that we can identify amongst religious and spiritual progressives across and beyond a range of traditions suggests that some caution may need to be taken about assuming too strong a boundary between institutional religion and the cultic milieu.

Fourthly, and finally, the phenomenon of progressive spirituality indicates that Linda Woodhead, Callum Brown, and others, are correct to suggest that gender plays a significant role beneath the surface of the changing patterns of western religion. As we noted earlier, Woodhead has argued that forms of religion are more likely to flourish in late modernity in the West if they provide women with resources for dealing with the challenges of negotiating new gender roles and identities for themselves. It is clear that the desire for such support – and the search for a constructive spirituality for women – have been important motivations in the development of many of the expressions of progressive spirituality. Pioneers of contemporary progressive spirituality have often been women who have found themselves on the margins of mainstream religious institutions and who have struggled with patriarchal attitudes and structures in wider society. The story of the emergence of this current phase of progressive religion in the West is bound up with the third wave of feminism, and its effects in creating new women-led movements both within mainstream religious institutions and beyond them. The emergence of contemporary forms of progressive spirituality is indicative of the struggles that mainstream religious institutions have had with the changing roles of women in modernity, and of the ways in which women have sought to create new religious forms that offer more constructive resources for their needs and concerns. It indicates that issues of gender have been deeply formative on changing patterns of western religion in the twentieth century – and this is likely to continue as we now enter the twenty-first.

In summary, then, by thinking about progressive spirituality in the wider context of theories about the changing nature of religion in modern western society, it is possible to see it as part of longer cultural and religious trends, and as a form of religion that has adapted to the social and cultural conditions of late modernity in the West. Whilst progressive spirituality will doubtless continue to evolve, and progressive religious groups and networks will come and go, it is reasonable to suggest that progressive spirituality will remain an ideological force in western religion for the foreseeable future. If progressive spirituality is going to be an enduring religious presence in the West, what can it contribute to the debate on the moral state of contemporary society? It is to this question that we will turn in the next chapter.

5 The collapse of civilization? Progressive spirituality and the demoralization debate

[Western] society, lacking a culture derived from its empty beliefs and desiccated religions, in turn, adopts as its norm the lifestyle of a cultural mass that wants to be 'emancipated' or 'liberated', yet lacks any sure moral and cultural guides as to what worthwhile experiences may be.

Daniel Bell[1]

It becomes increasingly clear that the lack of ethical behaviour in our world today stems from some fundamental rupture between us and a direct, non-institutionalized, and unmediated encounter with the divine.

Michael York[2]

There is a growing clamour of voices in the West suggesting that things are not as they should be. Despite the fact that large sections of the population of Western Europe and North America now enjoys levels of wealth, healthcare, educational standards, welfare provision, and comfort unimaginable even a hundred years ago,[3] there remains a sense of unease about the state of western society.

How can we explain this apparent disparity between the material comfort of the West and this sense of impending crisis? Perhaps we could see it as an expression of an enduring human capacity for moral anxiety and discontent that runs through all human civilizations. Francis Fukuyama, for example, suggests that this capacity for restlessness and discontent lies so deep in the human psyche that it may even lead to people rejecting the many benefits of liberal democracy in the search for something – if not better, then at least different.[4] Alongside this discontent is the apparent human attraction to narratives of history that imagine some kind of Golden Age in the past and depict the present as a process of ongoing decline. This is evident from high cultural, neo-classical wistfulness for the lost glories of Athens and Rome to the more mundane evidence of opinion polls which repeatedly demonstrate that people believe western society is becoming less decent, caring, and polite. 'Things aren't what they used to be', is a common enough human refrain.

Another possibility – linked to the apparent popularity of claims about moral and spiritual crisis – is that life for many in the West at the start of the twenty-first century is affluent, comfortable and, frankly, dull.[5] Norbert Elias described the civilizing process over recent centuries in the West as having produced individuals who are generally able to control their passions, fulfil their socially assigned roles, and enjoy life in an ordered society – yet who also feel cut off from something vital and exciting.[6] Certainly the sense of a yearning for greater spiritual meaning amidst the boredom of modern life works its way through to popular culture in films such as *American Beauty* and *Fight Club*. As Tyler Derden puts it in *Fight Club*, 'Our Great War is a spiritual war – our Great Depression is our lives.' The notion, then, that we are living through a time of moral and spiritual crisis could therefore be attractive because it gives a certain structure or even frisson to our daily lives – hence the popularity of books which draw attention to such crises.

Yet another possible effect of the civilizing process could be that our moral sensitivities are now higher than they were in previous times. In other words, perhaps we believe that society is getting worse because we care more about the state of society and apply higher standards in judging it.[7] Concern at the substantial inequalities between the West and the developing world, recently expressed through the Make Poverty History campaign and the Live8 events, could thus be seen as an indication of moral progress, given that such inequality in previous centuries may have been regarded with indifference or some form of pseudo-scientific justification.

It is possible, then, that a growing sense of concern about the moral decline of the West has its roots in perception as much as reality. Perhaps people are now more psychologically disposed towards moral anxiety and discontent. Perhaps we are becoming more morally scrupulous. Maybe claims about moral and spiritual crises have their own attraction for those suffering from the ennui of modern, comfortable life.

Those who support various forms of the demoralization thesis about contemporary western society argue, however, that their concerns are much more about social realities than neurotic perceptions. The exact nature of the hard data that people cite to demonstrate the weakening moral and cultural fabric of western society varies depending on the particular ideological assumptions underpinning the argument. And whilst statistical evidence is always more complex than broad generalizations allow, it is clear that there have been significant shifts in post-war British and American societies. On both sides of the Atlantic since 1950, for example, there have been substantial increases in reported violent crime, suicide amongst young people, births outside of marriage, rates of abortion, declining rates of marriage and increasing rates of divorce, growing inequalities between the richest and poorest members of society, and signs of growing public disengagement from political and other civic structures. Advocates of various theories of demoralization often argue that such trends demonstrate that life in today's society is more dangerous and more unstable and that people are less happy, less honest and less able to maintain moral commitments. On the social level, these trends are also seen as proving that society is becoming more unjust and less compassionate, and that people are becoming increasingly disengaged from civic and political structures that could effect any constructive social change. The overall picture that many critics paint from these trends is therefore one of a fragmenting society, ill at ease with itself, which is failing to nurture the moral and social resources needed to halt its decline. As Ralph Fevre observes, people in the West are currently experiencing affluence without necessarily enjoying it.[8]

These trends are not stable and consistent, nor can they necessarily be assumed to be symptoms of a deeper cultural process of demoralization. These trends can also look quite different depending on the historical framework one observes them in – today's homicide rate in Britain, for example, being a fraction of what it was at the start of the thirteenth century.[9] Such trends are inevitably affected by the loosening of legislative restrictions, for example, around abortion and divorce, and may not necessarily reflect so much a loss of cultural values as a society in which people have greater freedom for making certain kinds of choice about their lives. But, nevertheless, an awareness of these trends – fuelled by periodic moral panics over the attitudes and behaviour of young adults – provides the framework for an active debate about the weakening moral fabric of society. This debate is far from abstract – or the preoccupation of a small number of newspaper columnists and preachers – but has a significant impact on public life. Although the reality may have been more complex than this, voters' concern with 'moral issues' has often been cited as decisive in returning George W. Bush to office in the presidential election of 2004. And, when re-elected to government in 2005, Tony Blair declared that re-establishing a 'culture of respect' was to be a central concern of his next term of office (this, of course, being prior to the 'cash for peerages' scandal).

Debate about the demoralization of western society therefore forms an important part of the contemporary cultural and political landscape. The aim of this chapter is to explore the terms of this debate in more detail by highlighting four different versions of the demoralization thesis. I will then go on to explore how progressive spirituality (and wider thinking in the progressive milieu) can be understood in the context of this debate. In doing so, I will examine both theories of demoralization that are supported and rejected by particular writers in the progressive milieu, as well as considering what theories of demoralization and progressive spirituality may be able to learn from one another.

Four varieties of the demoralization thesis

Although the term 'demoralization' is not always used by those seeking to offer a critique of the moral and spiritual state of western culture, it is a useful umbrella term under which to cluster these critiques. 'Demoralization', as used by writers such as Gertrude Himmelfarb and Ralph Fevre, points to an important association between morality and well-being. Essentially the term 'demoralization' suggests that a crisis develops when people lack an adequate moral framework for living their lives, and that the lack of such a framework is not only a source of unethical behaviour, but also personal anxiety and unhappiness.[10] Demoralization thus carries a double sense of being de-moralized in the sense of lacking an adequate morality or spirituality by which to live one's life and demoralized in the sense of being anxious, confused and depressed as a consequence of this. Although the writers, theorists and public figures to be discussed in this part of the chapter do not all use the term 'demoralization' explicitly in their work, they do share a common belief in the important relationship between morality, the ability to understand life in true and meaningful ways, and happiness. Each of them also suggests that we are currently facing a problem in our ability to live in good, meaningful and fulfilled ways. In this sense, it is appropriate to see their ideas as representing different versions of a demoralization thesis of western culture.

At the outset, it is important to stress that the range of people who support some version of the demoralization thesis adopt a wide range of different moral, religious and political standpoints – including conservative, liberal and revolutionary perspectives. They all share the basic assumption of the demoralization thesis that there is something fundamentally awry with the moral and spiritual basis of western society, and that individual unhappiness and social decline is a direct consequence of this. Where they differ, however, is in their diagnosis of what is wrong at the heart of the moral and spiritual life of the West. For the purposes of our discussion here, I want to focus on four different diagnoses. This is not an exhaustive account of all the versions of the demoralization thesis that are currently in circulation, but the four versions we will turn to now represent some of the main lines of argument and help us to see some of the key issues at stake in this debate.

The four different versions of the demoralization thesis to be explored here variously suggest that:

- demoralization in the West is caused by the liberal, 'expressive' revolution of the 1960s which has had a devastating effect on moral attitudes and social policy.

- demoralization in the West is caused by the increasing secularization of western society which leaves people devoid of adequate moral and religious frameworks for their lives and which weakens the essential role that religious institutions play in the moral education of society.

- demoralization in the West is caused by the ideologies and lifestyles of contemporary capitalism which distort people's views of what is important in life, provide them with illusory forms of happiness and trap them in an exploitative and dehumanizing web of social and economic relationships.

- demoralization in the West is caused by the growing influence of rationality in modern societies which weakens our ability to think about our lives in morally adequate ways, traps us in inhumane and (ironically) irrational social systems, and separates us from a proper relationship with our emotional lives.

Let's now look briefly at each of these.

Demoralization and the liberal revolution of the 1960s

Over the past two decades there has been a growing suggestion that one of the primary causes of the recent moral and spiritual decline of the West lies in the liberal, 'expressive revolution' of the 1960s.

One version of this view suggests that the celebration of individual freedom, personal development, creativity and experimentation that characterized 1960s counter-culture, as well as particular 'person-centred' movements in therapy and education, led to a dangerous undermining of traditional moral restraints and guidelines. Bernice Martin, for example, argues that the Romantic pursuit of freedom and individuality underlying this expressive revolution only had the effect of 'releasing the terrors and the ennui of ultimate meaninglessness'.[11] In a similar vein, Daniel Bell has described the sensibility of the 1960s as 'the pathetic celebration of the self'.[12] From this perspective, the 1960s counter-culture was a confused, narcissistic and hedonistic movement that has done lasting damage to the social fabric of western culture.

A more nuanced version of this argument suggests that the expressive revolution of the 1960s was not simply an exercise in destroying traditional values, but was an attempt to build a new liberal moral ethos for western society. The problem with this project though, for conservative critics, was that it was both deeply influential upon many areas of society and also deeply flawed as a moral basis for that society. As a consequence, the values of the 1960s expressive revolution have become taken for granted in many parts of our social and cultural life – and we are too-often blind to their damaging effects.

Critics who have advanced this more nuanced critique have established themselves as doyennes of the political Right. Allan Bloom, for example, achieved considerable prominence for his best-selling critique of the effect of liberal values on American higher education, entitled *The Closing of the American Mind*. Gertrude Himmelfarb became well known for her support of Margaret Thatcher's call for a return to the moral standards of the Victorian era with her own historical analysis of why Victorian virtues were superior to contemporary liberal values.[13] Charles Murray became the talking point of broadsheet newspapers and social-policy specialists with his critique of liberal welfare policies and his highly controversial minimalist views on how much welfare provision governments should make for the poor.[14]

Each of these writers argued that the problem was not so much that the 1960s liberal revolution was devoid of any values, but that it offered an unbalanced perspective, emphasizing certain values too strongly and neglecting other key values altogether. For example, Bloom has argued that one of the key values of 1960s liberalism was 'openness', a tolerance of others' opinions, values and beliefs. Rather than functioning in a positive way to open up discussion and the free pursuit of truth, however, Bloom suggests that tolerance has become an institutionalized dogma that has degenerated into an uncritical relativism.[15] As a consequence of this new dogma of tolerance, it has become virtually unacceptable in public discourse to make evaluative judgements about whether one idea or action is truly better than another – with the exception of the moral censure of intolerance. One of the social effects of this over-extension of the value of tolerance is that, from the 1960s onwards, it became increasingly unfashionable to make negative judgements about others' lifestyle choices. As Himmelfarb argues, this had the effect of normalizing behaviour that would have been seen as deviant to previous generations.[16] Single parenthood and serial monogamy thus became seen as just as valid as any other lifestyle despite, some commentators would argue, clear evidence that nuclear families and lifelong marriage produce greater economic and emotional well-being for the adults involved as well as a much better environment for the raising of children.[17] Similarly, being an 'able-bodied pauper' would have been considered a source of shame in earlier generations. But Himmelfarb notes that welfare dependency has become seen as acceptable – even an entitlement – despite the social ills associated with the creation of an underclass chronically disinterested in being actively involved in the labour market.

Another seemingly positive value associated with the liberal ethos of the 1960s is that of equality. Charles Murray argues that an emphasis on equality arose in the 1960s partly through the profound influence of the civil rights movement and partly through growing middle-class concern about social inequality.[18] Again, far from being a positive influence, Murray argues that the post-1960s consensus on the need for social equality proved highly damaging. Taken together with the growing belief that social systems rather than individuals themselves were responsible for poverty, the drive for equality led to new approaches to social policy. These established welfare as a right, increased levels of welfare support and sought to avoid making distinctions between 'deserving' and 'undeserving' forms of poverty. By failing to treat people as if they were accountable for their own actions, Murray argues that these well-intentioned social policies actually had the effect of rewarding casual cohabitation, illegitimacy, educational underachievement, crime and welfare dependency.[19] Not only this, but these policies also took away any tangible material or social benefits that the 'decent' poor got from working hard and showing self-discipline. As a consequence, by treating the poor as a homogenous, 'equal' group, this new approach to welfare removed economic incentives to marry, raise children within marriage, work hard at school or find and keep a job.[20] The drive for equality, in Murray's view, thus took a wrong and dangerous turn when it overrode the importance of other traditional values in society.[21]

How did such an unbalanced view of moral values become so influential in western society, though? Murray and Himmelfarb place the blame for this squarely at the door of the comfortable middle classes for whom these liberal values have important uses. For example, Murray suggests that the liberal drive for equality is as much an expression of middle-class guilt about the inevitably inequitable nature of society as a genuine expression of concern for the well-being of the poor. In his view, this could be the only explanation for the continued middle-class support for a welfare system that produces such damaging effects in poor communities. He suggests that the current welfare system effectively functions as blood money, paid by the middle classes who seek absolution from the guilt they feel about their comfortable status. Murray suggests that the, 'the barrier to radical reform of social policy [i.e. radically reducing the extent of welfare support] is not the pain it would cause the intended beneficiaries of the present system, but the pain it would cause the donors… When reforms finally do occur, they will happen not because stingy people have won, but because generous people have stopped kidding themselves.'[22]

Himmelfarb similarly suggests the liberal revolution of the 1960s was one that was well-suited to the middle classes who had the financial and social security to enjoy the freedoms and opportunities that it brought. She accuses the middle classes of negligence, though, in failing to see that these same values would prove to be deeply damaging when applied to other, less privileged social groups. The 1960s liberal revolution was notable for challenging traditional, bourgeois values of 'deferral of gratitude, sobriety, thrift, dogged industry' – Weber's Protestant work ethic – yet it was precisely these values that the poor needed if they were to find the character to struggle out of their poverty.[23] According to Murray and Himmelfarb, the flawed moral project of 1960s liberalism became entrenched in society as a result of the neuroses and selfishness of the comfortable middle classes. Ironically, then, we see these right-wing critics berating middle-class liberals for being insufficiently responsible in their attitudes to wider society in general, and to the poor in particular.

In summary, writers such as Bloom, Murray and Himmelfarb do not argue that the liberal ethos arising out of the 1960s was completely bereft of values. Rather they suggest that this new moral order was damaging because it involved the overemphasis of certain values (e.g. tolerance and equality) to the exclusion of others (e.g. self-discipline and personal responsibility), and because it propagated values that reflected middle-class interests but which proved quite inadequate as a basis for life in poorer communities. As a consequence of this flawed moral project, these writers suggest that we are now facing a growing social crisis caused by the collapse of vital moral frameworks in poor communities – exemplified by rising rates of illegitimacy, violent crime and economic inactivity. This is mirrored by a collapse in the ability of the middle classes to face hard truths and to make discriminating moral judgements that could actually lead to the improvement of society. For such writers, the demoralization of society can only be reversed by an honest acknowledgement of the failings of 1960s liberalism, and a renewed moral discourse for personal and civic life. The battle between 'traditional' and 'progressive' values that provides the wider context for this critique of 1960s liberalism became one of the most important cultural tensions in *fin de siècle* western society.[24] Criticisms raised by writers such as Bloom, Himmelfarb and Murray are no longer simply the preserve of the political Right, however. Indeed, the emergence of third-way politics has seen parts of this agenda taken up by some people who would otherwise identify themselves with centre-left political views.[25] The critique of liberal values thus seems set to be a major theme in demoralization debates in the West for many years to come.

Demoralization and secularization

A second diagnosis of the demoralization of western society focuses on the increasing secularization of the West, and the effects this has on undermining important traditional moral and spiritual resources. At its simplest, this view sees the moral decay of society as a direct consequence of the declining significance of religion in western society. As Nicky Gumbel, the leading voice of the Alpha Course, one of most important evangelistic projects in contemporary western Christianity,[26] states:

> The vast majority of the population of the United Kingdom do not attend church, and of those who do, many only go at Christmas or Easter. Following in the wake of the decline in Christian belief, there has been a decline in the moral climate. The fabric of our society is unravelling. Every day in Britain at least 480 couples are divorced, 170 babies are born to teenage mothers and 470 babies aborted. In addition, at least one new crime is committed every six minutes. Although there are 30,000 clergy of all types, there are more than 80,000 registered witches and fortune tellers.[27]

The particular form that this version of the demoralization thesis takes will often depend on the beliefs, history and concerns of specific faith communities. There may be a more widely shared principle across such critiques that secular society is morally and spiritually flawed because it neglects the core truths of the critic's particular religious tradition (e.g. God's laws as revealed in the Torah, the Bible or the Qur'an). But faith traditions also shape the specific content of these critiques. Thus, the influential writing of the radical Islamist Sayyid Qutb discusses the demoralization of society not simply in terms of the neglected purity of the Qur'anic message, but also in terms of a reading of history that sees Islamic civilization as the moral and spiritual high-point of human society.[28] There are also significant differences in the extent to which such religious theories of demoralization support or challenge the basic ethos of western liberal democracy. Qutb's critique represents a fundamental challenge to western modernity. By contrast, Nicky Gumbel's Alpha Course offers a form of Christianity that is more accommodated to western liberal lifestyle culture. Religious critiques of the demoralization caused by an increasingly secular society may share a basic rhetoric about the effects of the vanishing religious and spiritual moorings of society, but beyond this can also take a wide variety of forms.

Religious critiques of secular society are usually intended to stir up the faithful to action – and may indeed be phrased in terms that make sense only to those able to hear them with the ears of faith. Not all such critiques are intended for just a religious audience, though. Indeed leading figures in the western monotheistic traditions of Judaism, Christianity and Islam have sought to present these critiques in the context of wider public debate about the state of society. An articulate example of this type of critique came in the 1990 BBC Reith Lectures delivered by the Chief Rabbi in Britain, Jonathan Sacks, and subsequently published under the title *The Persistence of Faith*. In these lectures, Sacks proposes two connected arguments as to why religion is essential to the moral well-being of western society. Firstly, he notes that religious values are grounded in an absolute reference point for existence beyond the self (i.e. God), and as such can be seen as an absolute, binding truth by which we should seek to live our lives.[29] If God is removed as the source of human values, then all values become relative – a matter of pragmatics, taste and choice. The logical end of this shift to non-religious ethics is Jean-Paul Sartre's claim that there is no human essence to which we are compelled to be true and that our moral lives are simply a matter of choice and invention.[30] According to Sacks:

> The values that once led us to regard one [choice] as intrinsically better than another... have disintegrated, along with the

> communities and religious traditions in which we learned
> them. Now we choose because we choose. Because it is what
> we want; or it works for us; or it feels right to me. Once we
> have dismantled a world in which larger values held sway,
> what remain are success and self-expression, the key values of
> an individualistic culture.[31]

Like other religious conservatives, Sacks sees religious tradition as
the only binding source of values and depicts a 'de-traditionalized',
individualistic moral relativism as the only logical alternative to
this. Whether this stark choice between lasting religious values or a
superficial, ethical narcissism is the most accurate way of depicting
the state of western modernity is a moot point – and is clearly a very
different view to that of Paul Heelas which we noted in the previous
chapter. Nevertheless, Sacks' belief in the importance of religious
tradition as the only substantial ground for human values is integral
to his analysis of the importance of religion for western society.

Sacks' first point is therefore that religion is the only really
adequate source of moral authority for our lives. His second point
is a sociological argument about the importance of religion for the
healthy functioning of society. He suggests that in the same way
that human existence is dependent on the physical ecology of the
environment, so human social life is dependent upon a moral ecology
which maintains healthy social bonds within society.[32] Religion
is essential to this moral ecology because it provides tradition,
authority and community that trains people in moral values and
provides communities that reinforce and celebrate these moral
commitments.[33] This role of shaping individuals' moral characters
is one that can only be maintained by intermediate social groups
such as families and religious organizations.[34] Individuals cannot,
by themselves, generate an adequate moral framework by which to
live their lives, nor is it feasible to imagine that the state can simply
legislate morality. Religion is therefore essential to the moral ecology
of western society not simply because it is the only possible source of
authoritative values, but because faith communities are able to play
an essential role in the moral education and formation of society.
Indeed Sacks argues that it is only through the moral influence of

religious communities that we can hope to have peaceful, pluralist societies.[35] For without religious communities who are committed both to their own religious traditions as well as to the wider social good, Sacks sees the only alternative as the rise of both the narcissistic ethics of secular consumer culture and the reactionary rise of the sectarian beliefs of religious fundamentalism.[36] In the same way that contemporary society is placing a heavy strain on the resources of our physical ecology, so Sacks argues that the secular refusal to recognize the social value of religion is draining away the moral resources built up by the religious culture of the West. As with the looming environmental crisis, Sacks therefore argues that we urgently need to address the impending crisis facing the moral ecology of the West. This can only be done, he suggests, by recognizing the importance of active engagement in religious traditions and communities for the maintenance of a healthy society.

Demoralization and capitalism

A third diagnosis of the demoralization of western society focuses on the damaging effects of global capitalism. Again the specific critiques of capitalism vary according to the interests and theoretical inclinations of the critic, but there are nevertheless some common themes. Contemporary capitalism, it is argued, reduces citizens into consumers, giving people a distorted view of the nature of happiness and society, and twists their desires to commodities and lifestyles that have little real benefit for them. Furthermore, global capitalism traps people in a system that values financial profit over human well-being, perpetuates injustice and exclusion, and gives work and consumption a degree of moral importance that is both undeserved and harmful. In sum, capitalist society reduces people's ability to approach life in free, authentic, imaginative and truly moral ways – and the increasing grip of the corporate world over many parts of society does not suggest an encouraging future.[37]

The work of Karl Marx is, inevitably, a significant influence for many people who have developed such critiques of contemporary capitalism. Whilst Marx's predictions about the collapse of the capitalist system have foundered in the post-Communist era, his ideas about the false consciousness generated by capitalism remain important. His concepts of ideology and the fetishism of the commodity reflected his conviction that capitalist societies encouraged their members to think in ways that both preserved that system and protected the interests of the dominant class within it. The freedom of capitalist societies is, in Marxist terms, an illusion. It is freedom simply to choose within the deadening constraints of the capitalist system – a case of having to be satisfied with the menu rather than the meal itself, as Theodore Adorno once said.[38] One of the effects of this distortion is to give people an unrealistic sense of what makes them happy. As the neo-Marxists of the Frankfurt School argued, such as Adorno and Herbert Marcuse, contemporary capitalist society does an excellent job in providing most of its members with small material comforts and undemanding entertainments. In doing so, it offers a palliative for the nagging sense that a life of compliant leisure and consumption fails to tap the true possibilities of the free and empowered human spirit.[39] This critique was taken up by the revolutionary movement, the Situationist International, in the 1950s and 1960s. Guy Debord, a founder of this movement, famously wrote about 'the society of the spectacle', in which authentic life finds itself squeezed out by the illusory happiness of modern bureaucratic, capitalist society. This is a society in which 'all that was once directly lived has become mere representation',[40] and in which this all-embracing and alienating spectacle 'is the sun that never sets on the empire of modern passivity'.[41] Whilst bleak, the vision of the Situationists was also a call to arms for radical cultural and political action (as well as a call to a radically authentic subjective life):[42] a call that ultimately found its expression in the Paris uprisings of 1968.[43]

Writers such as Adorno and Debord therefore criticized what they saw as the illusory freedoms and choices of capitalist society. Supplementing this critique, other writers have argued that consumer culture distorts people's desires by creating false needs which are perpetually unsatisfied. For example, Herbert Marcuse referred to the emotional state of modern, consumer society as one of 'euphoria in unhappiness'.[44] Although not writing from a Marxist perspective, J. K. Galbraith makes a similar point in his classic study, *The Affluent Society*. According to Galbraith, the emphasis on increased production – which has become a taken-for-granted good in mainstream economic thought – inevitably means that new and contrived needs have to be created for consumers in order to maintain this economic growth.[45] Although consumers may feel like they are making free and exciting choices, they are in reality simply cogs that keep the wheels of the capitalist system turning. And as writers across the years such as Vance Packard, George Ritzer and Douglas Rushkoff have suggested, advertising, marketing and shop design are carefully managed to encourage people to continue operating in this role.[46]

Global capitalism can be seen as a force for demoralization not only because it distorts people's ability to understand what it means to live free and happy lives, but also because it creates a dehumanizing social environment. Critics argue that capitalism produces a morally deformed society precisely because it places profit before human well-being.[47] The priorities of major social institutions which shape our daily lives are thus fundamentally out of sync with basic human values. To use the analogy from Joel Bakan's film, *The Corporation*, corporations could be seen as demonstrating all the emotional traits of a psychopath – concerned only with their own interests, uninterested in human suffering caused by the pursuit of their goals and unwilling to take responsibility for their harmful behaviour.

There are various ways in which capitalism produces a demoralized network of social relationships. Firstly, it perpetuates injustice in the processes by which material goods are produced and then consumed. The relative affluence of the western consumer lifestyle is made possible through inequities in both international trading systems, and through the use of cheap, non-unionized labour in the developing world. At the same time, the pleasures of this consumer lifestyle are generally unavailable to those who find themselves socially excluded through limited opportunities, a minimum-wage existence, unemployment or chronic ill-health.[48] Secondly, it distorts the moral and social environment in which children are raised, turning children into target markets through manipulative advertising practices and increasing the corporate influence over children's social and educational environments.[49] Thirdly, it undermines local communities by replacing them with simulated communities,[50] and in doing so weakens genuine social bonds. This is exemplified in the growth of out of town shopping malls which replace genuine local communities with simulated communities in which shoppers can sit in comfortable café zones but where they rarely meet their neighbours or foster local community relationships. Fourthly, it generates a cultural environment that intentionally undermines our sense of adequacy and well-being – illustrated by the work of graffiti artists, such as Ron English or Banksy, who seek to 'adapt' advertisements in public spaces in ways that highlight their damaging ideological effects.[51]

Finally, contemporary capitalism distorts social relationships though changing patterns in the workplace. For example, Richard Sennett has suggested that the effects of increasing flexibility in the marketplace (a.k.a. short-term contracts and job insecurity) corrodes moral virtues such as trust, loyalty and mutual commitment and makes it harder for people to fashion a meaningful long-term story for their lives.[52] Similarly, Arlie Russell Hochschild has noted both how the workplace is now being seen as more important than home life by both men and women (leaving family life increasingly marginalized and demoralized),[53] as well as how employees' emotional lives are now being colonized by employers who require the performance of 'emotional labour' as part of the normal working day.[54] The disproportionate importance of work in the lives of many adults in Britain and America has thus become another barrier to living balanced and truly fulfilled lives.

In summary, critiques of capitalism as a source of demoralization focus on both its potential to delude people about the nature of freedom and happiness and the ways in which it entraps people in harmful relationships, environments and lifestyles. As with all the other critiques discussed here, this analysis of the effects of capitalism on demoralization can be contested – in this case, by those who would argue for the benefits of global capitalism for raising standards of living, extending opportunities to growing numbers of people and stimulating cultural change.[55] Regardless of how convincing one finds the theoretical arguments of Adorno or Debord, these critiques of capitalism raise important questions about how the social and economic structures of society influence our values and our beliefs about what it is to live a meaningful life.

Demoralization and the dominance of rationality

A fourth diagnosis of the roots of demoralization highlights the damaging effects of the overemphasis on rationality in contemporary society. This diagnosis does not suggest that rationality is unimportant and can simply be discarded. Rather it suggests that rationality has become too important in western culture, squeezing out other ways of thinking about how society should work and how we should organize our personal lives.

How did rationality come to occupy such a central place in contemporary society? One of the most important writers to attempt to answer this question the sociologist Max Weber. Weber argued that the rise of rationality in western society was bound up with the interrelated growth of capitalism and the bureaucratic state in the period following the Reformation.[56] In *The Protestant Ethic and the Spirit of Capitalism*, Weber claimed that a new understanding of religious vocation arising out of the Protestant Reformation had led to a new attitude towards economic life, in which the pursuit of economic growth became valued as an end in itself. Within this new Protestant work ethic, the achievement of wealth became a sign of divine favour – however, this wealth was not to become a focus of pleasure in its own right, but was to be used to stimulate further economic growth. Weber suggests that this form of Protestant asceticism generated a historically unprecedented attitude to economics in which the pursuit of economic growth became the driving goal of western society. To achieve this goal, rational methods of economic planning and production became increasingly important. We can see this, for example, in the trend in seventeenth-century Britain for commonly owned agricultural land to be annexed into large privately owned farms on the grounds that this would represent a more efficient use of the land.[57] Over time, though, the religious values that underpinned the drive for economic efficiency and growth withered away as Christianity's role in public life declined. The end product of this process, Weber noted, has become an 'iron cage' of a rational bureaucratic and capitalist society, in which the goal of economic growth and the value of rational planning remain paramount in western society. But the religious values that made these goals so important have been forgotten. As a consequence, Weber suggested, we now live in a society in which 'the idea of duty in one's calling [in relation to work] prowls about in our lives like the ghost of dead religious beliefs'.[58] The moral and religious underpinnings of society have been lost, leaving only a rational, capitalist machine which will keep on running until it exhausts the natural resources it feeds on, or some new fundamental social revolution takes place.

According to Weber, then, rationality became central in western society as a result of the historical process of modernization – that is, the rise of modern capitalism and the national bureaucratic social structures that were required to support it. An alternative explanation for the rise of rationality in the West has been given by Alasdair MacIntyre in his highly influential study of ethics, *After Virtue*. In this book, MacIntyre traces the collapse of the coherent moral structure that underpinned medieval society. He suggests that the modern era sought to distinguish itself by pulling away the two key foundations of previous moral thought in the West, namely deference to the notion of God's law and an understanding of the intended purpose of the natural world that derived from Aristotelian philosophy.[59] Whilst this was intended as a project of intellectual liberation, it actually resulted in a collapse of any meaningful moral framework for western thought. As a consequence, MacIntyre suggests, contemporary moral arguments have become irresolvable conflicts between the subjective beliefs of individuals and groups. Any sense of a deeper, shared moral framework has been lost.[60] In the wreckage of the fragments of moral ideas left behind in western thought, MacIntyre argues that rationality has come to occupy an important role. The belief that the way we should morally guide our lives can be discovered through rational reflection has become a form of existential security blanket. We turn to rational reflection to make sense of our lives because it offers the promise of a deeper understanding of how we should approach life. But, MacIntyre argues, the belief that rational thought can be a sound basis for ordering our lives is a moral fiction. Rationality can help us think about how to achieve the values and goals to which we aspire, but it can never tell us which values and goals are the right ones.[61] The idea that rationality is some kind of objective path to the truth of how to live our lives also masks the fact that behind every 'rational' moral argument lies deeper interests and convictions. For both Weber and MacIntyre, then, the importance of rationality in modern society is not a sign of our moral freedom and maturity – far from it. Rather, the deference shown to rational thinking in all areas of social and cultural life is a symptom of the loss of deeper religious and moral foundations of society.

If rationality has come to occupy such a dangerously influential role in contemporary society, then what effect does this have on our lives? Firstly, it can be seen as reducing our capacity to approach our personal lives in genuinely moral ways. Ralph Fevre suggests that as rational calculation has become increasingly widespread in society, so we have learnt to see more and more parts of our lives as open to this kind of calculative thinking. So we find ourselves asking – should I stay at home to care for my young children or should I put them in day care in order to develop my career? Should I stay with my current partner or should I leave them in order to pursue the benefits and freedoms that single life might offer me? Thinking of our lives as a series of rational calculations, however, tends to lead to a weakening of commitments based on (non-rational) virtues such as love, loyalty and friendship. In addition, we tend to find that such a calculating approach either fails to provide answers to our moral quandaries or leaves us feeling demeaned or ashamed that our thinking about our most important relationships has been reduced to instrumental cost-benefit analyses.

Secondly, an emphasis on rationality can narrow the horizons of how we think about society. As economic rationality is increasingly relied upon to provide the core values for a society (e.g. economic efficiency and growth as the greatest social goods), it becomes harder to think critically about whether the goals of economic rationality are necessarily such a good thing.[62] Public debates often proceed on the basis of the assumption that wealth and job creation are unquestionably good (regardless of the moral and social effects of economic growth), and the social scientific study of economic life can be reduced to thinking about how the goals of efficiency and growth can best be served.[63] Wider moral questions about what kinds of society we want to create, or the nature of healthy social institutions, become lost when our moral imaginations shrink to the level of rational economic planning. Morality becomes displaced by economics.

Thirdly, the overemphasis on rationality leads to unhealthy social institutions run on the basis of rigid procedures and focused on the achievement of rationalized (rather than necessarily useful or humane) goals. The social theorist George Ritzer has become well known for advancing the McDonaldization thesis, in which he argues that increasingly large sections of society are modelled on the rationalized principles of the fast-food restaurant: efficiency, measurability, predictability and control through non-human technology.[64] When social institutions are organized along the lines of these principles, this has the effect of valuing measurable outcomes over the complex and unquantifiable human elements of the organization. Within a McDonaldized society, what matters is how long a hospital takes to process its patients, not how warm or sensitive the care the patients received during their treatment. Not only this but, as Ritzer notes, organizations which attempt to run on such rigid methods of rational planning and evaluation generate their own irrationalities. At a recent meeting at my former university, the Vice-Chancellor made it clear that it was more important for the university to pursue its standing in national league tables than to offer programmes to non-traditional students that might lower its results in those tables. The pursuit of arbitrarily fixed performance table indicators had come to be more important for that university than serving its core mission to provide important educational opportunities for a wide spectrum of society.

When McDonaldized systems are given a thin veneer of humanity in an attempt to disguise (or 're-enchant') their cold rationality, another degree of alienation is simply added to our social experience.[65] Travelling on the London Underground recently, I saw an advert for the most recent Microsoft Office software package. 'Your potential. Our passion™' ran the tag line of the ad. Potential and passion – the stuff of Romanticism – thus gets a trademark attached to it and is reduced to a thin marketing veneer designed to make a software package seem more exciting and inspirational. Concepts that refer to the depth of the human spirit thus become cultural ghosts surrounding the rationalized machinery of everyday life – a thin, sweet coating around a pill tasting of iron.

This notion has been developed by the social theorist Stjepan Mestrovic in his argument that we are now becoming a 'postemotional society', in which dead, abstracted and artificial emotions float over the surface of a McDonaldized world.[66] Emotions are thus no longer so much felt authentically by individuals, but are constructed and circulated through the mass media to suit wider social, commercial and political purposes.[67] One need only think about the synthetic rage and fury that drips from the pages of highly rationalized industries such as tabloid newspapers to see Mestrovic's point. Just as Arlie Russell Hochschild suggested that capitalism separates people from an authentic emotional life when it demands 'emotional labour' from them in their jobs, so Mestrovic points to a wider alienation from authentic emotions in our rationalized and commercialized culture. The overextension of rationality in contemporary society thus not only deepens our moral confusion, narrows our moral imagination and traps us in dehumanized, McDonaldized institutions – but the growth of this rationality is such that we become divorced from such basic human qualities as the capacity for true emotion.

Now, in describing these four variants of the demoralization thesis with reference to particular key thinkers, I may be in danger of conveying the impression that these theories are only significant for discussions amongst a small cadre of intellectuals and social commentators. The reality is quite different to this, however.

Each of these versions of the demoralization thesis has found broader support and expression amongst major social and cultural movements over the past forty years. The critique of 1960s moral liberalism has been central to the rise of the political and cultural Right in the United States and Britain since the late 1970s, including the New Christian Right in the United States. The notion that the decline of religion lies at the heart of moral collapse in the West finds support within a wide range of influential religious groups and institutions, from the Catholic Church, to the growing Evangelical movement and a range of different Muslim networks.

The critique of capitalism has been strongly taken up by the *alter mondialiste*[68] movement that has emerged out of anti-capitalist and anti-globalization protests at Seattle and Genoa and since coalesced into networks such as the European Social Forum and the World Social Forum.[69] The rejection of rationalized, McDonaldized society can also be seen in diverse cultural movements such as the fleeting celebratory parties of the rave movement,[70] the flourishing of neo-Paganism, Wicca and other forms of nature religion, as well as the Slow movement which aims to a return to a more human scale of living.[71] Far from being the preserve of idle academic chat, then, these varieties of the demoralization thesis represent some of the main forms that political and cultural organization and protest is taking at the start of the new century. Each of these different critiques has its own celebrity advocates, supportive media (whether TV programmes, newspapers, books or websites), campaign groups, and a significant base of support amongst different sections of the general public. By understanding more about these different ideas about demoralization, we can therefore develop a clearer picture about the nature of cultural conflict in western society today.

The progressive milieu, progressive spirituality and the demoralization debate

How, then, can we understand the progressive milieu and progressive spirituality in relation to this broader cultural debate? In the final part of this chapter, I want to explore this question by looking in turn at three issues. Firstly, how do the ideas of writers within the progressive milieu engage with arguments that are put forward in the demoralization debate? Secondly, what might writers in the progressive milieu have to learn from various forms of the demoralization thesis? Finally, what distinctive contribution could the ideology of progressive spirituality make to the re-moralization of society?

To begin with let us think about how the ideas and arguments of writers in the progressive milieu can be located in the context of the demoralization debate. It is worth saying at the outset that most writers in the progressive milieu would agree that western society is in the midst of a moral and spiritual crisis. Progressives may differ somewhat over the origins, causes and nature of this crisis, but it is hard to think of a significant writer in the progressive milieu at the moment who does not suggest that humanity is facing grave moral and spiritual challenges, exemplified not only by personal moral uncertainty, but also by environmental damage, economic injustice on a global scale, militarism, imperialism, and the threat posed by corporate globalization.

Given the left-leaning political sympathies of religious and spiritual progressives, it is unsurprising that they have little patience with the demoralization thesis and associated minimalist welfare policies advocated by writers like Murray and Himmelfarb. Jim Wallis, for example, notes that escaping the poverty trap is impossible simply through hard work and good moral character if healthcare and adequate housing is unaffordable and the poor are forced to do multiple jobs in a constant struggle for subsistence.[72] At the same time, however, where leading religious and spiritual progressives have written on social and welfare policy issues they have recently been careful not to adopt a simplistically oppositional view to such right-wing critiques. Writers like Wallis and Michael Lerner have been keen to stress that adequate responses to poverty and other social problems requires not only thoughtful policy intervention and welfare support, but also a strong emphasis on personal responsibility.[73] At times, Wallis' call for social liberals to stop simply 'servicing poverty'[74] through welfare programmes, or Lerner's objection to using structural oppression as an excuse for poor personal morality might sound close to the views of Murray and Himmelfarb. In practice, though, they reflect more the influence of third-way or communitarian politics on progressive thinkers like Wallis and Lerner that leads them to emphasize both personal responsibility and the need for fair social and economic structures.

Aside from analyses of questions of poverty and welfare support, the demoralization thesis, as advocated by Murray, Himmelfarb, and other figures on the cultural and political Right, rarely receives much detailed attention from religious and spiritual progressives. Where such progressive writers do address the question of the demoralization of society, it is far more common for them to do this in relation to issues raised by the other variants of the demoralization thesis that we noted earlier: secularization, capitalism and the dominance of rationality. Whilst it would be far too simplistic to suggest that there is anything like a clear consensus on the demoralization debate within the progressive milieu, it is nevertheless possible to identify a broadly similar response from a number of key writers within it. This response suggests that the demoralization of society arises out of the cultural dominance of an instrumental secular world view (or its 'other' – conservative, patriarchal religion) which upholds a rationalized, capitalist system that exploits humanity and the natural world as a whole. Within this response, then, there is a conflation of demoralization critiques of secular society, capitalism and the cultural dominance of rationality.

Let us unpack this progressive religious critique in more detail. As we noted back in Chapter Two, religious and spiritual progressives often express their opposition to a secular, instrumental world view. Whilst the secularization of the western mind might hold the promise of liberation from the constraints of religious dogma, in practice many progressives argue that it has contributed to a disenchantment of the world in which nature becomes no more than raw material for human projects.[75] In this sense, then, many religious and spiritual progressives would share Jonathan Sacks' doubt that mainstream secular values have the strength and depth to nurture an adequate resistance to the cultural and moral challenges of the new global capitalist society. Like Sacks, many religious and spiritual progressives also see a turn back to religious and spiritual resources as a central task for the re-moralization of society. Indeed Michael Lerner has argued that the success of the religious Right has been based precisely on its ability to meet people's desperate need for a sense of meaning and structure in modern, secular society. People need to feel part of a bigger picture and higher purpose, and conservative forms of religion appear to offer clear answers to this need.[76] Where progressives differ profoundly from Sacks' view, however, is on the issue of what kind of religious roots society should return to. As we noted earlier, Sacks has a high view of the value of traditional religious institutions as sources of moral wisdom and education – partly grounded in a functionalist view of sociology. From a progressive perspective, however, these long-standing religious institutions and traditions can be as much a part of the problem as a secular world view. Without a critique of the patriarchal assumptions and practices of these religious traditions, progressives argue that a return to the religious roots of western society will simply reinforce social patterns of dominance, oppression and exclusion – albeit with religious, rather than secular, justifications.[77] What is needed, William Bloom argues, is a spiritual 'third way' – an alternative between secularism and traditional, patriarchal religion.[78] This analysis has a particular resonance in the political context of the United States which, some progressives argue, has polarized between the equally flawed options of a religiously motivated Right and a secularist Left. Such an analysis is not completely new – with Jim Wallis giving his 1995 book, *The Soul of Politics*, the subtitle 'Beyond Religious Right and Secular Left'. But in the wake of the re-election of George W. Bush in 2004, on the back of the much-vaunted 'moral issues' factor, there has been renewed attention in the United States as to how social progressives can find a moral and religious language through which to articulate their political aspirations. What is needed – progressives argue – is an option beyond the choices of conservative religion and secular liberalism; a spirituality which is non-patriarchal, earth-centred and committed to social justice.[79]

Advocates of this progressive religious and spiritual stance see it as a critical step in the process of resisting the demoralizing effects of a rationalized, dehumanized, capitalist system. A central criticism of the current form of global capitalism made by religious and spiritual progressives is that it functions on the basis of the 'logic of domination' over both people and the natural world more generally. In historical terms, writers such as Thomas Berry and Rosemary Radford Ruether have argued that contemporary corporate globalization can be seen as the latest phase of a longer western colonial project.[80] An earlier phase of this project involved the direct military subjugation and political control of countries in the developing world. But the post-war era has seen such direct political colonialism replaced by an economic colonialism in which global banking and trade function in ways that are of direct benefit to a small number of wealthy nations and which often exploit or penalize developing economies.

Based on the central argument that contemporary global capitalism functions on the basis of patriarchal ideologies and structures, religious and spiritual progressives have advanced more specific criticisms of capitalism which reflect many of the objections to it that we noted earlier in the chapter. One such criticism is that contemporary capitalism undermines a sense of mutual interdependence by its overemphasis on rational principles of control and utility.[81] A mystical sense of the unity of existence thus becomes displaced by impersonal and calculating attitudes towards other people and nature as a whole. As Carol Christ argues – using Martin Buber's terms – patriarchal, capitalist society ends up producing I-It rather than I-Thou relationships.[82] Economic growth starts to be seen as a good in its own right – to the detriment of the environment – leaving the goals of transnational corporations too often at odds with principles of sustainability.[83] Alienated from our true selves and the natural world by the iron cage of the rational, capitalist system, we turn for consolation to the superficial pleasures of the consumer lifestyle – only to find ourselves further distanced from our genuine physical, emotional and spiritual needs.[84] As Satish Kumar states, 'obsessive attachment to acquisition leads to poverty of spirit and imagination'.[85] We forget that money has its cultural origins in human rituals of gift and exchange that have profound moral and spiritual significance, seeing it instead simply as an instrumental device which greases the wheels of the capitalist machine.[86] Even the promise of McDonaldized, rational systems to produce a better standard of living proves illusory. As Satish Kumar has often commented, the mass production of food has produced food that is environmentally costly and not particularly nutritious, displacing our sacred bond with simple, nutritious food which is organically grown, locally sourced and made with our own hands.[87]

Some writers within the progressive milieu argue that underlying this patriarchal capitalist system is a fundamental existential anxiety. Charlene Spretnak suggests that attempts to distance humanity from nature – for example, by construing nature as a 'resource' to be exploited to serve human needs and goals – reflects a deeper anxiety of engulfment in the face of recognizing the unitive ground of existence.[88] This pathological desire for control can even find expression in apparently spiritual forms. Carol Christ, for example, critically notes how the illusory notion of the autonomous, human agent in control of their world finds expression in New Age spiritualities which suggest that an individual's life circumstances is entirely of their own choosing and that one's spiritual outlook can change one's external situation.[89]

Advocates of progressive spirituality argue that it is only through cultivating such a non-patriarchal, earth-centred spirituality focused on the immanent divine that we can hope to find the resources to move beyond this neurotic, controlling and alienating phase of global capitalism. This is not simply about changing individual attitudes towards consumption or the environment, but creating a new discourse for public life. Michael Lerner, for example, has used his most recent book to argue for the development of 'a new bottom line', in which social and economic relationships based, simply on 'rational' principles of control and efficiency, are replaced by a new political calculus that operates on principles of justice, compassion and awe at the grandeur of the universe.[90] As we noted back in Chapter Three, religious and spiritual progressive organizations are also involved in various forms of direct action and political protest at the effects of corporate globalization: from participating in public demonstrations for third-world debt relief and against neo-liberal globalization, to practising sustainable approaches to agriculture. Through changing personal spiritual outlooks and behaviours, the terms of public debate, and approaches to production and consumption, religious and spiritual progressives offer their own contribution to the debate about the demoralization and re-moralization of society.

From this overview, it is clear that writers in the progressive milieu tend to connect with aspects of the demoralization debate that relate to secularization, capitalism and the overextension of rationality in economic and cultural life. But what might religious and spiritual progressives have to learn from a deeper engagement with the literature on demoralization, and what might they distinctively have to contribute to this debate?

In terms of learning from the broader literature on demoralization, there is scope for writers on progressive spirituality to engage in more depth with social theory, in particular in debates on capitalism and globalization. As we have just noted, advocates of progressive spirituality typically criticize global corporate capitalism for its inherently patriarchal ideologies and structures. At times, however, this critique can be phrased in rather vague terms, and it is not always clear how the charge of patriarchy maps onto specific economic and global institutions and structures. Given that much of the literature on progressive spirituality has been concerned so much with defining its theological/thealogical position, it is perhaps not surprising that writers on progressive spirituality have not always gone on to offer so much by way of detailed social and economic analysis. If the oppositional stance towards corporate globalization in the progressive milieu is to move beyond identity politics to a substantial critique of the structures and processes of contemporary capitalism, then organic intellectuals within the progressive milieu will need to continue to hone their critiques. This will entail developing more sophisticated analyses of how contemporary capitalism operates – in terms of systems of production and consumption – as well as how it functions in ways that are alienating, unjust and harmful to the natural world. An example of good practice in this regard is Rosemary Radford Ruether's recent book, *Integrating Ecofeminism, Globalization and World Religions*. Here Radford Ruether offers a clear summary of the origins and effects of institutions such as the World Bank, the International Monetary Fund and the World Trade Organization, noting how their policies have historically been detrimental to economies in the developing world. Radford Ruether also sets out clear examples of resistance and alternatives to corporate globalization based around principles such as participatory democracy, subsidiarity, ecological sustainability, common wealth, bio-diversity, human rights and equity.[91] Work such as this is helpful in setting out a specific alternative agenda to current forms of corporate globalization, and offers the potential for a clearer political agenda for the nascent social movement of religious and spiritual progressives. It also sets an agenda in which religious and spiritual progressives can find a place within the broader *alter mondialiste* movement of organizations and networks concerned with corporate globalization. Some writers and organizations within the progressive milieu already have contacts with this wider movement.[92] But given that the position on the demoralization debate taken by many advocates of progressive spirituality emphasizes a critique of capitalism, there is arguably scope for progressive spirituality to be located more explicitly in relation to a broader social movement of fellow travellers – including networks such as the European Social Forum and the World Social Forum, as well as the International Forum on Globalization.

What might progressive spirituality have to offer the contemporary debate on demoralization, though? If we are indeed experiencing a crisis of demoralization in western society, then arguably progressive spirituality could offer a viable approach to the construction of a moral sensibility which is grounded in a sense of the sacred whilst still embracing the values of liberal society. Progressive spirituality may represent a solution to some of the challenges noted in this chapter by, as Carol Christ suggests, providing both a mythos and ethos for a demoralized culture.[93] These terms – mythos and ethos – drawn from Clifford Geertz's theory of culture, point to two important elements of a culture's moral outlook. 'Mythos' is the story within which the members of a culture locate themselves – a story bound up with particular cultural symbols and rituals. 'Ethos' is the moral sensibility – the values, sentiments and motivations – that are generated through immersion in that mythos. Progressive spirituality offers a particular mythos through its turn to the story of the unfolding universe as the grounding narrative within which human existence makes sense. Unlike a secularist world view that depicts human life as devoid of meaning and value other than that created by humans themselves, the universe story places humanity as one small element in a grander narrative of cosmic unfolding. Within this story, human consciousness is seen not as a site for nihilism or existential despair, but as a symptom of the universe becoming conscious of itself. Human consciousness finds its meaning as it is used to deepen awareness of the cosmos of which we are a part. It finds its moral significance when it is used to reflect on how humans can act constructively within the cosmic drama into which they have been invited to take part. Far from being atomized, isolated individuals caught in a meaningless universe, we find ourselves born into a story that gives us both pleasures and obligations. As Thomas Berry puts it, 'we are... thrown into existence with a challenge and a role that is beyond any personal choice. The nobility of our lives, however, depends on the manner in which we come to understand and fulfil our assigned role.'[94]

This mythos of the universe story has the potential to give rise to a particular ethos. The moral sensibility celebrated by progressive spirituality is one of a deeply felt participation in the unity and interdependence of the whole of existence.[95] According to Carol Christ, 'the source of morality is the deep feeling of connection to all people and to all beings in the web of life'.[96] This sense of connection is not simply an intellectual assent to principles of the interdependence of life, but needs to be – as Christ and Charlene Spretnak argue – a felt reality. To quote Christ again: 'our ethics must be grounded in our love for life. When we are in touch with our feelings, we know that our joy in living can only exist in inter-dependence with the joy of other people and all beings.'[97] Phrased simply in this way, this moral sensibility can appear idealistic but, as writers like Christ, Starhawk and Matthew Fox readily recognize, this love of life is nurtured in the context of the ever-present shadows of vulnerability, pain, suffering and death. It is a love of life as we find it in this lifetime and this cosmos, as opposed to some idealized life that is located in another time and realm beyond death. Far from being a vacuous sentiment, this sense of deep connection with the web of life finds expression through particular ethical principles. Carol Christ summarises these as: 'nurture life; walk in love and beauty; trust the knowledge that comes through the body; speak the truth about conflict, pain and suffering; take only what you need; think about the consequences of your actions for seven generations; approach the taking of life with great restraint; practice great generosity; and, repair the web.'[98]

If progressive spirituality, in principle, offers resources for the re-moralization of society through its mythos of the universe story and its ethos of deeply felt interdependence, how will this mythos and ethos be practically cultivated? Michael Lerner suggests that this can happen through progressive spirituality serving as a basis for constructive dialogue and collaboration between members of existing religious and spiritual traditions. As he sees it, the role of progressive spirituality is not to replace religion, but to 'bring religious traditions together in dialogue, to learn from all of them, and to selectively adopt ritual activities from each that seem to bind together a more universal movement'.[99] Lerner's vision here seems more realistic than other claims that progressive spirituality can form the basis of a new religious movement that will increasingly become the shared religion of western societies. But even Lerner's vision is still very much a work in progress. As we have already noted, there are significant barriers that hinder collaboration between religious and spiritual progressives, and even if these are broken down this is a process which will be many years in the making. If progressive spirituality is to be a force for the re-moralization of the West, it will not achieve this in the near future by creating inclusive sacred spaces and rituals that draw people together within a new common religion. Rather, progressive spirituality's influence will be more fragmented, finding expression through a diverse range of individuals, groups and organizations, across different religious and spiritual traditions, and worked out through many different therapeutic, artistic, educational, political, economic and religious activities. This is not to diminish the potential influence of progressive spirituality as a source of moral values and sentiments for contemporary living, but equally is not to fall into grandiose claims about progressive spirituality as the irresistible force behind a new spiritual renaissance of western culture. Progressive spirituality may prove to be an inspirational and transformative resource for some people – but not for everyone, or indeed for most people in the West. The future influence of progressive spirituality will depend on a number of uncertain factors, however, and it is to an assessment of these that we will now finally turn.

6 Future prospects for progressive spirituality and the progressive milieu

In drawing this book to a close, I want to take stock and reflect about the current position and possible future for progressive spirituality and the wider progressive milieu. Assessments of the future of the progressive milieu by some insiders are rosy, if not to say bullish. David Tacey, for example, in *The Spirituality Revolution*, regularly uses metaphors such as the flooding back of the tide of faith or the overwhelming of our cultural river-banks by the growing torrent of the new, mystical spirituality.[1] Similarly, William Bloom argues that principles of holistic spirituality are now accepted by a substantial part of society and that it forms an increasingly influential part of the religious landscape of the West.[2] Only a small part of the progressive milieu expresses the explicitly millennialist belief that the world is on the verge of a radical spiritual transformation – bound up, in particular, with various predictions and claims focused around the year 2012.[3] But there is, nevertheless, a sense of expectation amongst many religious and spiritual progressives that they are part of a wider, and deeply significant, cultural and religious movement.

It is worth saying at the outset here that, whilst I am sympathetic to the concerns and activities of the progressive milieu, I am less convinced by some of the more overly optimistic assessments of its future. Religious progressives have often tended to overestimate the size and prospects of their religious movements. As Leigh Schmidt comments, Thomas Jefferson confidently predicted in 1822 that Unitarianism would become the 'general religion' of the United States within his lifetime – and such false optimism has been demonstrated by many others since Jefferson's time.[4] In this conclusion, I want to offer an assessment of the significance and future prospects of progressive spirituality and the progressive milieu which is more cautious and notes both its potential and its limitations in the emerging landscape of twenty-first-century religion in the West.

A starting point for this assessment is to recognize that the preceding chapters have identified something of a paradox in relation to progressive spirituality and the progressive milieu. On the one hand, there is good ground for seeing these progressive religious and spiritual developments as an important part of contemporary religion, and for believing that the expansion of progressive faith is an inevitable aspect of the longer social, cultural and political turn towards progressive, liberal democratic societies. As we noted back in Chapter Four, progressive spirituality is a contemporary expression of deeper religious trends in modern western society, such as the cult of the individual, the turn to experience, the sacralization of nature and the rise of the new mysticism. Again, as we saw in Chapter Two, it also forms part of deeper post-Reformation cultural traditions in the West – the rise of the self, Romanticism and Modernism – and is the heir of a well-established tradition of western liberal religion. Not only does progressive spirituality have secure and well-established cultural roots, but it also seems well adjusted to the cultural conditions of late modernity – offering a sacralized framework for valuing personal development, social concern and respect for nature as well as a range of secondary institutions which support people's spiritual development in this vein. It also has potential ideological and ethical resources to offer a coherent and spiritually grounded response to putative sources of demoralization in contemporary society. All of these factors suggest that progressive spirituality is a logical religious expression of key trends, values and concerns in late modern western society, in the same way that conservative religious reactions against late modernity are also an integral part of this same process of social, cultural and political development. The place and significance of progressive spirituality and the progressive milieu in the coming decades of western religion seems secure.

At the same time, however, progressive spirituality and the progressive milieu face significant limitations. The numbers of people actively involved as members or supporters of the new generation of religious and spiritual progressive organizations identified in Chapter Three remain relatively small. Measuring the size of the progressive milieu is a complex task, and one which needs more work beyond this current study. Any successful measurement of this kind would need to take into account the different levels of involvement that people have in the progressive milieu. At the nucleus of the progressive milieu are people who are active members of organizations and networks which engage in various forms of personal development work, therapy, performance of sacred rituals, education, sustainable agriculture and political action from a progressive religious or spiritual perspective. The membership of such organizations is relatively small – occasionally in the thousands, often in the hundreds, and quite often only in double figures. Beyond this small nucleus of people – who are probably too small to measure sensibly as a percentage of the whole population in Britain or America – lies a larger group of people who participate in progressive religious denominations such as the Religious Society of Friends, the Metropolitan Community Church, the Unitarian Universalist Association, or other analogous 'denominational' structures such as the Pagan Federation or Covenant of the Goddess.[5] In the UK, total membership of such progressive denominations stands somewhere between 50–100,000, and in the United States somewhere between 500,000 and 1,000,000. Beyond this lies a larger pool of people in other religious institutions (or none) who might think of themselves broadly as religious or spiritual progressives, or who are creators and consumers of various media that support the ideology of progressive spirituality (whether they be books, magazines, tapes or websites). This larger group is much harder to quantify, and to measure it will require much more detailed analysis of, for example, website hits, mailing lists, organizational affiliates to networks such as the Center for

Progressive Christianity, and sales figures for progressive books. Broadly speaking, though, this group is perhaps in the region of 4–6 million people in the US (around 1.5–2 per cent of the total population), and perhaps around three quarters of a million people in the UK (a little more than 1 per cent of the population). Finally, there is a pool of people who are sympathetic to progressive values, such as tolerance, diversity, personal autonomy, social justice, and respect for nature – or who may be sympathetic to understanding the divine in terms of the latent, life-giving intelligence and energy of the cosmos. This group is larger still – perhaps representing around 30–40 per cent of the population, in the case of the USA.[6] But those within it are not actively engaged with progressive spirituality or the progressive milieu, and have quite probably never even heard of or encountered the ideas of progressive spirituality or progressive religious and spiritual organizations. This larger group is a latent source of potential support for progressive spirituality, but there are no guarantees that this latency will translate into active involvement with progressive spirituality or the progressive milieu in the coming years.

As we have previously noted, the fact that many religious and spiritual progressive organizations operate with very limited human and financial resources means that their activities are therefore fairly tightly circumscribed. Again, there is also the range of structural and attitudinal factors which makes close collaboration across the wide range of different progressive organizations difficult, varying from different priorities, adverse reactions to such collaboration amongst members of one's particular religious tradition, and different perceptions about the merits of mainstream religious traditions and institutions. As a consequence the social, cultural and political impact of the progressive milieu is, at best, mixed. At the moment, when compared to the Religious Right in America – or indeed with conservative forms of religion more generally – the progressive milieu is less well funded, often has less influence on public policy, and has less effective publicity and recruitment strategies. Compared to the most recent high point in terms of the influence of progressive religion on public life in America – the civil rights and anti-war movements of the 1960s – the progressive milieu has since then rarely been able to mobilize significant levels of public support around a transformative social agenda. Campaigns for trade justice and international debt relief are perhaps the one significant exception to this.

So we are ultimately faced with the puzzling question of why – if progressive spirituality is so well attuned to the cultural conditions and moral sensibilities of late modernity – so few people actively engage with progressive spirituality or participate in the progressive milieu. One explanation of this paradox is that whilst progressive spirituality fits certain cultural and religious trends in late modern western society, the organizational base of the progressive milieu is still relatively weak. The progressive milieu is still institutionally marginalized and organizationally fragmented, and only a small minority of the population in the West are likely to even have the opportunity to get drawn into progressive religious groups and activities. This tension between the potential ideological appeal of progressive spirituality to a wider population at ease with liberal, post-materialist values, and the organizational limitations of the progressive milieu, should provide the context for any balanced assessment of the current situation and future prospects for progressive faith in the West. But organizational limitations are perhaps not the whole story. Put crudely, we still need to understand more about why there aren't more Quakers, Unitarians and Pagans in contemporary western society. Perhaps, to go back to my very opening comments in the Introduction, religious beliefs and identities simply aren't important or useful enough for most people in the West for progressive religious organizations to be able to capitalize on broader public sympathy for their ethos and values. If religions really are 'cultural tool-kits', then perhaps the identities, communities and activities that progressive spirituality generates simply aren't compelling enough as tools for the kinds of things that most people in the West want to do with their lives. In a society in which very few people now to get to live their lives in an assumed and unchallenged religious belief-system (Wuthnow's 'spirituality of dwelling'), perhaps the hard work needed to negotiate and maintain any kind of personal religious identity and belief-system is simply too much for most people.

The future for progressive spirituality is not easy to predict, though. The shape, size and influence of the progressive milieu in the West in coming decades will be subject to a number of unpredictable factors. Firstly, as some Christian denominations (notably the Episcopalian Church in the United States of America) move towards schism along progressive and conservative lines, it is possible that the coming years may see the emergence of a new generation of progressive congregations and denominational structures which are not tied to more conservative co-religionists. What this might mean in terms of new forms of collaboration between religious progressives across and beyond different religious traditions is hard to judge at this stage. But it is conceivable that within ten and certainly within twenty years, we will see more Christian congregations in America (and probably other English-speaking countries) with explicitly progressive identities and affiliations. This may give progressive Christianity, at least, a stronger and more distinct organizational base from which to operate.

Secondly, the future of the progressive milieu will also depend on whether it is able to develop effective ways of recruiting and retaining members. A number of sociologists have argued that conservative religious groups have proven to be far more effective in creating ideological and psychological conditions for people to join and remain committed to them. By contrast, it has often been argued that liberal values of tolerance, diversity and encouraging the pursuit of the individual path, tend to be corrosive to long-term commitments to liberal religious organizations. Whether a conservative religious ideology is inherently more congenial to recruiting and sustaining religious organizations is an open question. Certainly liberal churches have fared particularly badly since the 1960s. But whether this is necessarily an inevitable sociological consequence of liberal theology or more to do with the particular demographics, ethos and cultural conditions of those churches over the past four decades remains to be seen. Whether a new generation of progressive religious congregations and other organizations can find ways of recruiting and sustaining their membership will prove highly significant for the future shape and influence of the progressive milieu. In part, this will also mean that religious progressives will need to find ways of communicating the core ideas of progressive spirituality in a less technical way than is often adopted by its leading intellectual advocates. There are already creative attempts being made at encoding progressive spirituality into ritual, music, dance and visual culture, and such moves to create experiential and emotional engagements with core tenets of progressive spirituality will be vital to the future life and growth of the progressive milieu.

Thirdly, the wider public appeal of progressive spirituality is likely to be heavily influenced by the ways in which western consciousness and lifestyles change in the face of the growing threat of global warming and other pressures on natural resources. There seems little doubt that the coming decades will require significant changes globally in terms of the ways in which natural resources are used in processes of industrial production, energy generation and travel – as well as the consumption of energy and other natural resources in individual households. Certainly, without such changes, it is difficult to see a viable ecological future for much of life on this planet. Whether such changes will be undertaken on a pragmatic basis of self-interest, or whether they may prompt deeper questioning about the relationship between humanity and the natural world remains to be seen. But if there is a cultural turn towards the sacralization of nature amongst the wider public, as part of a growing environmental consciousness, then we could well see a broader public engagement with progressive spirituality.

Finally, the factor that will probably have most bearing on the wider cultural and political influence of the progressive milieu will be the extent to which it is able to find points of connection with others sympathetic to progressive values and political perspectives, with whom it can mobilize on clear points of shared concern. Initiatives such as Tikkun's 'Spiritual Covenant with America' or the Sojourners' 'New Covenant with America' (whilst noting the apparent lack of coordination between the two) may go some way towards achieving this. But such progressive mobilizations are more likely to be successful if they are focused on a specific cause, and there appears to be little consensus at the moment of what this might prove to be.

With all of this in mind, let me offer some final broad predictions, by way of conclusion:

- The progressive milieu will be remain an integral part of the religious landscape of western society, and its significance and public profile will be consolidated as western religion continues to restructure itself along conservative and progressive lines. There are other forms of religion that will continue to survive and flourish as the century progresses: local, congregational religion that attracts people because of its various social capital benefits, prosperity religion that offers the socially and economically disenfranchised the hope of greater material well-being, and diffuse spiritual technologies (e.g., astrology, crystals, angelology, etc.) which offer therapeutic benefits or a sense of control over one's life without the structure of formal religious affiliations or beliefs. But, alongside these, the emerging divide between progressive and conservative religious responses to late modern, liberal democratic societies will be a defining feature of the years ahead.

- Progressive spirituality will continue to develop within the broad framework of values and beliefs that were identified in Chapter Two. This religious ideology will continue to be used by a number of people as a source of religious belief and identity, and as a framework for various forms of ritual and other religious practices, as well as social and political action. Progressive spirituality will play an important role as one source of collective identity amongst religious and spiritual progressives. However, only a small minority of people in the West will have any active involvement with groups or media advocating progressive spirituality – reflecting the fact that only a small proportion of the population in the West will have an active religious identity, affiliation or belief-system of *any* kind.

- Progressive spirituality will not become an identifiable 'religion' or new religious movement in its own right for the foreseeable future, but people will engage with progressive spirituality within the structures of a range of different religious or spiritual traditions and identities. Progressives across these different traditions will continue to develop a greater sense of collective identity with religious and spiritual progressives from traditions other than their own.

- Despite this, however, practical collaboration across the spectrum of the new generation of progressive religious and spiritual organizations will be slow to develop. The relative infancy of many of these organizations, and the fact that many of them are in the early stages of clarifying their identities, aims and activities, makes more ambitious levels of collaboration across a wide range of such organizations difficult to envisage in the next few years. From the early 1970s, it took the Christian Right in America at least a decade to organize into a more cohesive religious and political movement, and the progressive milieu probably faces some greater challenges in developing this kind of collaborative activity than was faced by a more homogenous group of conservative Evangelicals.

- In the United Kingdom, progressive religious organizations will attract little interest from the Government because policy-makers in Britain at present are largely interested in religious organizations either as mechanisms of delivering policy on community development and social cohesion, or, more negatively, as potential sources of anti-western radicalism and politically motivated violence. Because the progressive milieu in Britain has neither the constituency behind it to act as a significant source of community development provision – and is not a terrorist risk – it will attract little interest from policy-makers. In America, with religious organizations and discourse having more influence on public life, it is conceivable that the progressive milieu may achieve more political influence in the future, largely depending on the nature of the leadership and electoral success of the Democrat Party. Rather like the religious Right, though,[7] religious progressives may struggle to fully realize their political ambitions. But again, like religious conservatives, they may come to have a significant effect on American politics by forming part of a broader coalition of political interest groups. The influence of the progressive milieu on American politics will therefore depend largely on whether religious progressives are able to build effective coalitions with fellow travellers in the Democrat Party – as well as the outcome of the next Presidential election and its implications for progressive politics in America.

All this remains to be seen, however. The future of progressive spirituality and the progressive milieu rests partly in the hands of religious and spiritual progressives themselves, and the organizational and strategic choices they make, but also in wider economic, cultural and political factors beyond their control. And perhaps their future – as for all of us – lies in the divine impetus towards life and the unfolding of the miracle of the cosmos, which may be our ultimate hope.

Appendix

An illustrative sample of progressive religious organizations formed since 1991

The Centre for Progressive Christianity www.tcpc.org
The Progressive Muslim Union of North America www.pmuna.org
CrossLeft www.crossleft.org
The Westar Institute www.westarinstitute.org
Al Fatiha www.al-fatiha.org
The Living Spirituality Network http://www.ctbi.org.uk/lsn/welcome.htm
The Progressive Christian Network for Great Britain and Ireland www.pcnbritain.org.uk
The Meta-Net Roundtable Network www.meta-net.info/index.shtml
Integral Spiritual Center http://integralspiritualcenter.org/
The Tikkun Community www.tikkun.org
Soul Force www.soulforce.org
The Cultivate Centre www.sustainable.ie
Progressive Islam.org www.progressiveislam.org
Centre for Earth and Spirit http://www.centreforearthandspirit.org
Enlightennext http://www.enlightennext.org
Christians Awakening to a New Awareness www.canaweb.info
Greenspirit www.greenspirit.org.uk
The Holism Network www.holism.info

The SnowStar Institute www.snowstarinstitute.org
The Progressive Spirituality Network www.progressivespirituality.net
Canadian Centre for Progressive Spirituality www.progressivespirituality.ca
Faith Futures Foundation www.faithfutures.org
Christian Alliance for Progress www.christianalliance.org
Integral Institute http://www.integralinstitute.org/
Progressive Christians Uniting www.progressivechrisiansuniting.org
Faithful America www.faithfulamerica.org
The Dragon Environmental Network http://www.dragonnetwork.org
The University for Spirit Forum www.ufsforum.org
An Tairseach – Centre for Ecology and Spirituality http://www.ecocentrewicklow.com/

Notes

1   Capra, *Tao of Physics*, pp.374f.
2   Radford Ruether, *Goddesses and the Divine Feminine*, p.308.
3   Crowley, *Way of Wicca*, p.175
4   Maslow, *Toward a Psychology of Being*, p.iv.
5   Walsch, *Tomorrow's God*, p.3.

Introduction

1   Lynch, *After Religion*, pp.90ff.
2   Lynch, *Understanding Theology and Popular Culture*, pp.166ff; Lynch and Badger, 'The post-rave dance scene as secondary institution'.
3   See Luckmann, *The Invisible Religion*.
4   The American Religious Identification Survey is a telephone survey that involved over 50,000 respondents. For more information see http://www.gc.cuny.edu/faculty/research_briefs/aris/key_findings.htm.
5   For a summary of Gallup polls on religion, see http://poll.gallup.com/topics/.
6   As the ARIS poll indicated, only around 1.3 per cent of the US population identify themselves as Jews.
7   Working with smaller sample sizes than the ARIS poll, Gallup have recorded that, between 1945–70, 95 per cent+ of the American population identified with a particular religious group. Since 1990 this figure more typically falls in a range between 88–90 per cent – with around 82–84 per cent typically identifying with some form of Christianity. Studies by the Pew Research Council in 1996–2002 also returned scores of 82–84 per cent of respondents identifying with some form of Christianity. The NRSI survey of 1990 (comparable to ARIS in its scale) also indicated that 91 per cent of Americans identified with some form of religion.
8   The ARIS survey suggested that reported religious membership may have

fallen to 54 per cent. There is a debate about actual levels of church attendance in the US, with recent studies suggesting that actual weekly attendance at churches and synagogues may now have fallen to around 20–25
per cent of the US population. See Heelas and Woodhead, *The Spiritual Revolution*, p.57.

9   When respondents to the ARIS poll were invited to state whether their
outlook on life was essentially religious or secular, 37 per cent stated that
they were religious and 38 per cent that they were somewhat religious, as
opposed to only 16 per cent of respondents who said they were secular or
somewhat secular.

10   In the ARIS poll, 23 per cent of people aged 18–34 identified their outlook
as secular or somewhat secular – more than the average for the general
population, and 35 per cent of those who claimed to have no religion
were aged 18–29. The General Social Survey of 2002 also indicated that
respondents aged 18–30 were nearly four times more likely to say that
they had no religion than those aged 65 and over, and half as likely to say
that they were strongly religious. See cross-tabulation of data on strength
of religion and age for the General Social Survey (2002) at www.thearda.
com.

11   The demographics of all of the major Christian denominations are ageing, with mainstream denominations such as the Catholics, Methodists,
Lutherans, United Church of Christ and Presbyterians seeing a fall of the
proportion of their membership made up by young adults. Compare the
demographic profiles of those claiming membership of religious organizations in the 1990 NRSI poll with the 2001 ARIS poll. All of the Christian
denominations – even independent Evangelical and Pentecostal – show
some signs of ageing demographics

12   In the National Census of the United Kingdom in 2001, 72 per cent of
respondents identified themselves as Christian, with a total of 76.8 per
cent identifying with a particular religious tradition and only 15.5 per cent
identifying themselves as having no religion. In the British Social Attitudes
Survey, however, the percentage of respondents identifying themselves as
having no religion was much higher – rising from 31 per cent in 1983 to
43 per cent in 2003. Over the same period, the number of respondents
identifying themselves as Christian fell from 65 per cent to 48 per cent,
and the number identifying with any religious tradition fell from 67 per
cent to 54 per cent. The difference between the Census and BSA results is
almost certainly a reflection on the different ways in which the question of
religious identity is put to respondents.

13   Brierley, *UK Christian Handbook Religious Trends 2000/2001*. See also http://
www.cofe.anglican.org/info/statistics/churchstatistics2002. Survey data
on self-reported religious membership is less common in the UK. However, in a MORI poll in 2003, 18 per cent of respondents reported that they

were active members of a religious organization and a further 25 per cent said that they were non-active members. In terms of self-reported regular religious observance, the British Social Attitudes Survey has shown that since 1989 around 20 per cent of respondents claim to attend services or meetings connected with their religion at least once a month, and that around 13–14 per cent typically report attendance on a weekly basis. The discrepancy between these self-reported figures and the headcount figures reported by Brierley reflects the possible discrepancy of self-reported and headcount figures of church attendance in the US. If the English Church Attendance Survey results can be generalized to the UK as a whole, then this means that probably no more than 10–12 per cent of the UK population attend any kind of religious service on a more or less weekly basis.

14 Over the past ten years, the British Social Atttitudes Survey has shown consistently shown that around 60 per cent people aged 18–34 identify themselves as having no religion compared to only around 25 per cent of those aged 55 and over. Similarly, in 2003, the same survey showed that only 12 per cent of those aged 18–34 identified themselves as belonging to the Church of England, compared to 40 per cent of those aged 55 and over. The English Church Attendance Survey has also shown that the percentage of children in the total English population who attend church on a regular basis fell from 14 per cent in 1989 to 7 per cent by 1998, whilst the proportion of church congregations made of those in later life has significantly increased. Brierley, *UK Christian Handbook Religious Trends 2000/2001*. Lambert similarly provides evidence from the European Values Study that whilst some young adults are demonstrating increased levels of religious commitment, in general young adults in Western Europe are increasingly disengaged from traditional, institutional religion. Lambert, 'A turning point in religious evolution in Europe'.

15 See http://www.mori.com/polls/2003/bbc-heavenandearth-top.shtml.

16 Smith et al., *Soul Searching*, p.31.

17 See Smith et al., *Soul Searching*.

18 Ibid., p.131. See also Davies, *Death, Ritual and Belief*, pp.168ff.

19 Ibid., pp.162ff.

20 See Chaney, *Cultural Change and Everyday Life*, p.13.

21 Woodhead, 'Introduction: Studying religion and modernity'.

22 Tacey, *Spirituality Revolution*.

23 Herrick, *The Making of the New Spirituality*.

24 Carrette and King, *Selling Spirituality*.

25 Drane, *Do Christians Know How to Be Spiritual?*

26 See, for example, Lynch, *After Religion; Losing My Religion?*

27 Melucci, 'The process of collective identity', pp.58–60.

28 See Partridge, *The Re-Enchantment of the West*.

Chapter 1

1   See Wuthnow, The Restructuring of American Religion, pp.140–2.
2   Ibid., pp.142ff.
3   Ibid., pp.215ff. See also Bates, Church at War.
4   See, for example, Davis and Robinson, 'Religious orthodoxy in American society'; Smith, Christian America?; Hoge et al., Vanishing Boundaries, pp.179ff.
5   See http://www.acn-us.org.
6   Interview, 27 February 2006.
7   See, for example, www.wupj.org; www.liberaljudaism.org.
8   See www.pmuna.org.
9   See www.tcpc.org.
10   See www.sojo.net; see especially the Sojourners' statement of faith, http://www.sojo.net/index.cfm?action=about_us.community.
11   See, for example, the Christian Alliance for Progress (www.christianalliance.org), Cross Left (www.crossleft.org) and Progressive Christians Uniting (www.progressivechristiansuniting.org).
12   See Rountree, Embracing the Witch and the Goddess, p.5, for a helpful summary of the progressive milieu.
13   See Queen, Engaged Buddhism in the West.
14   Diarmuid O'Murchu, for example, sees emerging forms of progressive spirituality as a distinctive step beyond interfaith dialogue towards the clarification of a global spirituality. Interview, 27 February 2006.
15   See http://www.matthewfox.org/sys-tmpl/door/; http://www.dioceseofnewark.org/jsspong/reform.html.
16   See, for example, Walsch, What God Wants, pp.19–57; Tacey, The Spirituality Revolution, pp.36ff; Holloway, Doubts and Loves, pp.4ff.
17   Tacey, ibid., p.2.
18   See www.progressivespirituality.net.
19   Tomlinson, The Post-Evangelical, p.3.
20   Wuthnow, The Restructuring of American Religion, pp.153ff.; Kemp, The Christaquarians?, p.238; Jorgensen and Russell, 'American Neo-Paganism'; Eller, Living in the Lap of the Goddess, p.18; Rountree, Embracing the Witch and the Goddess, p.10.
21   See, for example, Tacey, The Spirituality Revolution, pp.39ff.
22   O'Murchu, Reclaiming Spirituality, pp.2–5.
23   See https://www.tcpc.org/about/the_8_points_6.html. See also Pilgrim, 'The Quakers'.
24   See, for example, Smith, Tomorrow's Faith, p.ix; Freitas, Becoming a Goddess of Inner Poise, p.66.
25   Holloway, Doubts and Loves, pp.45ff.
26   See, for example, Eller, Living in the Lap of the Goddess, pp.15ff.

27 Tacey, The Spirituality Revolution, p.39.
28 See, for example, Sjoo and Mor, The Great Cosmic Mother, p.6; Eller, Living in the Lap of the Goddess, p.48.
29 See, for example, Christ and Plaskow, Womanspirit Rising, p.5.
30 Eaton, Introducing Ecofeminist Theologies, p.7.
31 See ibid., p.1.
32 See Daly, Quintessence, p.15.
33 Christ, Diving Deep and Surfacing, pp.133ff; Radford Ruether, Goddesses and the Divine Feminine, pp.288ff; Ind, Fat is a Spiritual Issue.
34 Daly, Beyond God the Father, p.40.
35 Christ and Plaskow, Womanspirit Rising, p.5.
36 Daly, Beyond God the Father, p.32ff.
37 See, for example, Neu, Return Blessings.
38 See, for example, Christ, Rebirth of the Goddess; Raphael, Introducing Thealogy.
39 Christ (ibid., p.60) criticises the use of the term 'matriarchy' to describe pre-biblical culture as it implies women ruling through patriarchal structures rather than an egalitarian culture in which women played a key role.
40 See, for example, Gimbutas, Civilisation of the Goddess.
41 Sjoo and Mor, The Great Cosmic Mother, p.8.
42 See, for example, Radford Ruether, Goddesses and the Divine Feminine, pp.3, 6. See also Hutton, 'The discovery of the modern goddess'; Eller, The Myth of Matriarchal Prehistory.
43 Radford Ruether, Goddesses and the Divine Feminine, pp.3ff., 297ff.
44 Daly, Beyond God the Father, pp.xviiiff.
45 Starhawk, The Spiral Dance, p.34.
46 See Christ and Plaskow, Womanspirit Rising, pp.5ff.
47 Carol Christ, Laughter of Aphrodite, p.xv.
48 See Christ's critique of magic in Radford Ruether, Goddesses and the Divine Feminine, p.290.
49 Radford Ruether, Goddesses and the Divine Feminine, pp.5f.
50 Robinson, Honest to God, pp.11–18; see also Holloway, Doubts and Loves, p.37.
51 Bloom, SOULution, p.84.
52 Ibid., p.17.
53 Capra, Tao of Physics, p.11.
54 Bohm, Wholeness and Implicate Order, pp.xiff.
55 Ibid., pp.236ff.
56 Davies, The Mind of God, pp.226ff.
57 'Authentic science can and must be one of humanity's sources of wisdom for it is a source of sacred awe, of childlike wonder, and of truth.' No.87 of Matthew Fox's recent 95 theses for a new reformation, http://www.mat-

thewfox.org/sys-tmpl/htmlpage19/.

58   Berry, The Dream of the Earth, pp.123ff.
59   Ibid., pp.14ff.
60   See Jencks, The Language of Post-Modern Architecture.
61   Jencks, What is Post-Modernism?, pp.70ff; Jencks cites Swimme and Berry's The Universe Story in developing this argument.
62   See Jencks, The Garden of Cosmic Speculation.
63   Ibid., p.20.
64   See, for example, Davies, Origin of Life, pp.xviiiff.
65   Capra, The Tao of Physics, pp.141ff.
66   The theory of non-local relations between subatomic particles is, for example, a significant challenge to the notion of local causal effects at the quantum level (see, for example, Bohm, Wholeness and Implicate Order, p.236).
67   Jencks, The Garden of Cosmic Speculation, pp.104ff. Bohm, Wholeness and Implicate Order, p.242.
68   Capra, The Tao of Physics, pp.361ff.
69   Ibid., pp.209ff.
70   Bohm, Wholeness and Implicate Order, p.12.
71   Young, The Unfinished Universe.
72   As Paul Davies observes, the differences between these two scientific perspectives can have quite profound cultural and philosophical implications. Origin of Life, pp.255ff.
73   Davies, The Mind of God, p.195.
74   Young, The Unfinished Universe, pp.42ff.
75   Ibid., pp.43ff. See also Jencks, What is Post-Modernism?, pp.75ff.
76   As Paul Davies puts it, 'It is then highly significant, surely, that the products of nature's complexifying trend – intelligent beings like Homo Sapiens – are able to understand the very laws that have given rise to "understanding" in the first place.' Origins of Life, p.254.
77   Roberts, 'The chthonic imperative', p.60.
78   Capra, Tao of Physics, pp.370ff.
79   Jencks, The Garden of Cosmic Speculation, p.19.
80   See Radford Ruether, Integrating Ecofeminism, p.45; see also Eaton, Introducing Eco-Feminist Theologies, p.98.
81   See http://environment.harvard.edu/religion/main.html.
82   Ibid., pp.46ff.
83   Eaton, Introducing Ecofeminist Theologies, p.102.
84   See, for example, Naess, Ecology, Community and Lifestyle.
85   See, for example, Capra, Web of Life, pp.7ff.
86   Fox, Creation Spirituality.
87   Ibid., p.26.
88   See Guha and Martinez Alier, Varieties of Environmentalism, pp.92ff.

89 This notion of the 'new' spirituality being 'new' because it engages with the intellectual currents, and social and cultural challenges of the day, has a long history to it. At the turn of the twentieth century, Horatio Dresser defined the religious liberalism that was, in time, to produce progressive spirituality, commenting that 'to be liberal is to be of the new age'. Cited in Schmidt, Restless Souls, p.12.

90 See, for example, Rountree, Embracing the Witch and Goddess, p.5.

91 See, for example, MacKinnon and McIntyre, Readings in Ecological and Feminist Theology; Eaton, Introducing Ecofeminist Theologies.

92 Sanders, Wicca's Charm, p.xi.

93 Radford Ruether, Goddesses and the Divine Feminine, p.6. Matthew Fox had also referred to this 'deep ecumenism' some ten years before, in Creation Spirituality, p.31.

94 Ibid., p.296.

95 See Plaskow, The Coming of Lilith, pp.110–3.

Chapter 2

1 See, for example, Geertz, *The Interpretation of Culture*; Luckmann, *The Invisible Religion*; Berger, *The Sacred Canopy*; Roof, *Spiritual Marketplace*; York, 'New age and Paganism'.

2 See, for example, the critique of Geertz's definition of religion, in Miller, *Consuming Religion*, pp.20ff.

3 See, for example, Stringer, *An Ethnography of Worship*.

4 See, for example, Frykholm, *Rapture Culture*; Schofield Clark, *From Angels to Aliens*, pp.10ff.

5 Reports of the activities of the PCN local group meeting in Sedbergh, Cumbria (see, for example, PCN Britain newsletter, December 2005, p.8) illustrate this by emphasizing that whilst all the group members welcome its open spirit of discussion, not all of them embrace the 'radical' theology of writers associated with PCN Britain such as John Shelby Spong or Richard Holloway.

6 See, for example, Schofield Clark, *From Angels to Aliens*, p.10ff.

7 Albanese, *Nature Religion in America*, pp.200ff.

8 Eller, *Living in the Lap of the Goddess*, p.39; Bloch, 'Individualism and community', pp.296ff.

9 Albanese, *Nature Religion in America*, p.7.

10 Crowley, 'Wicca as a mystery religion'.

11 There are, for example, monotheist Pagans and Wiccans. See Harvey, *Listening People, Speaking Earth*, p.168; Michael York, *Pagan Theology*, p.158.

12 See, for example, Chopra, *The Seven Spiritual Laws*, p.10; Emerson, *Nature and Selected Essays*, p.60.

13 Smith, *Tomorrow's Faith*, p.40. See also Matthew Fox on 'Jesusolatry', *Creation Spirituality*, p.55.

14   See Crowley, *Way of Wicca*, pp.102ff.

15   Ibid., p.171. See also Christ, *Laughter of Aphrodite*, p.110.

16   Walsch, *What God Wants*, p.111.

17   Moore, *The Soul's Religion*, p.133. Note that Starhawk grounds her polytheism in a recognition of the ineffability of the divine, in *Earth Path*, p.30. See also Emerson, *Nature and Selected Essays*, p.71.

18   Christ, *Laughter of Aphrodite*, p.110.

19   Chopra, *How to Know God*, pp.14, 30ff.

20   See, for example, O'Donohue, *Anam Cara*, p.76; Lerner, *Jewish Renewal*, p.415; Christ, *Rebirth of the Goddess*, p.105; Fox, *Creation Spirituality*, pp.63–5.

21   See, for example, Daly, *Quintessence*, p.11; Lerner, *Jewish Renewal*, pp.410ff.

22   See, for example, Pearson, 'Assumed affinities', p.45; Harvey, *Listening People, Speaking Earth*, p.219; Fox, *Creation Spirituality*, pp.19ff.

23   Starhawk, *Spiral Dance*, p.27; O'Murchu, *Reclaiming Spirituality*, p.95.

24   Ward, *Pascal's Fire*.

25   Frequent reference is made in progressive spirituality literature to Lovelock's thesis of Gaia as an interconnecting process of ecological sustainability and development. See, for example, Crowley, *Way of Wicca*, p.22; Samuel, 'Paganism and Tibetan Buddhism', p.135.

26   Bloom, *SOULution*, pp.134ff.

27   See, for example, Lerner, *Jewish Renewal*, p.411; also the teachings of Andrew Cohen, http://www.andrewcohen.org.

28   Compare Arne Naess's guiding maxim that 'the unfolding of potentialities is a right'. *Ecology, Community and Lifestyle*, p.164.

29   See, for example, Starhawk, *Earth Path*, pp.41ff.

30   See, for example, Eaton, *Introducing Eco-Feminist Theologies*, pp.95ff.

31   See, for example, O'Donohue, *Anam Cara*, p.62: 'In the human mind, the universe first becomes resonant with itself... In the human person, creation finds the intimacy it mutely craves. Within the mirror of the mind it becomes possible for diffuse and endless nature to behold itself.'

32   See, for example, Fox, *Toward a Transpersonal Ecology*, pp.199ff.

33   Lerner, *Jewish Renewal*, pp.415ff.

34   See, for example, O'Murchu, *Reclaiming Spirituality*, p.41.

35   Ibid., p.42; Crowley, *Way of Wicca*, pp.36ff; Shallcrass, 'A priest of the goddess', p.168.

36   See Daly, *Quintessence*.

37   See, for example, Jones, 'Pagan theology', p.34; York, *Pagan Theology*, p.162.

38   See O'Donohue, *Anam Cara*, pp.84ff.

39   See, for example, Lerner, *Jewish Renewal*, p.414.

40   See, for example, Crowley, 'Wicca as a mystery religion', p.83; Bloom,

SOULution, p.92; Shallcrass, 'A priest of the goddess', p.164; Walsh, *What God Wants*, pp.98ff; Bloch, 'Individualism and community', p.296.

41 Ibid., p.96.

42 Walsh, *What God Wants*, p.61.

43 See, for example, Borg, *The God We Never Knew*, pp.32ff.

44 See http://wildfaith.homestead.com/mcdaniel.html.

45 See, for example, Michael York, *Pagan Theology*, p.60.

46 See, for example, Borg, *The God We Never Knew*, pp.34ff; Radford Ruether, *Goddesses and the Divine Feminine*, p.308; Christ, *Rebirth of the Goddess*, pp.104–7.

47 Crowley, 'Wicca as nature religion', p.178.

48 Crowley, *Way of Wicca*, p.171.

49 See Christ, *Rebirth of the Goddess*, pp.101ff.

50 O'Murchu, *Quantum Theology*, p.56.

51 Ali, 'How I met God', p.34.

52 Radford Ruether, *Goddesses and the Divine Feminine*, p.308; Geoffrey Samuel, 'Paganism and Tibetan Buddhism', p.134.

53 Christ, *Rebirth of the Goddess*, pp.105–7.

54 See Schmidt, *Restless Souls*, p.25ff, on the significance of mysticism in the longer tradition of progressive western faith.

55 Bloom, *SOULution*, pp.62ff.

56 Ibid., p.77.

57 Chopra, *Seven Spiritual Laws*, pp.14ff. See also Schmidt, *Restless Souls*, pp.143ff; Wilber, *The Essential Ken Wilber*, p.5.

58 Daly, *Beyond God the Father*, p.xxv.

59 See, for example, Crowley, 'Wicca as a mystery religion'; Starhawk, *Spiral Dance*.

60 Cited in Crowley, 'Wicca as nature religion', p.175.

61 See Eller, *Living in the Lap of the Goddess*, pp.58ff; Rountree, *Embracing the Witch and the Goddess*, p.8.

62 In Kemp's 'Christaquarian' groups, for example, women typically outnumbered men by three to one. *The Christaquarians?*, p.237.

63 See, for example, the stories of American women's engagement with Kwan Yin, in Boucher, *Discovering Kwan Yin*, pp.59ff.

64 Shallcrass, 'A priest of the goddess'.

65 O'Murchu, *Reclaiming Spirituality*, pp.52ff.

66 Lerner, *Jewish Renewal*, p.313.

67 Ibid., p.311.

68 See, for example, Carol Christ's account of the difficulty of getting goddess language accepted amongst feminist theologians in the 1970s, in *Laughter of Aphrodite*, pp.105–7.

69 York, *Pagan Theology*, pp.159ff.

70 Chopra, *Seven Spiritual Laws*, p.4.

71   Crowley, *Way of Wicca*, p.7.

72   Borg, *The God We Never Knew*, p.77.

73   Eliade, *The Sacred and the Profane*, pp.14ff.

74   See, for example, Starhawk, *Spiral Dance*, p.35. See also Harris, 'Paganism as sacred ecology'.

75   See, for example, Rosemary Radford Ruether's description of the environmental activism of Starhawk, in *Integrating Ecofeminism*, p.96; or the sacred rituals performed by the Dragon Environmental Network http://www.dragonnetwork.org/.

76   This reflects Emerson's definition of nature as 'essences unchanged by man'. *Nature and Selected Essays*, p.36.

77   Bloom, *SOULution*, p.78.

78   Crowley, *Way of Wicca*, p.29.

79   See, for example, Bloom, *SOULution*, pp.104ff.

80   See Ward, *Pascal's Fire*.

81   Shallcrass, 'A priest of the goddess', pp.158ff. Unlike some esoteric forms of New Age thinking, this divine spark does not require liberation from the lower, material body. See Sutcliffe, 'Between apocalypse and self-realization', on the tensions between idealist and materialist accounts of nature and the self in New Age thought.

82   Freitas, *Becoming a Goddess of Inner Poise*, pp.48ff.

83   O'Donohue, *Anam Cara*, p.85.

84   See Christ, *Rebirth of the Goddess*, p.147.

85   Starhawk, *Spiral Dance*, p.37; Walsch, *What God Wants*, p.164.

86   Bloom, *SOULution*, p.119; Christ, *Rebirth of the Goddess*, pp.147ff.

87   Dianne Neu, *Return Blessings*, p.27.

88   Ibid., p.85.

89   Ibid., p.120. See also Paul Heelas, *The New Age Movement*, p.37.

90   See, for example, Bloom, *SOULution*, pp.110ff; Pearson, 'Assumed affinities', p.52; Chopra, *How to Know God*, p.17; Bloch, 'Individualism and community', p.293.

91   Christ, *Rebirth of the Goddess*, pp.31ff. Again this progressive emphasis on the authority of personal experience can be located in a longer tradition of the writing of Emerson and Whitman: Emerson once wrote that 'what [another person] announces, I must find true in me, or wholly reject'. Cited in Schmidt, *Restless Souls*, p.33. In his 'Song of Myself', Whitman declared 'You shall no longer take things at second or third hand, nor look through the eyes of the dead, nor feed on the spectres in books, You shall not look through my eyes either, nor take things from me, You shall listen to all sides and filter them from yourself.' Whitman, *Collected Poems*, pp.64ff.

92   Neu, *Return Blessings*, p.27.

93   O'Donohue, *Anam Cara*, p.83.

94   Walsch, *What God Wants*, p.155.

95   Restall Orr, 'The ethics of Paganism', pp.6ff.

96   See the interview with Donna Freitas at http://www.beliefnet.com/story/170/story_17078_2.html?rnd=60.

97   Starhawk, *Spiral Dance*, p.32.

98   Ibid., p.35.

99   See Crowley, *Way of Wicca*, p.163. See also Wilber, *The Essential Ken Wilber*, p.3, on meditation as a spiritual practice whose truth is to be tested through experience. Adrian Smith's book contains a blank page titled 'My creed is…', which allows readers space to articulate their own personal beliefs. *Tomorrow's Faith*, p.97.

100 Jones, 'Pagan theology', pp.37ff.

101 William Bloom, for example, writes about human development as a 'moral imperative'. *SOULution*, pp.142ff.

102 Chopra, *How to Know God*, p.181; Freitas, *Becoming a Goddess of Inner Poise*, pp.163ff.

103 See Heelas, *The New Age Movement*, p.19.

104 O'Donohue, *Anam Cara*, p.118; Wilber, *The Essential Ken Wilber*, pp.3ff. See also http://www.andrewcohen.org/teachings/.

105 See Crowley, 'Wicca as a mystery religion'; Pearson, 'Assumed affinities', p.49.

106 Freitas, *Becoming a Goddess of Inner Poise*, p.xxii.

107 See, for example, Chopra, *Seven Spiritual Laws*, pp.93ff; O'Donohue, *Anam Cara*, p.160.

108 Bloom, *SOULution*, pp.165ff.

109 Crowley, 'Wicca as a mystery religion'; Starhawk, *Spiral Dance*.

110 See, for example, Wilber, *The Essential Ken Wilber*, pp.13ff.

111 Chopra, *How to Know God*, p.145.

112 See Daly, *Beyond God the Father*, p.29.

113 Fox, *Toward a Transpersonal Ecology*, p.198.

114 See, for example, Bloom, *SOULution*, pp.69ff; Lerner, *Jewish Renewal*, p.409; Walsch, *What God Wants*, pp.154ff.

115 See, for example, Crowley, *Way of Wicca*, p.103; Chopra, *How to Know God*, pp.47ff.

116 See, for example, Daren Kemp, *The Christaquarians?*, pp.250ff.

117 Walsch, *What God Wants*, p.152. Walsch's statement is reminiscent of an epigraph that appeared on the programme book of the Greenacre meeting in 1897: 'All religions are true. They are like so many rivers flowing towards the one ocean of Light and Love infinite.' Schmidt, *Restless Souls*, p.136.

118 Bloom, *SOULution*, p.22.

119 Heelas, *The New Age Movement*, pp.27ff.

120 See, for example, Crowley, *Way of Wicca*, p.15.

121 Crowley, 'Wicca as nature religion', pp.174ff; Sutcliffe, *Children of the New*

Age, pp.107ff; Greenwood, 'The nature of the goddess'.

122   Bloom, *SOULution*, p.71.

123   Neo-traditionalist critiques of progressive spirituality demonstrate that the ideological differences between the two are very real. See, for example, http://www3.telus.net/st_simons/arm15.html; http://www.vow.org/feminism/feminism_menu.html.

124   The progressive construct of this secular philosophy is illustrated in Ray and Anderson's description of the core beliefs of 'moderns'. *Cultural Creatives*, pp.26ff.

125   See, for example, Lerner, *The Left Hand of God*.

126   See York, *Pagan Theology*, pp.159ff.

127   Starhawk, *Spiral Dance*, p.36; Bloom, *SOULution*, p.72; Puttick, 'Goddesses and Gopis', pp.114ff.

128   See, for example, Sjoo, *New Age and Armageddon*, pp.119ff. See also Harvey, *Listening People, Speaking Earth*, pp.219ff; and Pearson, 'Assumed affinities'.

129   Some members of Greenspirit have suggested that its name possibly has unhelpful 'New Age' connotations – indicating that they wish to distinguish themselves clearly from a New Age identity. Interview with Chris Clarke, 2 March 2006. As Chris Clarke observed to me, the emphasis on the 'natural' in New Age spirituality can still be fundamentally anthropocentric.

130   See Carrette and King, *Selling Spirituality*.

131   See, for example, Drane, *Do Christians Know?*, pp.2ff.

132   Campbell, *The Romantic Ethic*, pp.99ff.

133   Taylor, *Sources of the Self*, pp.355ff.

134   Taylor, *Modern Social Imaginaries*, pp.3ff. See also Heelas, 'De-traditionalisation of religion and self', p.76.

135   Heelas, 'De-traditionalisation of religion and self', p.71.

136   David Harvey, *The Condition of Postmodernity*, p.10. Harvey recalls Baudelaire's observation that one half of art is concerned with the transient, the fleeting and the contingent, and the other half with the eternal and the immutable. Harvey suggests that cultural modernism also strove to negotiate between these two poles – of the transient, fleeting nature of modern life and of ultimate states of truth and beauty.

137   See, for example, Golding, *Paths to the Absolute*.

138   See Bell, *Art*.

139   Gablik, *Has Modernism Failed?*, pp.124ff.

140   See Schmidt, *Restless Souls*, p.12. Elsewhere Schmidt describes key tenets of this nineteenth-century liberal faith as emphases on 'divine immanence, Inner Light mysticism, social service, and cosmopolitan openness to "many roads"'. Ibid., p.147.

141   Many contemporary advocates of progressive spirituality would, for ex-

ample, be sympathetic to the views of Thomas Wentworth Higginson, expressed in his 1854 tract on *Scripture Idolatry*: 'The soul needs some other support also; it must find this within – in the cultivation of the Inward Light; in personal experience of Religion; in the life of God in the human soul; in faith in God and love to man; in the reverent study of the vast and simple laws of Nature… [I]n these, and nowhere else, lies the real foundation of all authority; build your faith here, and churches and Bibles may come or go, and leave it undisturbed.' Ibid., pp.110ff.

142 Ibid., p.28.
143 Ibid., pp.54ff.
144 Emerson, *Nature and Selected Essays*, p.57.
145 Schmidt, *Restless Souls*, pp.289ff.

Chapter 3

1   See http://www.cog.org/05poll/poll_results.html.
2   See http://www.st-james-piccadilly.org/.
3   See http://www.theriversidechurchny.org/.
4   See http://www.glide.org/.
5   See http://www.fellowshipsf.org/.
6   See http://www.beyttikkun.org.
7   See http://www.quaker.org.uk.
8   See http://www.unitarian.org.uk/.
9   See http://www.uua.org/.
10 See http://www.mccchurch.org/.
11 See http://www.paganfed.org/index.php.
12 See http://www.cog.org/.
13 See Heelas and Woodhead, 'Homeless minds today?'; see also Albanese, *Nature Religion in America*, p.13.
14 See http://www.woodbrooke.org.uk/.
15 See http://www.pendlehill.org/.
16 See http://www.iona.org.uk/.
17 See http://www.scargillhouse.co.uk.
18 See http://www.sojo.net.
19 See http://www.movement.org.uk.
20 See, for example, Schmidt, *Restless Souls*, for his detailed discussion of the Greenacre community, a pioneering venture in progressive interfaith dialogue and collaboration, which was founded by Sarah Farmer in 1894 and finally collapsed when she died in 1916.
21 See http://www.cpwr.org/.
22 See http://www.interfaithalliance.org/.
23 See, for example, http://www.commonspirit.org/.
24 See http://www.canaweb.info/index.shtml.
25 See http://www.snowstarinstitute.org/AboutSIR.htm.

26 See http://www.livingfusion.org.

27 Specialist media providers also provide a range of such resources, including specialist publishing houses and imprints such as The Beacon Press (www.beacon.org), the publishing division of the Unitarian Universalist Association in the US, and HarperCollins San Francisco (http://www.harpercollins.com/imprints.asp?imprint=HarperSanFrancisco). Specialist independent magazines and e-zines also feed the wider progressive milieu, notably *What is Enlightenment?* (http://www.wie.org), and Resurgence (http://www.resurgence.org.uk/).

28 See, for example, the activities of the Westar Institute, the Faith Futures Foundation, the Living Spirituality Network and Breathing Space (http://www.breathingspace.org.uk).

29 See http://www.livingthequestions.com/. Living the Questions has, for example, been taken up as a study resource by a number of local groups in the PCN Britain network.

30 See http://www.nvo.com/thequest/homepage/.

31 See http://www.wisdomuniversity.org/; www.integraluniversity.org. For similar, more advanced, educational programmes within the progressive milieu see, for example, the MA in Religion and Ecology taught at the Irish Missionary Union at Dalgan Park or the PG Certificate in Spiritual Development and Facilitation at the University of Surrey.

32 See, for example, http://www.greenspirit.org.uk/about/index.htm; http://www.progressivechristianity.ca/ccpc/mission.aspx.

33 See, for example, participants' feedback response sheets from day conferences organized by the Living Spirituality Network in Durham and Salisbury in autumn 2005.

34 For example, Eley McAinsh commented how reading books on spirituality often formed an important part of the intellectual and emotional support structures that supporters of the LSN built up for themselves. Other media can also contribute to these social and ideological support structures. For example, McAinsh herself produces the successful BBC Radio 4 programme, *Something Understood*, which offers a weekly exploration of a particular spiritual theme. Interview with Eley McAinsh, 13 February 2006.

35 See, for example, the Vine and Fig Tree bookstore in Vancouver (http://www.vineandfig.ca/).

36 I'm grateful to Chris Clarke for a description of the Cosmic Walk. Interview with Chris Clarke, 2 March 2006. Diarmuid O'Murchu also mentioned to me that a similar Cosmic Walk has been established by Maryknoll Sisters based in the Philippines, and a version of the Cosmic Walk is given on O'Murchu's website (http://www.diarmuid13.com). Interview with Diarmuid O'Murchu, 27 February 2006.

37 See, e.g, http://www.tcpc.org/about/mission.html; http://www.progres-

sivechristianity.ca/ccpc/mission.aspx.

38   http://www.christianalliance.org/site/c.bnKIIQNtEoG/b.592941/k.CB7C/Home.htm.

39   http://www.inclusivechurch.net/; http://www.changingattitude.org/;

40   http://www.crosswalkamerica.org/index.php.

41   http://www.democracyinaction.org/dia/organizations/Sojo/.

42   See http://www.holism.info.

43   Interview with Hugh Dawes, 27 February 2006.

44   http://www.tikkuninstitute.org/.

45   http://www.americanprogress.org/site/pp.asp?c=biJRJ8OVF&b=86591.

46   See   http://www.faithfulamerica.org/display_articlelist.php?article_type=action.

47   See http://www.sojo.net/index.cfm?action=action.home.

48   http://www.jubileedebtcampaign.org.uk/.

49   See http://www.cluela.org.

50   See http://www.sustainable.ie; interview with Ben Whelan, Cultivate Centre, 31 March 2006.

51   See http://www.genesisfarm.org/.

52   See http://www.ecocentrewicklow.com/.

53   See http://www.spiritualprogressives.org/.

54   See http://www.crossleft.org/.

55   See http://www.meta-net.info/index.shtml.

56   See http://www.ufsforum.org/.

57   See Nip, 'Queer sisters', p.256.

58   See, for example, Forman, *Grassroots Spirituality*.

59   See Sutcliffe, *Children of the New Age*. See also York, *The Emerging Network*; Redden, 'The New Age'.

60   See http://www.interdependencedeclaration.org/.

61   See della Porta and Diani, *Social Movements*, pp.69ff.

62   Taylor and Whittier, 'Collective identity in social movement communities', pp.104ff.

63   Castells, *Power of Identity*; Stalder, *Manuel Castells*; see also Melucci, *Playing the Self*, pp.31–3, and *Challenging Codes*, p.73.

64   A sense of identity gained from participation in a social movement may, however, be only one of many identities that an individual has. See della Porta and Diani, *Social Movements*, p.93.

65   See Melucci, *Nomads of the Present*, pp.45ff, 55. For a fuller discussion of such conflict around cultural values and meanings, see Hunter, *Culture Wars*.

66   Melucci, 'The process of collective identity', pp.50ff.

67   Taylor and Whittier, 'Collective identity in social movement communities', p.110. See also Melucci, *Nomads of the Present*, p.29, and Melucci, 'The process of collective identity', pp.48ff.

68   Melucci, *Challenging Codes*, p.74.

69   A striking example of this was provided by my conversation with Sister Marian O'Sullivan, director of the Centre for Ecology and Spirituality at An Tairseach. During the course of our conversation, Sr Marian talked about the influence of the Genesis Farm project and the Sophia Center at Holy Names University on her thinking (she had studied at both places over the course of a year in 1998/99). She also demonstrated an understanding of how her Christian identity dovetailed with native, Celtic spiritual traditions and sacred sites in Ireland, talking, for example, about her engagement with the work of John O'Donohue and Maria Gimbutas. She was able to identify an international network of women in religious orders with an interest in living out the implications of the Universe Story, as well as other ventures beyond the Christian tradition with an interest in evolutionary spirituality – such as the Cultivate Centre. Far from seeing her ideas and work as an isolated venture, Sr Marian clearly identified herself with a growing global movement. Interview with Sister Marian O'Sullivan, 3 April 2006.

70   Interview with Janice Dolley, 11 April 2006.

71   Interview with Adrian Alker, 18 March 2006.

72   Interview with Sister Marian O'Sullivan, 3 April 2006.

73   Interview with Ben Whelan, 31 March 2006.

74   Melucci laments the facile use of such broad descriptions of social movements which fail to recognize their complexity and the multiplicity of perceptions, structures and activities within them. *Nomads of the Present*, pp.28–30.

75   See, for example, Melucci, *Nomads of the Present*, p.26; 'The process of collective identity', *Challenging Codes*, p.70.

76   Ibid., p.71.

77   For example, Janice Dolley explained that the work of the Wrekin Trust is dependent on two paid workers (whose remuneration only formally covers a total of three days a week) and a larger group of voluntary workers. From this organizational base, it is highly demanding for the Wrekin Trust to maintain even its own programme of conferences, and to extend much beyond this is very difficult. The University for Spirit Forum has provided a structure within which the Wrekin Trust has been able to build up links with other people interested in spirituality in education, but to develop significant new collaborative ventures within this structure would be very resource intensive. Interview with Janice Dolley, 11 April 2006.

78   Janice Dolley of the Wrekin Trust commented that, since the 1970s, progressive organizations (such as Findhorn) had often developed clearer and more specific organizational goals as they came to recognize the unlikeliness of achieving broad, and undifferentiated, aims for global spiritual transformation. As Janice commented to me, getting to the stage of being

prepared to give up the particulars of one's identity and aims in order to find the universal is a difficult process. Interview with Janice Dolley, 11 April 2006.

79 See http://www.crosscurrents.org/HarrisSpring2005.htm.

80 Interview with Janice Dolley, 11 April 2006.

81 Interview with Janice Dolley, 11 April 2006.

Chapter 4

1 See, for example, Bruce, *God is Dead*.

2 See Martin, *A General Theory of Secularization*; Berger, *The Desecularization of the World*; Davie, *Europe: The Exceptional Case*, pp.156ff; Woodhead, 'Introduction: Studying religion and modernity', pp.3ff; Eisenstadt, 'Multiple modernities'.

3 See in particular the Preface to the 1902 edition of Durkheim's *The Division of Labour*, the concluding chapter of *Suicide*, the concluding chapter of *The Elementary Forms of the Religious Life* and his article 'Individualism and the intellectuals'. See also Pickering, *Durkheim: Essays on Morals and Education*, pp.3–27; and Bellah, *Emile Durkheim*, pp.ix-lv.

4 See Durkheim, *The Division of Labour*; see also Bellah, *Emile Durkheim on Morality and Society*, pp.xxivff.

5 Durkheim, *Suicide*. See also Heelas, 'On things not being worse', p.211; and Mestrovic, *Emile Durkheim and the Reformation of Sociology*, p.135.

6 See, for example, Mestrovic, *Emile Durkheim and the Reformation of Sociology*, pp.128–41 (esp. p.136). Durkheim recognized, though, that some measure of anomie was an inevitable part of a society in which people had intellectual freedom and were free to pursue their desires – as he commented in *Suicide* (p.331), 'the entire morality of progress and perfection is thus inseparable from a certain amount of anomie'. See also Bellah, *Emile Durkheim*, p.xxix.

7 See Mestrovic, *Emile Durkheim and the Reformation of Sociology*, pp.139, 141.

8 Durkheim, *The Division of Labour in Society*, pp.407ff. See also Bellah, *Emile Durkheim*, p.xxvi.

9 In his lectures on 'The nature of morals and of rights', Durkheim argued that the modern State had proven to be an important support for the rise of the cult of the individual precisely because the State had curtailed the power of social collectivities such as families, guilds, etc., that were able to place restraints on individual freedoms.

10 See Vogt, 'Durkheim's sociology of law'.

11 See Durkheim's Preface to the 1902 edition of *The Division of Labour*. See also Bellah, *Emile Durkheim*, p.xxxiii; Vogt, 'Durkheim's sociology of law', p.86.

12 'We erect a cult in behalf of personal dignity... [which has become] a

common cult, but it is possible only by the ruin of all others and, consequently, cannot produce the same effects as the multitude of extinguised beliefs. There is no compensation for that.' Durkheim, *The Division of Labour*, p.172) See also Bellah, *Emile Durkheim*, p.xxvff.

13   See Mestrovic, *Emile Durkheim and the Reformation of Sociology*, p.139; Bellah, *Emile Durkheim*, p.xl.

14   See Bellah, *Emile Durkheim*, pp.xlii, xlvii. Durkheim also saw flaws within this new cult as well. Writing about the cult of the individual, Durkheim notes that 'it is still from society that it takes all its force, but it is not to society that it attaches us; it is to ourselves'. *The Division of Labour in Society*, p.172.

15   Cited in Bellah, ibid., p.xlvii.

16   See Durkheim, *The Elementary Forms of Religious Life*, pp.322ff. See also Bellah, ibid., pp.xlviff.

17   Simmel, 'The crisis of culture', p.259; Troeltsch, *The Social Teaching of the Christian Churches*, vol.2, p.997.

18   See, for example, Kandinsky, *On the Spiritual in Art*.

19   Simmel, *Essays on Religion*, p.21.

20   Simmel, 'The crisis of culture', p.259.

21   Simmel, *Essays on Religion*, p.23.

22   Troeltsch, *The Social Teaching of the Christian Churches*, vol.2, pp.1001, 1006–10.

23   Ibid., vol.1, p.381; ibid., vol.2, p.992.

24   Ibid., vol.2, p.1001.

25   Simmel, *Essays on Religion*, p.25.

26   Bell, *The Cultural Contradictions of Capitalism*.

27   Sorokin, *Social and Cultural Dynamics*, p.622.

28   Ibid., p.625.

29   Ibid., pp.699ff.

30   Ibid., p.701.

31   Luckmann, *The Invisible Religion*, p.28ff.

32   Ibid., pp.109ff.

33   Ibid., pp.104ff.

34   Ibid., pp.98ff.

35   Ibid., p.27. See also Berger, *Sacred Canopy*, pp.141ff.

36   Berger, *Heretical Imperative*, p.3ff.

37   Ibid., pp.12ff.

38   Ibid., p.16ff.

39   Ibid., p.17.

40   See ibid., pp.21ff.

41   Berger, *Sacred Canopy*, p.141.

42   Berger, *The Desecularization of the World*, p.2.

43   See ibid., p.11; see also Berger, 'Postscript', pp.194ff.

44   Berger, 'Postscript, p.194; see also Bruce, 'The curious case of the unnecessary recantation'.

45   For examples of work in this area, see Wuthnow, *The Consciousness Reformation*.

46   Campbell, ibid., p.122. See also Partridge, *The Re-Enchantment of the West*, vol.1, pp.62–6.

47   Campbell, ibid., pp.122ff.

48   Campbell, ibid., p.131.

49   Partridge, *The Re-Enchantment of the West*, vols.1 & 2.

50   See Partridge, ibid., vol.1, p.67.

51   Campbell, 'The Easternization of the West'.

52   Bruce, *God is Dead*.

53   See also Hoge, Johnson and Luidens, *Vanishing Boundaries*.

54   Roof, *Spiritual Marketplace*, pp.6ff.

55   Roof, ibid., pp.8ff.

56   Roof, ibid., p.10.

57   See Wuthnow, *After Heaven*; and Wuthnow, *The Restructuring of American Religion*.

58   For a more detailed account of 1950s religion in America, see Ellwood, *The Fifties Spiritual Marketplace*.

59   Wuthnow cites a 1978 survey of baby boomers which indicated that most had lived in their local neighbourhoods for less than five years. *After Heaven*, p.75.

60   College enrolments in America in 1960 totalled 3.6 million; by 1970, this had increased to 8.6 million. Wuthnow, ibid., p.68.

61   In the 1950s, the average period for young people between confirmation and the birth of their first child was seven years; by the late 1960s this had more than doubled to 15 years. Wuthnow, ibid., p.67.

62   See also Roof, *Spiritual Marketplace*, p.48.

63   Roof's view of social factors that have encouraged the spiritual-quest culture is very similar to that of Wuthnow. Roof cites immigration, shifts in values and beliefs, a changing intellectual culture (encouraging personal knowledge), the increasing role of the media, the rise of a consumer culture which focuses on the self as a target for marketing and the erosion of local communities as all factors which, from the 1960s onwards, changed the face of American religion. Roof, *Spiritual Marketplace*, p.8.

64   Again, in the 1978 survey of baby boomers, 86 per cent of respondents said they had received religious training as children but only around 50 per cent said that they were making sure their own children also had some grounding in a particular religious faith. Wuthnow, *After Heaven*, p.76.

65   Ibid., p.4.

66   Wilson, 'Salvation, secularization and de-moralization', p.40.

67   Ibid., p.49.

68   See, for example, Cupitt, *Taking Leave of God*.

69   Fenn, *Beyond Idols*, p.8.

70   Ibid., p.10.

71   Fenn, *Time Exposure*, p.14.

72   See, for example, Martin, *A General Theory of Secularization*.

73   Martin, *On Secularization*, pp.17ff.

74   Ibid., pp.3ff. Martin refers to this process of oscillation between the Christianization and de-Christianization of society as a 'dialectic of faith and nature'.

75   Ibid., p.5.

76   Ibid., p.12.

77   Davie, *Religion in Britain since 1945*, p.76.

78   Ibid., p.83.

79   Davie, 'Europe: The exception that proves the rule?', p.82.

80   Or again, as Davie puts it, 'Europeans... remain very largely as passive members of their majority churches.' Davie, *Europe: The Exceptional Case*, p.139.

81   See ibid., pp.19ff., 40ff.

82   Tacey, *The Spirituality Revolution*, pp.78ff.

83   Heelas and Woodhead, *The Spiritual Revolution*, pp.78ff.

84   Ibid., pp.2ff.

85   See Heelas, 'On things not getting worse', and 'The spiritual revolution: From "religion" to "spirituality"'.

86   The phrase, 'the subsumed self' is not one that Heelas and Woodhead explicitly use, but it is one that I have borrowed from David Lyon, *Jesus in Disneyland*.

87   See, for example, Heelas and Woodhead, *Religion in Modern Times*, pp.2ff; *The Spiritual Revolution*, pp.6ff.

88   Heelas, *The New Age Movement*, pp.18ff.

89   See Heelas, 'Expressive spirituality and humanistic expressivism: Sources of significance beyond church and chapel'.

90   See, for example, Heelas and Woodhead, 'Homeless minds today'.

91   Heelas and Woodhead refer to these types of more subjectively oriented forms of religions as 'religions of experiential difference'. *Religion in Modern Times*, pp.2ff.

92   See, for example, Miller, *Reinventing American Protestantism*.

93   Heelas and Woodhead, *The Spiritual Revolution*, pp.33ff.

94   Indeed Woodhead has criticized large swathes of the literature on the sociology of religion for being 'gender-blind'. 'The impact of feminism', pp.72ff.

95   Woodhead, 'Women and religion', pp.334ff.

96   Woodhead, 'The impact of feminism', p.75.

97   See, for example, Ozorak, 'The power but not the glory'.

98   Ibid., pp.338ff. See also Woodhead, who observes that spiritualities of life have attracted women because 'they downplay the authority of spheres and offices in which men have traditionally been dominant.' Woodhead, 'The impact of feminism', p.71. See also Palmer, *Moon Sisters*.

99   Heelas and Woodhead, *The Spiritual Revolution*, pp.94ff.

100   See also Brown, *The Death of Christian Britain*.

101   Heelas, 'Sources of significance beyond church and chapel', p.251.

102   Heelas, 'On things not being worse', pp.251ff.

103   This finding is similar to that of Zinnbauer et al., who demonstrated that, in a sample of respondents to a questionnaire on religious and spiritual beliefs and attitudes, mental health workers were more likely to identify as 'spiritual but not religious', and to reject organized religion, think in terms of personalized spirituality, be interested in mysticism and alternative spiritualities, and be less likely to have been raised in religious homes. Zinnbauer et al., 'Religion and spirituality: Unfuzzying the fuzzy'.

104   Bellah et al., *Habits of the Heart*, p.221.

105   Heelas and Woodhead, 'Homeless minds today', pp.60ff.

106   Heelas and Woodhead, *The Spiritual Revolution*, p.11.

107   Compare, for example, Simmel's notion of the turn to life; and Neale Donald Walsh's observation that in the new spirituality, 'for people everywhere, life itself will become the prime value'. *What God Wants*, p.160.

108   Gellner, *Postmodernism, Reason and Religion*; Giddens and Pierson, *Conversations with Anthony Giddens*.

109   The Pagan Anti-Defamation Network website, for example, illustrates the degree of hostility felt by some Pagans towards Christian-Pagan dialogue. See http://www.patregan.freeuk.com/panpage.htm.

110   See, for example, Heelas, 'De-tradionalisation of religion and self', p.67.

Chapter 5

1   Bell, The Cultural Contradictions of Capitalism, p.145.

2   York, Pagan Theology, p.168.

3   See, for example, Simon, The State of Humanity; Halsey, Trends in British Society since 1900.

4   Fukuyama, End of History, pp.338ff.

5   See, for example, Vaneigem, The Revolution of Everyday Life.

6   Elias, The Civilizing Process.

7   See, for example, Riesman, The Lonely Crowd, p.xxix.

8   Fevre, Demoralization of Western Culture.

9   Simon, The State of Humanity, pp.91–6.

10   See also Fevre, The Demoralization of Western Culture, p.1.

11   Martin, A Sociology of Contemporary Cultural Change, p.12.

12   Bell, The Cultural Contradictions of Capitalism, p.144.

13   Himmelfarb, The Demoralization of Society.

14   Murray, Losing Ground.

15   Nietzsche's critique on the objectivity of morals as reflecting underlying interests is seen both by Bloom and Himmelfarb as highly influential on this drift towards relativism. See, for example, Bloom, ibid., pp.217ff; Himmelfarb, The Demoralization of Society, pp.10ff. On the relativism on contemporary expressive culture, see Bell, The Cultural Contradictions of Capitalism, p.134.

16   Himmelfarb, ibid., pp.221ff.

17   See, for example, Myers, The American Paradox.

18   Murray, Losing Ground, pp.15ff.

19   See Murray, ibid., pp.56–142.

20   Murray, ibid., pp.178ff.

21   For a critique of this interpretation of the effects of changes in American welfare policy, see, for example, Bellah et al., Habits of the Heart, pp.xiv–xvi.

22   Murray, Losing Ground, p.236.

23   Himmelfarb, The Demoralization of Society, p.244.

24   See, for example, Hunter, Culture Wars. See also Sacks, The Persistence of Faith, p.96.

25   See, for example, Myers, The American Paradox.

26   See Hunt, *The Alpha Phenomenon*.

27   Cited in Hunt, *The Alpha Phenomenon*, p.9.

28   Qutb, Milestones, p.194ff. Qutb regarded Islamic civilization as the only period in human history in which true human values were properly attained. Whilst having respect for the technological advancement of western modernity, he regarded it as morally and ideologically bankrupt (see pp.12ff) and was equally critical of modern Islamic societies which diluted the truth of God's message. Ibid., pp.21ff, 173ff.

29   Sacks, The Persistence of Faith, pp.36ff.

30   Sartre, Existentialism and Humanism.

31   Sacks, The Persistence of Faith, p.32.

32   Sacks takes the term 'moral ecology' from Bellah et al., Habits of the Heart.

33   See Bell, The Cultural Contradictions of Capitalism, p.154; Bryan Wilson, 'Salvation, secularization and de-moralization'.

34   Sacks, Persistence of Faith, pp.45, 48ff, 90.

35   Ibid., p.94.

36   Ibid., pp.59–94.

37   An eloquent example of this kind of critique can be found in Philip Wander's Introduction to Lefebvre, Everyday Life in the Modern World.

38   Adorno, The Culture Industry, p.10.

39   As Guy Debord put it, 'comfort will never be comfortable enough for those who seek what is not on the market – or rather that which the mar-

ket eliminates'. Debord, 'The decline and fall of the "spectacular" commodity-economy', p.101.

40   Debord, Society of the Spectacle, p.12.

41   Ibid., p.15.

42   Vaneigem, The Revolution of Everyday Life, pp.236ff.

43   See Greil Marcus' articulate essay, 'The long march of the Situationist
International'; Dark Star, Beneath the Paving Stones; Gray, Leaving the
20th Century; McDonough, Guy Debord and the Situationist International;
and Sadler, The Situationist City.

44   Marcuse, One-Dimensional Man, p.7.

45   Galbraith, The Affluent Society, pp.130ff.

46   Packard, The Hidden Persuaders; Ritzer, Enchanting a Disenchanted
World; Rushkoff, Coercion.

47   See, for example, Miller, 'The unintended political economy'.

48   See Lynch, Understanding Theology and Popular Culture, pp.65–8.

49   Critics of the corporate influence on children's lives have raised a number
of points including the intentional targeting of children by advertisers
keen to induct them into a consumer lifestyle and to exploit their nagging
potential to influence the purchases of adults. See Quart, Branded; Schor,
Born to Buy. For more on the increasing privatization of state education
associated with a target-centred, reductionist approach to education, see
Giroux, Stealing Innocence, pp.83ff. On the influence of large corporations over children's diets both in educational and wider social contexts
(effectively explored by Morgan Spurlock's film Super Size Me as well as
celebrity chef Jamie Oliver's campaign for healthy school dinners in the
UK), and the growing profile of corporate logos and commodities in educational materials as well as the increasing use of advertising in American
schools, see Giroux, Stealing Innocence, pp.94ff; Klein, No Logo, pp.87ff.

50   See, for example, Ritzer, Enchanting a Disenchanted World, pp.104ff.

51   Banksy, Cut It Out, p.33; also http://www.popaganda.com.

52   See, for example, Sennett, The Corrosion of Character, pp.26ff.

53   See Hochschild, The Second Shift and The Time Bind; Fevre, The Demoralization of Contemporary Society; Fevre, The New Sociology of Economic Behaviour, pp.36–56.

54   Hochschild, The Managed Heart.

55   See, for example, North, Wealth: A Very Personal Defence.

56   See, for example, Giddens, Capitalism and Modern Social Theory,
pp.178ff.

57   Meiksins Wood, The Origin of Capitalism, pp.83ff.

58   Weber, The Protestant Work Ethic, p.124.

59   MacIntyre, After Virtue, p.68.

60   Ibid., pp.6ff.

61   Ibid., p.54.

62   In Weberian terms, this represents the shift from formal rationality (the use of rationality as a means of securing certain goals – and even the codification of rational processes into fixed rules and protocols) to a form of substantive rationality in which rationality itself defines the goals which are sought; see Giddens, Capitalism and Modern Social Theory, pp.183ff.

63   See Fevre, The New Sociology of Economic Behaviour.

64   Ritzer, The McDonaldization of Society; and The McDonaldization Thesis.

65   Ritzer, Re-Enchanting a Dis-Enchanted World.

66   'Thus postemotionalism refers to the use of dead, abstracted emotions by the culture industry in a neo-Orwellian, mechanical and petrified manner.' Mestrovic, Postemotional Society, p.26.

67   This is not to suggest that people are cultural dopes, governed by emotions manufactured by the culture industry. If anything, people are increasingly aware of how the emotional environment in which they live is manipulated by political and commercial interests, and are thus increasingly sceptical of such emotions – reflecting David Riesman's notion of the 'inside-dopester'. See Postemotional Society, p.58. But this cynicism leads to a deeper rift in people's ability to experience and trust their own emotions. Ibid., pp.118ff.

68   The term 'alter mondialiste' is a reference to the slogan emerging out of the meeting of the World Social Forum in Porto Alegre, Brazil in 2002: 'Another world is possible'.

69   See, for example, Callinicos, An Anti-Capitalist Manifesto.

70   See, for example, St John, Rave Culture and Religion.

71   See Honoré, In Praise of Slow.

72   Wallis, God's Politics, pp.222, 228.

73   Ibid., pp.4–6; Lerner, The Left Hand of God, pp.245ff.

74   Wallis, God's Politics, p.226.

75   See, for example, Lerner, Jewish Renewal, p.265.

76   Lerner, The Left Hand of God, pp.39ff.

77   See, for example, Walsch, What God Wants, pp.2ff; O'Murchu, Reclaiming Spirituality, p.173.

78   Bloom, SOULution, p.4.

79   Michael Lerner's position in this regard is somewhat more nuanced than that of Jim Wallis. Lerner, Left Hand of God, pp.217, 227.

80   Berry, The Great Work, pp.xiff, 8; Radford Ruether, Integrating Ecofeminism, pp.1–3.

81   Christ, Rebirth of the Goddess, pp.144ff.

82   Ibid., pp.113ff; see also Spretnak, 'Earthbody and personal body as sacred', p.271.

83   Ibid., pp.263ff; Berry, The Great Work, pp.108ff.

84   Christ, Rebirth of the Goddess, pp.146, 172.

85   Kumar, No Destination, p.303.

86   Bloom, SOULution, pp.215ff.

87   See, for example, Kumar, No Destination, pp.307ff.

88   Spretnak, 'Earthbody and personal body as sacred', p.266.

89   Christ, Rebirth of the Goddess, pp.124ff.

90   Lerner, Left Hand of God, pp.227ff.

91   Radford Ruether, Integrating Ecofeminism, pp.164ff.

92   See, for example, Starhawk's anti-globalization activism; Diarmuid O'Murchu also told me that he regarded the work of the International Forum on Globalization as an important resource for his own thinking. Interview with Diarmuid O'Murchu, 27 February 2006.

93   Christ, Rebirth of the Goddess, pp.160ff.

94   Berry, The Great Work, p.7.

95   See, for example, Spretnak, 'Earthbody and personal body as sacred', p.265.

96   Christ, Rebirth of the Goddess, p.156.

97   Ibid., p.157.

98   Ibid., p.167.

99   Lerner, Jewish Renewal, p.270.

Chapter 6

1   See, for example, Tacey, The Spirituality Revolution.

2   Bloom, SOULution, pp.8ff.

3   See, for example, http://www.diagnosis2012.co.uk.

4   Schmidt, Restless Souls, pp.13ff.

5   MCC reported their global membership in 2004 to be around 16,000. Total membership of British Quaker meetings in 2004 was reported by the British Yearly Meeting to be 15,558. Reported membership of the Friends' General Conference in the United States in 2006 was around 30,000 (see http://www.fgcquaker.org/info/). In 2005, the Unitarian Universalist Association had a total of 218,519 members (159,383 adults and 59,136 enrolled in Sunday schools), and an estimated total global membership of 350,000. Statistics provided by UUA Public Information Office.

6   This rough estimate is based partly on Ray and Anderson's (The Cultural Creatives) claim that there are over 50 million people in the US who share broadly progressive moral and religious attitudes, and on Gallup polls on progressive moral issues which, for example, consistently show that between 35–45 per cent of Americans are supportive of gay rights. Ray and Anderson, The Cultural Creatives. See also Wuthnow, Restructuring of American Religion, p.133, on similar polling in the USA in the 1980s, which showed that around 40 per cent of the American population identified themselves as liberals.

7   See, for example, Bruce, Politics and Religion, pp.142ff.

Bibliography

Adorno, T. (2001) *The Culture Industry*. London: Routledge.

Alcock, P. (1996) 'Back to the future: Victorian values for the twenty-first century', in *Charles Murray and the Underclass: The Developing Debate*. London: Institute of Economic Affairs (IEA) Health & Welfare Unit.

Ali, S. (2005) 'How I met God', in S. Abdul-Ghafur (ed.), *Living Islam Out Loud: American Muslim Women Speak*. Boston, MA: Beacon Press: 19–35.

Banksy (2005) *Cut It Out*. No place of publication, published by Banksy.

Bartholomew, C. and T. Moritz (2000) *Christ and Consumerism: A Critical Analysis of the Spirit of the Age*. Carlisle: Paternoster.

Bates, S. (2004) *A Church at War: Anglicans and Homosexuality*. London: Hodder & Stoughton.

Bell, C. (1914) *Art*. London: Chatto & Windus.

Bell, D. (1976) *The Cultural Contradictions of Capitalism*. London: Heinemann.

Bellah, R. (1973) *Emile Durkheim: On Morality and Society*. Chicago, IL: University of Chicago Press.

Bellah, R., R. Madsen, W. Sullivan, A. Swidler and S. Tipton (1996) *Habits of the Heart*. Updated edition. Berkeley, CA: University of California Press.

Benson, J. (2005) *Affluence and Authority: A Social History of 20th Century Britain*. London: Hodder Arnold.

Berger, P. (1967) *The Sacred Canopy: Elements of a Sociological Theory of Religion*. New York: Doubleday.

Berger, P. (1979) *The Heretical Imperative: Contemporary Possibilities of Religious Affirmation*. New York: Doubleday.

Berger, P. (ed.) (1999) *The Desecularization of the World: Resurgent Religion and World Politics*. Grand Rapids, MI: Eerdmans.

Berger, P. (2001) 'Postscript', in L. Woodhead (ed.), with D. Martin and P. Heelas, *Peter Berger and the Study of Religion*. London: Routledge: 189–98.

Berry, T. (1988) *The Dream of the Earth*. San Francisco, CA: Sierra Club Books.

Berry, T. (1999) *The Great Work: Our Way Into the Future*. New York: Bell Tower.

Bloch, J. (1998) 'Individualism and community in alternative spiritual magic'. *Journal for the Scientific Study of Religion*, 37 (2): 286–302.

Bloom, A. (1987) *The Closing of the American Mind*. New York: Simon & Schuster.

Bloom, W. (2004) *SOULution: The Holistic Manifesto – How Today's Spirituality Changes Everything*. London: Hay House.

Bohm, D. (1980) *Wholeness and Implicate Order*. London: Routledge.

Borg, M. (1994) *Meeting Jesus Again for the First Time: The Historical Jesus and the Heart of Contemporary Faith*. San Francisco, CA: HarperSanFrancisco.

Borg, M. (1997) *The God We Never Knew: Beyond Dogmatic Religion to a More Authentic Contemporary Faith*. New York: HarperCollins.

Boucher, S. (1999) *Discovering Kwan Yin, Buddhist Goddess of Compassion: A Path Toward Clarity and Peace*. Boston, MA: Beacon Press.

Brabazon, T. (2005) *From Revolution to Revelation: Generation X, Popular Memory and Cultural Studies*. Aldershot: Ashgate.

Bruce, S. (2001) 'The curious case of unnecessary recantation: Berger and secularization', in L. Woodhead (ed.), with D. Martin and P. Heelas, *Peter Berger and the Study of Religion*. London: Routledge: 87–100.

Bruce, S. (2002) *God is Dead: Secularization in the West*. Oxford: Blackwell.

Callinicos, A. (2003) *An Anti-Capitalist Manifesto*. Cambridge: Polity.

Campbell, C. (1972) 'The cult, the cultic milieu and secularization', in M. Hill (ed.), *A Sociological Yearbook of Religion in Britain*, 5. London: SCM Press: 119–36.

Campbell, C. (1987) *The Romantic Ethic and the Spirit of Consumerism*. Oxford: Blackwell.

Campbell, C. (1999) 'The Easternisation of the West', in B. Wilson and J. Creswell (eds.), *New Religious Movements: Challenge and Response*. London: Routledge: 35–48.

Capra, F. (1975/1982) *The Tao of Physics: An Exploration of the Parallels between Modern Physics and Eastern Mysticism*. (3rd edition) London: Flamingo.

Capra, F. (1997) *The Web of Life: A New Synthesis of Mind and Matter*. London: Flamingo.

Carette, J. and R. King (2005) *Selling Spirituality: The Silent Takeover of Religion*. London: Routledge.

Carson, R. (1962/2002) *The Silent Spring*. (40th anniversary edition) Boston, MA: Houghton Mifflin.

Castells, M. (2004) *The Power of Identity* (2nd edition) Oxford: Blackwell.

Chaney, D. (2002) *Cultural Change and Everyday Life*. Basingstoke: Palgrave.

Chopra, D. (1997) *The Seven Spiritual Laws of Success: A Practical Guide to the Fulfilment of Your Dreams*. London: Bantam.

Chopra, D. (2000) *How to Know God: The Soul's Journey into the Mystery of Mysteries*. London: Rider.

Christ, C. (1987) *Laughter of Aphrodite: Reflections on a Journey to the Goddess.* San Francisco, CA: HarperSanFrancisco.

Christ, C. (1989) 'Rethinking theology and nature', in J. Plaskow and C. Christ (eds.), *Weaving the Visions: New Patterns in Feminist Spirituality.* San Francisco, CA: HarperSanFrancisco: 314–25.

Christ, C. (1995) *Diving Deep and Surfacing: Women Writers on Spiritual Quest.* (3rd edition) Boston, MA: Beacon Press.

Christ, C. (1997) *Rebirth of the Goddess: Finding Meaning in Feminist Spirituality.* New York: Routledge.

Christ, C. and J. Plaskow (1979) *Womanspirit Rising: A Feminist Reader in Religion.* San Francisco, CA: HarperCollins.

Cohen, S. (2002) *Folk Devils and Moral Panics.* (3rd edition) London: Routledge.

Crowley, V. (1998) 'Wicca as nature religion', in J. Pearson, R. Roberts and G. Samuel (eds.), *Nature Religion Today: Paganism in the Modern World.* Edinburgh: Edinburgh University Press: 170–9.

Crowley, V. (2000) 'Wicca as a mystery religion', in G. Harvey and C. Hardman, *Pagan Pathways: An Introduction to the Ancient Earth Traditions.* London: HarperCollins.

Crowley, V. (2001) *Way of Wicca.* London: Thorsons.

Cupitt, D. (2001) *Taking Leave of God.* London: SCM Press.

Dark Star (ed.) (2001) *Beneath the Paving Stones: Situationists and the Beach, May 1968.* Edinburgh: AK Press.

Daly, M. (1973/1986) *Beyond God the Father: Towards a Philosophy of Women's Liberation.* London: Women's Press.

Daly, M. (1999) *Quintessence... Realizing the Archaic Future: A Radical Elemental Feminist Manifesto.* London: Women's Press.

Davie, G. (1994) *Religion in Britain since 1945: Believing Without Belonging.* Oxford: Blackwell.

Davie, G. (1999) 'Europe: The exception that proves the rule?', in P. Berger (ed.), *The Desecularization of the World.* Grand Rapids, MI: Eerdmans: 65–83.

Davie, G. (2000) *Religion in Modern Europe: A Memory Mutates.* Oxford: Oxford University Press.

Davie, G. (2002) *Europe: The Exceptional Case. Parameters of Faith in the Modern World.* London: Darton, Longman and Todd Ltd.

Davies, D. (2002) *Death, Ritual and Belief.* (2nd edition) London: Continuum.

Davies, P. (1993) *The Mind of God: Science and the Search for Ultimate Meaning.* London: Penguin.

Davies, P. (2003) *The Origin of Life.* London: Penguin.

Davis, N. and R. Robinson (1996) 'Religious orthodoxy in American society: The myth of a monolithic camp'. *Journal for the Scientific Study of Religion*, 35 (3): 229–45.

Debord, G. (1965/2001) 'The decline and fall of the "spectacular" commodity-economy', in Dark Star (ed.), *Beneath the Paving Stones: Situationists and the*

Beach, May 1968. Edinburgh: AK Press: 98–104.

Debord, G. (1995) *The Society of the Spectacle.* New York: Zone Books.

Della Porta, D. and M. Diani (2005) *Social Movements: An Introduction.* (2nd edition) Oxford: Blackwell.

Drane, J. (2005) *Do Christians Know How to Be Spiritual? The Rise of New Spirituality, and the Mission of the Church.* London: Darton, Longman and Todd Ltd.

Durkheim, E. (1893/1933) *The Division of Labour in Society.* New York: Free Press.

Durkheim, E. (1897/2002) *Suicide: A Study in Sociology.* London: Routledge.

Durkheim, E. (1912/2001) *The Elementary Forms of the Religious Life.* Oxford: Oxford University Press.

Eaton, H. (2005) *Introducing Ecofeminist Theologies.* London: T & T Clark.

Eisenstadt, S. (2000) 'Multiple modernities'. *Daedalus,* 129 (1): 1–28.

Elaide, M. (1957) *The Sacred and the Profane: The Nature of Religion.* San Diego, CA: Harcourt.

Eller, C. (1995) *Living in the Lap of the Goddess: The Feminist Spirituality Movement in America.* Berkeley, CA: University of California Press.

Eller, C. (2000) *The Myth of Matriarchal Prehistory: Why an Invented Past Won't Give Women a Future.* Boston, MA: Beacon Press.

Elias, N. (1994) *The Civilizing Process.* Oxford: Blackwell.

Ellwood, R. (1997) *The Fifties Spiritual Marketplace: American Religion in a Decade of Conflict.* New Brunswick, NJ: Rutgers University Press.

Fenn, R. (2001) *Beyond Idols: The Shape of a Secular Society.* Oxford: Oxford University Press.

Fenn, R. (2001) *Time Exposure: The Personal Experience of Time in Secular Societies.* Oxford: Oxford University Press.

Fevre, R. (2000) *The Demoralization of Western Culture.* London: Continuum.

Fevre, R. (2003) *The New Sociology of Economic Behaviour.* London: Sage.

Forman, R. (2004) *Grassroots Spirituality: What it Is, Why it is Here, Where it is Going.* London: Academic Imprint.

Fox, M. (1991) *Creation Spirituality: Liberating Gifts for the Peoples of the Earth.* San Francisco, CA: HarperCollins.

Fox, W. (1990) *Toward a Transpersonal Ecology.* Boston, MA: Shambhala.

Freitas, D. (2005) *Becoming a Goddess of Inner Poise: Spirituality for the Bridget Jones in All of Us.* San Francisco, CA: Jossey Bass.

Fukuyama, F. (1992) *The End of History and the Last Man.* London: Penguin.

Gablik, S. (2004) *Has Modernism Failed?* (Revised edition) London: Thames & Hudson.

Galbraith, J. K. (1999) *The Affluent Society.* (Revised edition) London: Penguin.

Gellner, E. (1992) *Postmodernism, Reason and Religion.* London: Routledge.

Giddens, A. (1971) *Capitalism and Modern Social Theory.* Cambridge: Cambridge University Press.

Giddens, A. and C. Pierson (1998) *Conversations with Anthony Giddens: Making*

Sense of Modernity. Cambridge: Polity.

Gimbutas, M. (1992) *Civilisation of the Goddess*. San Francisco, CA: HarperSanFrancisco.

Giroux, H. (2000) *Stealing Innocence: Corporate Culture's War on Children*. Basingstoke: Palgrave.

Golding, J. (2002) *Paths to the Absolute: Mondrian, Malevich, Kandinsky, Pollock, Newman, Rothko and Still*. London: Thames & Hudson.

Gray, C. (1998) *Leaving the 20th Century: The Incomplete Work of the Situationist International*. London: Rebel Press.

Guha, R. and J. Martinez Alier (1997) *Varieties of Environmentalism: Essays North and South*. London: Earthscan.

Hanegraff, W. (1998) 'Reflections on new age and the secularization of nature', in J. Pearson, R. Roberts and G. Samuel (eds.), *Nature Religion Today: Paganism in the Modern World*. Edinburgh: Edinburgh University Press: 22–32.

Hardt, M. and A. Negri (2000) *Empire*. Cambridge, MA: Harvard University Press.

Harvey, D. (1990) *The Condition of Postmodernity: An Enquiry into the Origins of Cultural Change*. Oxford: Blackwell.

Harvey, G. (1997) *Listening People, Speaking Earth: Contemporary Paganism*. London: Hurst & Co.

Heelas, P. (1996) *The New Age Movement: The Celebration of the Self and the Sacralization of Modernity*. Oxford: Blackwell.

Heelas, P. (1996) 'On things not being worse, and the ethic of humanity', in P. Heelas (ed.), *Detraditionalization*. Oxford: Blackwell: 200–18.

Heelas, P. (2000) 'Expressive spirituality and humanistic expressivism: Sources of significance beyond church and chapel', in S. Sutcliffe and M. Bowman (eds.), *Beyond New Age: Exploring Alternative Spirituality*. Edinburgh: Edinburgh University Press: 237–54.

Heelas, P. (2002) 'The spiritual revolution: From "religion" to "spirituality"', in L. Woodhead, P. Fletcher, H. Kawanami and D. Smith (eds.) (2002) *Religions in the Modern World*. London: Routledge: 357–78.

Heelas, P. and L. Woodhead (2002) 'Homeless minds today?', in L. Woodhead (ed.), with P. Heelas and D. Martin, *Peter Berger and the Study of Religion*. London: Routledge: 43–72.

Heelas, P., L. Woodhead, B. Seel, B. Szernszynski and K. Tusting (2005) *The Spiritual Revolution: Why Religion is Giving Way to Spirituality*. Oxford: Blackwell.

Herrick, J. (2003) *The Making of the New Spirituality: The Eclipse of Western Religious Tradition*. Leicester: Inter-Varsity Press.

Himmelfarb, G. (1995) *The De-Moralization of Society: From Victorian Virtues to Modern Values*. London: Institute of Economic Affairs (IEA) Health & Welfare Unit.

Hoge, D., B. Johnson and D. Luidens (1994) *Vanishing Boundaries: The Religion of*

Mainline Protestant Baby Boomers. Louisville, KY: Westminster/John Knox.

Holloway, R. (2001) *Doubts and Loves: What is Left of Christianity?* Edinburgh: Canongate.

Honoré, C. (2004) *In Praise of Slow: How a Worldwide Movement is Challenging the Cult of Speed*. London: Orion.

Hunt, K. (2003) 'Understanding the spirituality of people who do not go to Church', in G. Davie, P. Heelas and L. Woodhead (eds.), *Predicting Religion: Christian, Secular and Alternative Futures*. Aldershot: Ashgate: 159–69.

Hunt, S. (2005) *The Alpha Phenomenon: Some Tentative Observations*, paper presented at the annual conference of the British Sociological Association Sociology of Religion study group, University of Lancaster, 11–13 April.

Hunter, J. D. (1991) *Culture Wars: The Struggle to Define America*. New York: Basic Books.

Hutton, R. (1998) 'The discovery of the modern goddess', in J. Pearson, R. Roberts and G. Samuel (eds.), *Nature Religion Today: Paganism in the Modern World*. Edinburgh: Edinburgh University Press: 89–100.

Ind, J. (1993) *Fat is a Spiritual Issue*. London: Continuum.

Inglehart, R. (1990) *Culture Shift in Advanced Industrial Society*. Princeton, NJ: Princeton University Press.

Inglehart, R. (1997) *Modernization and Postmodernization*. Princeton, NJ: Princeton University Press.

James, W. (1902) *The Varieties of Religious Experience*. London; Longmans Green.

Jameson, F. (1991) *Postmodernism, or the Cultural Logic of Late Capitalism*. London: Verso.

Jencks, C. (1977) *The Language of Post-Modern Architecture*. Chichester: Academy Editions.

Jencks, C. (1996) *What is Post-Modernism?* (4th edition) Chichester: Academy Editions.

Jencks, C. (2005) *The Garden of Cosmic Speculation*. London: Frances Lincoln.

Jorgensen, D. and S. Russell (1999) 'American Neo-Paganism: The participants' social identities'. *Journal for the Scientific Study of Religion*, 38 (3): 325–38.

Kemp, D. (2003) *The Christaquarians? A Sociology of Christians in the New Age*. Sidcup: Kempress.

Klein, N. (2000) *No Logo*. London: Flamingo.

Lambert, Y. (2004) 'A turning point in religious evolution in Europe'. *Journal of Contemporary Religion*, 19 (1): 29–45.

Lefebvre, H. (1999) *Everyday Life in the Modern World*. New Brunswick, NJ: Transaction Publishers.

Le Grignou, B. and C. Patou (2004) 'ATTAC(k)ing expertise: Does the internet really democratize knowledge?', in W. van de Donk, et al. (eds.), *Cyberprotest: New Media, Citizens and Social Movements*. London: Routledge: 164–79.

Lerner, M. (1994) *Jewish Renewal: A Path to Healing and Transformation*. New York:

HarperPerennial.

Lerner, M. (2006) *The Left Hand of God: Taking Back Our Country From the Religious Right*. San Francisco, CA: HarperSanFrancisco.

Lipset, S. (1996) *American Exceptionalism: A Double-Edged Sword*. New York: Norton.

Lovelock, J. (1979/2000) *Gaia: A New Look at Life on Earth*. Oxford: Oxford University Press.

Luckmann, T. (1963/1967) *The Invisible Religion*. New York: Macmillan.

Luckmann, T. (1983) *Life-World and Social Realities*. London: Heinemann.

Lynch, G. (2002) *After Religion: 'Generation X' and the Search for Meaning*. London: Darton, Longman and Todd Ltd.

Lynch, G. (2003) *Losing My Religion? Moving Away From Evangelical Faith*. London: Darton, Longman and Todd Ltd.

Lynch, G. and Badger, E. (2006) 'The mainstream post-rave club scene as secondary institution: a British perspective'. *Religion and Culture*, 7 (1), pp.27–40.

Lynch, G. (2005) *Understanding Theology and Popular Culture*. Oxford: Blackwell.

MacKinnon, M. and M. McIntyre (1995) *Readings in Ecology and Feminist Theology*. Kansas City: Sheed & Ward.

MacIntyre, A. (1985) *After Virtue: A Study in Moral Theory*. London: Duckworth.

Marcus, G. (2002) 'The long march of the Situationist International', in T. McDonough (ed.), *Guy Debord and the Situationist International: Texts and Documents*. Cambridge, MA: MIT Press: 1–20.

Marcuse, H. (1991) *One-Dimensional Man*. (2nd edition) London: Routledge.

Martin, D. (1978) *A General Theory of Secularization*. Oxford: Blackwell.

Martin, D. (2005) *On Secularization: Towards a Revised General Theory*. Aldershot: Ashgate.

Maslow, A. (1982) *Toward a Psychology of Being*. (2nd edition) Princeton, NJ: D. Von Nostrand.

McDonough, T. (ed.) (2002) *Guy Debord and the Situationist International: Texts and Documents*, Cambridge, MA: MIT Press.

Meiksins Wood, E. (1999) *The Origin of Capitalism*. New York: Monthly Review Press.

Mestrovic, S. (1988) *Emile Durkheim and the Reformation of Sociology*. Lanham, MD: Rowan & Littlefield.

Mestrovic, S. (1991) *The Coming Fin de Siecle*. London: Routledge.

Mestrovic, S. (1997) *Postemotional Society*. London: Sage.

Miller, D. (2002) 'The unintended political economy', in P. du Gay and M. Pryke (eds.), *Cultural Economy*, London: Sage: 166–84.

Miller, V. (2004) *Consuming Religion: Christian Faith and Practice in a Consumer Culture*. New York: Continuum.

Moore, T. (2002) *The Soul's Religion*. New York: HarperCollins.

Murray, C. (1994) *Losing Ground: American Social Policy, 1950–1980*. (2nd edition)

New York: Basic Books.

Naess, A. (1989) *Ecology, Community and Lifestyle*. Cambridge: Cambridge University Press.

Nip, J. (2004) 'The Queer Sisters and its electronic bulletin board: A study of the internet for social movement mobilization', in W. van de Donk, et al. (eds.), *Cyberprotest: New Media, Citizens and Social Movements*. London: Routledge: 233–58.

O'Donohue, J. (1997) *Anam Cara: Spiritual Wisdom from the Celtic World*. London: Bantam.

O'Murchu, D. (1997) *Reclaiming Spirituality: A New Spiritual Framework for Today's World*. Dublin: Gateway.

O'Murchu, D. (2004) *Quantum Theology: Spiritual Implications of the New Physics*. (Revised edition) New York: Crossroad.

O'Murchu, D. (2005) *Consecrated Religious Life: The Changing Paradigms*. Maryknoll, NY: Orbis.

Ozorak, E. (1996) 'The power but not the glory: How women empower themselves through religion'. *Journal for the Scientific Study of Religion*, 35 (1): 17–29.

Palmer, S. (1994) *Moon Sisters, Krishna Mothers, Rajneesh Lovers: Women's Roles in New Religions*. Syracuse, NY: Syracuse University Press.

Partridge, C. and T. Gabriel (2003) *Mysticisms East and West*. Carlisle: Paternoster.

Partridge, C. (2004) *The Re-Enchantment of the West (Vol. 1)*. London: Continuum.

Pearson, J. (1998) 'Assumed affinities: Wicca and the New Age', in J. Pearson, R. Roberts and G. Samuel (eds.), *Nature Religion Today: Paganism in the Modern World*. Edinburgh: Edinburgh University Press: 45–56.

Philips, M. (1996) 'Where are the New Victorians?', in *Charles Murray and the Underclass: The Developing Debate*. London: Institute of Economic Affairs (IEA) Health & Welfare Unit: 156–60.

Pickering, W. (ed.) (1979) *Durkheim: Essays on Morals and Education*. London: Routledge & Kegan Paul.

Pilgrim, G. (2003) 'The Quakers: Toward an alternate ordering', in G. Davie, P. Heelas and L. Woodhead (eds.), *Predicting Religion: Christian, Secular and Alternative Futures*. Aldershot: Ashgate: 147–58.

Plaskow, J. (2005) *The Coming of Lilith: Essays on Feminism, Judaism and Sexual Ethics, 1972–2003*. Boston, MA: Beacon Press.

Putnam, R. (2001) *Bowling Alone: The Collapse and Revival of American Community*. New York: Simon & Schuster.

Puttick, E. (1998) 'Goddesses and Gopis: In search of new models of female sexuality', in J. Pearson, R. Roberts and G. Samuel (eds.), *Nature Religion Today: Paganism in the Modern World*. Edinburgh: Edinburgh University Press: 111–22.

Queen, C. (ed.) (2000) *Engaged Buddhism in the West.* Somerville, MA: Wisdom Publications.

Qutb, S. (1988) *Milestones.* Delhi: Ishaat-e-Islam Trust Publications.

Radford Ruether, R. (2005) *Goddesses and the Divine Feminine.* Berkeley, CA: University of California Press.

Radford Ruether, R. (2005) *Integrating Ecofeminism, Globalization and World Religions.* Lanham, MD: Rowan & Littlefield.

Raphael, M. (1999) *Introducing Thealogy: Discourse on the Goddess.* London: Continuum.

Ray, P. and S. Anderson (2000) *The Cultural Creatives: How 50 Million People Are Changing the World.* New York: Three Rivers Press.

Redden, G. (2005) 'The New Age: Towards a market model'. *Journal of Contemporary Religion,* 20 (2): 231–46.

Riesman, D. (1964) *Abundance for What? And Other Essays.* London: Chatto & Windus.

Ritzer, G. (1998) *The McDonaldization Thesis.* London: Sage.

Ritzer, G. (1999) *Enchanting a Disenchanted World: Revolutionizing the Means of Consumption.* Thousand Oaks, CA: Pine Forge Press.

Ritzer, G. (2000) *The McDonaldization of Society.* Thousand Oaks, CA: Pine Forge Press.

Roberts, R. (1998) 'The chthonic imperative: Gender, religion and the battle for the Earth', in J. Pearson, R. Roberts and G. Samuel (eds.), *Nature Religion Today: Paganism in the Modern World.* Edinburgh: Edinburgh University Press: 57–73.

Robinson, J. (1963/2002) *Honest to God.* (40th anniversary edition) London: SCM.

Roof, W.C. (1999) *Spiritual Marketplace: Baby Boomers and the Re-making of American Religion.* Princeton, NJ: Princeton University Press.

Rountree, K. (2004) *Embracing the Witch and the Goddess: Feminist Ritual-Makers in New Zealand.* London: Routledge.

Rushkoff, D. (1999) *Coercion: Why We Listen to What "They" Say.* New York: Riverhead.

Rushkoff, D. (2003) *Nothing Sacred: The Truth About Judaism.* New York: Crown Publishers.

Sacks, J. (2005) *The Persistence of Faith.* (2nd edition) London: Continuum.

Sadler, S. (1998) *The Situationist City.* Cambridge, MA: MIT Press.

Samuel, G. (1998) 'Paganism and Tibetan Buddhism: Contemporary Western religions and the question of nature', in J. Pearson, R. Roberts and G. Samuel (eds.), *Nature Religion Today: Paganism in the Modern World.* Edinburgh: Edinburgh University Press: 123–40.

Sanders, C. E. (2005) *Wicca's Charm: Understanding the Spiritual Hunger Behind the Rise of Modern Witchcraft and Pagan Spirituality.* Colorado Springs, CO: Shaw Books.

Schofield Clark, L. (2004) *From Angels to Aliens: Teenagers, the Media and the*

Supernatural. New York: Oxford University Press.

Schor, J. (2004) *Born to Buy: The Commercialized Child and the New Consumer Culture*. New York: Schriber.

Sennett, R. (1998) *The Corrosion of Character: The Personal Consequences of Work in the New Capitalism*. New York: W.W. Norton & Co.

Shallcrass, P. (1998) 'A priest of the goddess', in J. Pearson, R. Roberts and G. Samuel (eds.), *Nature Religion Today: Paganism in the Modern World*. Edinburgh: Edinburgh University Press: 157–69.

Simmel, G. (1976) 'The crisis of culture', in P. Lawrence (ed.), *Georg Simmel: Sociologist and European*. Sunbury-on-Thames: Nelson: 253–66.

Simmel, G. (1997) *Essays on Religion*. New Haven, CT: Yale University Press

Simon, J. (ed.) (1995) *The State of Humanity*. Oxford: Blackwell.

Sjoo, M. (1992) *New Age and Armageddon*. London: Women's Press.

Sjoo, M. and B. Mor (1991) *The Great Cosmic Mother: Rediscovering the Religion of the Earth*. (2nd edition) San Francisco, CA: HarperCollins.

Smith, A. (2005) *Tomorrow's Faith: A New Framework for Christian Belief*. Ropley: O Books.

Smith, C. (2000) *Christian America? What Evangelicals Really Want*. Berkeley, CA: University of California Press.

Smith, C. and M. Denton (2005) *Soul Searching: The Religious and Spiritual Life of American Teenagers*. Oxford and New York: Oxford University Press.

Sorokin, P. (1957) *Social and Cultural Dynamics*. (Abridged version) London: Peter Owen Ltd.

Spong, J. (1998) *Why Christianity Must Change or Die: A Bishop Speaks to Believers in Exile*. San Francisco, CA: HarperSanFrancisco.

Spretnak, C. (1993) 'Earthbody and personal body as sacred', in C. Adams (ed.), *Ecofeminism and the Sacred*. New York: Continuum: 261–80.

Stalder, F. (2006) *Manuel Castells*. Cambridge: Polity Press.

Starhawk (1999) *The Spiral Dance: A Rebirth of the Ancient Religion of the Great Goddess*. (20th anniversary edition) San Francisco, CA: HarperSanFrancisco.

St John, G. (2004) *Rave Culture and Religion*. London: Routledge.

Sutcliffe, S. (1998) 'Beyond apocalypse and self-realization: "Nature" as an index of new age religiosity', in J. Pearson, R. Roberts and G. Samuel (eds.), *Nature Religion Today: Paganism in the Modern World*. Edinburgh: Edinburgh University Press: 33–44.

Sutcliffe, S. (2003) *Children of the New Age: A History of Spiritual Practices*. London: Routledge.

Swimme, B. and T. Berry (1992) *The Universe Story: From the Primordial Flaring Forth to the Ecozoic Era – A Celebration of the Unfolding of the Cosmos*. San Francisco, CA: HarperCollins.

Tacey, D. (2004) *The Spirituality Revolution: The Emergence of Contemporary Spirituality*. Hove: Brunner-Routledge.

Taylor, C. (1989) *Sources of the Self: The Making of Modern Identity*. Cambridge:

Cambridge University Press.

Taylor, C. (2004) *Modern Social Imaginaries*. Durham: Duke University Press.

Tolle, E. (2005) *A New Earth: Awakening to Your Life's Purpose*. London: Dutton.

Troeltsch, E. (1911/1931) *The Social Teaching of the Christian Churches*. (2 vols.) London: George Allen & Unwin.

Underhill, E. (1911) *Mysticism: A Study in the Nature and Development of Man's Spiritual Consciousness*. London: Dover.

van de Donk, W., B. Loader, P. Nixon and D. Rucht (2004) 'Introduction: Social movements and ICTs', in W. van de Donk et al. (eds.), *Cyberprotest: New Media, Citizens and Social Movements*. London: Routledge: 1–25.

Vaneigem, R. (2003) *The Revolution of Everyday Life*. London: Rebel Press.

Vogt, W. (1993) 'Durkheim's sociology of law: Morality and the cult of the individual', in S. Turner (ed.), *Emile Durkheim: Sociologist and Moralist*. London: Routledge: 71–94.

Wallis, J. (2005) *God's Politics: Why the American Right Gets It Wrong and the Left Doesn't Get It*. Oxford: Lion.

Walsch, N. D. (2005) *What God Wants: A Compelling Answer to Humanity's Biggest Question*. London: Hodder Mobius.

Ward, K. (2006) *Pascal's Fire*. Oxford: One World.

Weber, M. (1930/1992) *The Protestant Ethic and the Spirit of Capitalism*. London: Routledge.

Wilson, B. (2001) 'Salvation, secularization and de-moralization', in R. Fenn (ed.), *The Blackwell Companion to Sociology of Religion*. Oxford: Blackwell: 39–51.

Woodhead, L. and P. Heelas (2000) *Religion in Modern Times*. Oxford: Blackwell.

Woodhead, L. (2001) 'The impact of feminism on the sociology of religion: From gender-blindness to gendered difference', in R. Fenn (ed.), *The Blackwell Reader for the Sociology of Religion*. Oxford: Blackwell: 67–84.

Woodhead, L. (2002) 'Introduction: Studying religion and modernity', in L. Woodhead, P. Fletcher, H. Kawanami and D. Smith (eds.), *Religions in the Modern World*. London: Routledge: 1–14.

Woodhead, L. (2002) 'Women and religion', in L. Woodhead, P. Fletcher, H. Kawanami and D. Smith (eds.), *Religions in the Modern World*. London: Routledge: 332–56.

Wuthnow, R. (1976) *The Consciousness Reformation*. Berkeley, CA: University of California Press.

Wuthnow, R. (1988) *The Restructuring of American Religion: Society and Faith Since World War II*. Princeton, NJ: Princeton University Press.

Wuthnow, R. (1998) *After Heaven: Spirituality in America since the 1950s*. Berkeley, CA: University of California Press.

York, M. (1995) *The Emerging Network: A Sociology of New Age and Neo-Pagan Movements*. Lanham, MD: Rowman & Littlefield.

York, M. (2003) *Pagan Theology: Paganism as a World Religion*. New York: New

York University Press.

Young, L. (1986) *The Unfinished Universe*. Oxford: Oxford University Press.

Zinnbauer, B. (1997) 'Religion and spirituality: Unfuzzying the fuzzy'. *Journal for the Scientific Study of Religion*, 36 (4): 549–64.

Index